G000161253

THE STORY OF NOEL MELLISH VC, MC

The Story of
Noel Mellish VC, MC

A Chaplain's War

HUGH MONTELL

SERENDIPITY

© Hugh Montell, 2002

First published in 2002 by
Serendipity
Suite 530
37 Store Street
Bloomsbury
London

All rights reserved.
Unauthorised duplication
contravenes existing laws.

British Library Cataloguing-in-Publication data
A catalogue record for this book is available from the British Library

ISBN 1-84394-008-6

Printed and bound in the UK by Alden Digital, Oxford

Contents

Introduction

IN 1952 WHILE AT BALTONSBOROUGH near Glastonbury, Noel Mellish was immobilised by a badly poisoned knee. Unable to get about on his usual parish rounds he took the opportunity to write something of his early life and experiences – a task that had been earnestly and repeatedly requested by his family for a long time. He had brought this account up to 1910 or thereabouts when he recovered and returned to his pastoral work, leaving the story unfinished and with many unanswered questions.

My original plan when I started to write about Noel Mellish was simply to publish his account of the war with extracts from contemporary letters to present a broader picture. But on seeing the chapter on his early life it seemed possible to put this together with the war story, and then with a great deal of help from the family, to cover the whole of this remarkable man's life.

The typescript of his personal account of the war which follows was found among Noel Mellish's papers after his death. Not even his beloved wife with whom he shared his life's work and thoughts for over forty years had any idea that he had written it.

Chapter One

Early Life

O N 28 AUGUST 1878 EDWARD MELLISH was married at St John's Church, Holloway to Mary Coppin, a 26-year-old girl from Plymouth. Mellish was then aged 44, a successful and much-travelled businessman who had already been married twice before. The first marriage was to an Australian girl in Sydney who bore him three children between 1855 and 1859. Mellish never talked about this marriage to his later family, possibly because he was ashamed of marrying again comparatively soon after the death of his first wife. The second marriage to Sara Waterworth took place in Hong Kong in 1863 and this produced five children.

A photograph of Edward Mellish a few years later shows a strong, self-confident face, full-bearded and perhaps somewhat arrogant. He was a discount broker by profession, and clearly a very successful one who worked in the Far East for some years and continued his dealings there after he returned home. He had also worked in Mauritius and in 1861 between his first and second marriages, Mellish was invited by the Governor to join an expedition of congratulation to King Rhadama II of Madagascar, on his succession to the throne after Queen Radavani. 'If ever there was a fiend in human form, she was one,' his diary records. The diary which Mellish kept of this expedition reveals a clear, observant mind and a fine talent for colourful description. It also shows his interest in education and in the teaching of Christianity although his primary function was to represent the Chamber of Commerce to whom he reported.

These qualities were later borne out by one of his daughters by the second marriage, Alice, who was a brilliant classical scholar and schoolteacher and successively headmistress of Guernsey Ladies College and Jerusalem College. She used to relate that at the age of six her father considered her rather stupid because she could only read Latin and not Greek.

And so a picture emerges of the man who married for the third time in 1878. Experienced, well educated, shrewd, probably impatient of less successful people, a proud and self-reliant Victorian businessman who had carried the banner overseas and won riches and material possessions. But there was one critical failing in his make-up which had disastrous effects on his career. During his trips overseas, Mellish had perforce to leave the operation of his London office in the hands of partners, and though he could assess a man's commercial ability accurately, he proved to be a poor judge of character. As a result his fortunes waxed and waned and though Mellish himself built up a very prosperous business more than once, he also lost most of it at least twice through unscrupulous partners.

The marriage to Mary Coppin produced five children. Mary, the eldest, born in 1879, married a young banker, Walter Hodson who retired early and made quite a good living from doing up houses and moving every few years. He was a delightful Edwardian gentleman, most punctilious in manner, an excellent raconteur and a connoisseur of early prints and etchings. The eldest son was born on Christmas Even, 1880 and was duly christened Noel. A second girl, Margaret, was born on 12 May 1883, but she contracted typhoid very young and though she recovered partially, she was never strong and died at the age of 29, in 1912. Another son, Charles, also caught typhoid at Launceston, and died after only two months. Finally Richard was born in 1890. When he left school he went out to Canada but returned in 1914 to join up and was killed in action on 25 September 1915, leading his platoon of the Middlesex Regiment.

Noel was born at Oakley Park in North London, but when he was five the family moved to Launceston in Cornwall where Edward Mellish hoped to retire, on one of the upturns in his fortunes. But by 1890 the tide had turned again and the whole family moved back to a small house in Lewisham and once more money was very scarce. Noel went to a small local school until he was 13 and was then entered into King Edward's School, Saffron Walden. At that time the school was in good hands and its reputation was high. A report from a visiting examiner in 1894 states: 'Throughout my visit I was very favourably impressed by the gentlemanly conduct of the boys. I may add that everything I saw and heard testified to the efficient discipline and excellent tone of the school.' The report goes on to deal with each subject examined, and among the best three or four in each subject Noel is named for Scripture, in which he won a prize, English Grammar, Latin translation, grammar and composition. He also received a special commendation for his work in botany and for the neatness of his spare-time collection of local flora. This is the first mention of his great love for flowers, so often shown in his later writing and letters, and it is no surprise to find gardening was one of his lifelong hobbies. Of the other boys mentioned in the report, one, Bob Scruby, became a staunch friend of Noel's for life and was best man at his wedding. Sadly the school went down badly when the original headmaster died, and Noel was glad to leave just before his sixteenth birthday, but whatever its failings then, he was certainly soundly educated and prepared to tackle the far harder examinations of a degree course later.

There is an unhappy sequel to the Launceston period in the family history. Tom, the second son of Edward Mellish's first marriage, had set up as a solicitor in the town after some time in India. In August 1893 he took part in the local tennis tournament with his sister and young half-sister Adelaide. The following Saturday a party of seven went out for a boating trip at Boscastle, but as the tide was out and the boats could not launch they went for a walk on the cliffs. Tom slipped on the rocks and apparently walked to the edge to bathe his face which was bleeding. A sudden freak wave washed him off the rock and a friend from India, Dr Anstead, went to his rescue. He in turn was swept off the rocks. Adelaide then went to help and tried to pull them out with her umbrella but she too was sucked in and all three were drowned before help could reach them. Tom Mellish was then aged 36 and Adelaide 24.

Edward Mellish and two of his daughters attended the triple funeral at Boscastle where there were apparently 800–900 people in the churchyard – a striking tribute to Tom and his sister, since Dr Anstead was from India and presumably only his immediate family was present.

On leaving school, Noel joined his father's firm which was now again fairly prosperous. But money-making held no attraction for him and he had little in common with his father, who was devoted to commerce and probably did not appreciate a son whose interests lay in craftwork with his hands, and nature. Apart from this, Noel soon found that his father's partner was, if not crooked, at least unscrupulous in his methods. Rather than precipitate a family row which would have caused his gentle mother much distress and would anyway have left him the outsider in the firm, Noel resigned without making any charges, and found himself a job with the Big Tree Wine Company. At the same time he enlisted in the Artists Rifles, a territorial recruiting regiment serving the London area.

Many years later, at the urgent request of his family, Noel Mellish started to write an account of his early life. The first instalment covers his childhood and school years and takes us to the point where he sailed for South Africa on a cattle boat in December 1900.

You asked me to write to you something of my earlier life, so here goes. There isn't much to say about childhood. Mary, Margaret and I were born at Oakley Park, near Finsbury Park, then fairly out of London. My father bought a large house at Launceston in Cornwall and we moved when I was about five. We had a large garden and a fine old gardener called Connett, who lived in a cottage near the stable. We had a pony and a little chaise, and we sometimes used to go with Mother to call and have tea in some of the big houses. For the most part it was quite uneventful and we played in the garden and had a good nursery. At about six I went to a small school presided over by two Miss Smiths in the town. I don't remember much about it except that I had a very good grounding in Latin, was much afraid of dogs, and also of the small boys who used to call out at me as they passed to their school, one way, as I went the other. When I was about nine my father had a bad collapse in his business: he was a discount broker and had hoped to retire when we went to Cornwall, leaving his partner to run the business. But Bruce, the partner, was a terrible gambler in stocks, and broke up the business, making my father bankrupt and getting off himself.

So the house was sold in the winter and the furniture and stuff went for almost nothing and we rented a small house in South London, Brockley. I had forgotten to say that another little brother called Charlie, born at Launceston, died of typhoid and Margaret caught it too, but recovered, though it left her very delicate. Mother had a terrible time all the way through the illness and the anxiety of it all. We were very poor indeed, but she was a very brave and wonderful woman and we managed to get along with the money which came in from my father's life insurance, which he converted to cash, and I think with help from a Mrs Dobbing, an old school friend of mother's. She was a rich woman and was very good. I went to a little boys' school owned by a tiny little woman called Miss Bailey near our home. There I learnt a good deal. I remember our next door neighbours, a large family, with whom we had long talks over the wall. There were lots of girls. I remember on one birthday they gave me *Treasure Island*, always a great joy. The older families, for my father had married three times, were away from home so we never saw much of them after Launceston, except Alice, who was always wonderful to us children. Tom was in India, Arthur in America. I don't think I ever saw him. Edith went to New Zealand where for twenty-five years or so she did wonderful work as a deaconess at Christchurch. Agnes married a coffee planter, Bob Sidgwick, who was Jack Sidgwick's father and lived in Jamaica. Lilian married Frank Collins, science master at Tonbridge. A few years later Addie and Tom, who was home from India, were drowned at Boscastle; they tried to save a friend who had slipped off the rocks. So except for Alice, who was teaching at Cheltenham after taking her BA at 19, we were more or less only ourselves. Cecil was at Sherborne, and then went to the Civil Service. He was 25 years in Jamaica and was a long time a magistrate at Montego Bay. Richard was born when I was about ten.

After leaving Miss Bailey's I went to another local school which was not much good and then went to Saffron Walden when I was thirteen. It was a good school, run on public school lines and for the first year I was very happy, but after the Headmaster died of diphtheria, I wonder we didn't all get it, as the stink from the drains was awful. The school went down a lot, after his death, under his successor, who had a rather terrible wife, probably an early suffragette; she was very mean and the food was pretty bad. After the elder boys left, most of them for Cambridge, it was not a happy school and I was glad to leave before I was sixteen.

I had a taste for mechanics and carpentering, which my mother encouraged. She wanted me to be apprenticed, but father wanted me to go into his office. This was a mistake and I wasn't much good there. His next partner was the reverse of Bruce, he was all too careful and timid and at length committed suicide. That didn't help the business. But an old clerk of father's, who knew the business very well, offered to join him and built it up again. I came into the office when he was there for £3 a month, living at home. He was a little, sharp tempered man and drank too much but knew the work and steered it along. It really wasn't the place for me but there it was, and as a clerk I suppose I wasn't worse than many, but I hadn't any head or heart for it either. I used to get home soon after five and in the summer Mary and I used to play tennis in a local club where all the men wore immensely high collars and the girls long skirts, but it was good fun, though the tennis would have made anyone laugh these days. Wimbledon hadn't come into focus. Then Mary got engaged to Walter and we were very good friends. Walter was one of the smartest dressed young men you could find. Very high collars, trousers so tight you could imagine he had to use a shoehorn to get into them. He was in the Bank of England and had a good position. His father was the Rector of St Paul's Deptford but lived in a large rectory in the more fashionable top part called Brockley, near where we lived. We had moved into a rather larger house and knew them well.

I had been confirmed at school without it leaving much impression on me. Now I became a regular communicant, usually going with mother to a Mission Church about a mile away and it was through her that my communion became a matter of real importance in my life. She did not talk religion but she lived it with a tremendous faith, with a quiet and wonderful reality in everything she did. Margaret was not very strong but was one of the saints who never grumbled and was a great example to everybody. I don't remember when it happened, but I was away, perhaps after I went to South Africa or when I was at school, but while she was getting into a bus, the driver went off and she was dragged for some time. This wrenched her right arm very badly and she suffered very much and it gradually became worse, so that she was unable to use it at all, but she wrote with her left hand and became very proficient in doing most beautiful drawn-thread embroidery in linen, and used to get orders for her work which was much admired. I joined the choir at the Church of the Transfiguration which was very keen and we had an orchestra of strings.

About this time, 1899, the quarrel in South Africa came to a head with the result that war broke out after the Jameson Raid and for the first year we suffered many heavy disasters, until Lord Roberts went out in command and the Boers surrendered and Paul Kruger, the stubborn old President of the Transvaal, escaped. But the war continued, a much wider and more difficult business against brave leaders like Smuts and Botha. And we had to pour troops and guns and thousands of horses into a very hard fought struggle against determined guerillas who knew every inch of their country and were independent of heavy and slow moving transport.

In 1899 I joined the Artists, then one of the crack volunteer regiments who were brigaded with the London Scottish, Inns of Court, and Queen's Westminsters. I had my first camp at Aldershot and enjoyed it. I suppose it was about that year that an event happened which changed my life. I had passed my recruit firing course and had done very well at the short ranges, and hoped to win the recruits spoon, which was given for a good standard of shooting. I had arranged to go on a Saturday afternoon to Runnymede, where the long range was, and asked my father if I could get off a bit early; the office closed on Saturdays at 2. We were not very busy and I was going off, when the irascible little man, Stewart, my father's partner, got on to me and said I was getting off behind his back. So we had some words, as it was quite unmerited. I went down to shoot but it was a dark winter day and the light was very bad and I daresay the row with Stewart had upset me; at any rate I shot very badly so did not win my spoon. The upshot of the row was that I had to leave the office and after a week or so got a job as clerk in a wine merchants, "The Big Tree Wine Co." on Waterloo Bridge, at £1 a week.

Meanwhile I wrote for advice to a few friends and a cousin of my mother, Major Hicks, a regular soldier, who later commanded the 1st Hants and died of wounds after Mons, in 1914. He suggested that I should join one of the irregular corps than forming for South Africa. Meanwhile I took a course of riding at Woolwich, pretty rough and I had a most awful sore bottom and wounds in my legs where the stirrup leathers had cut in, but I survived, got through the riding test, and went up to the office where they were recruiting and enlisted as a trooper at 5/- a day in a police corps, then called Baden Powells' Police, afterwards SA Constabulary, and went out in the first draft of about 70 men in a cattle boat called the Idaho. We picked up drafts of the 17th Lancers and 6th Inniskilling Dragoons with a lot of horses at Queenstown and then away. It was a roughish boat, iron decked, and very hot and the horses suffered miserably from sea sickness. We sailed on 15th December and landed at Capetown on 9th January 1901.

Well, I think this an appropriate place to end this chapter, and will continue, if you like next week, being now, 505 Trooper Mellish aged 20.

Chapter Two

South Africa

THE SERVICE RECORDS SHOW THAT Mellish landed in January 1901 and was attested at Bloemfontein. On 20 July 1902 he was promoted from 3rd to 2nd class trooper. On 9 January 1903 Mellish applied to re-engage for a further term of two years at an extra 3d per day. His troop commander, Captain Dawson, forwarded this application with the following endorsement:

> No.E465, Cpl. M. Hanson and E505 2nd cl. Tpr E. N. Mellish apply for permission to re-engage and I attach application from the latter for three months leave to England. I see by DO's 525 para 1 that re-engagements will cease except in very special cases. If the applications hitherto sent in by me [the underlining is Capt. Dawson's] are disallowed, Sgt. Norman will be the only NCO left in the Troop. These men came out from England with the first draft of SAC. They are a much better class than the majority of those who have joined since and are literally the backbone of the troop. It is quite impossible for me to replace them and I would much prefer to discharge any four other men rather than one of these. Former applications to re-engage have been sent to the Adjutant.
>
> 22.12.02 F. S. Dawson Capt.

The application was forwarded to SAC headquarters with a memo from Dawson's superior: 'Forwarded for favour of early orders on these and previous cases referred to (of which I have no knowledge). If desirable men wish to re-engage I should suppose it to be most desirable that they should be permitted to do so, from every point of view.'

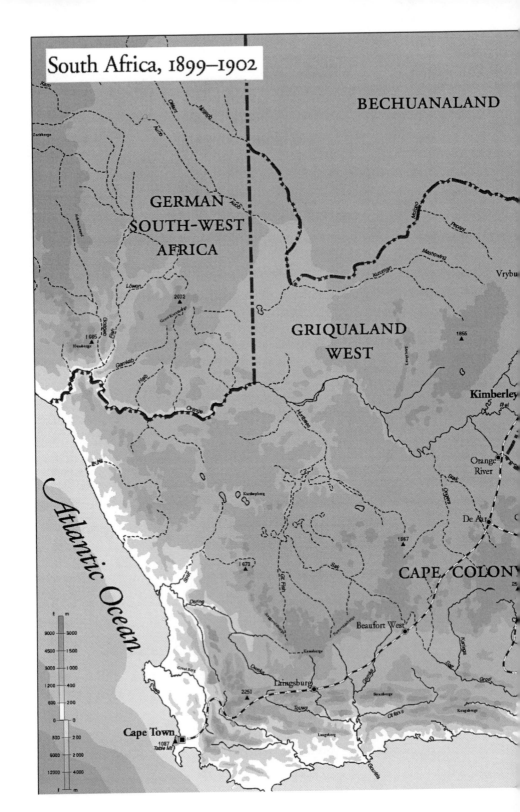

South Africa, 1899–1902

BECHUANALAND

GERMAN SOUTH-WEST AFRICA

GRIQUALAND WEST

Vrybu

Kimberley

Orange River

De Aar

CAPE COLONY

Atlantic Ocean

Beaufort West

Laingsburg

Cape Town

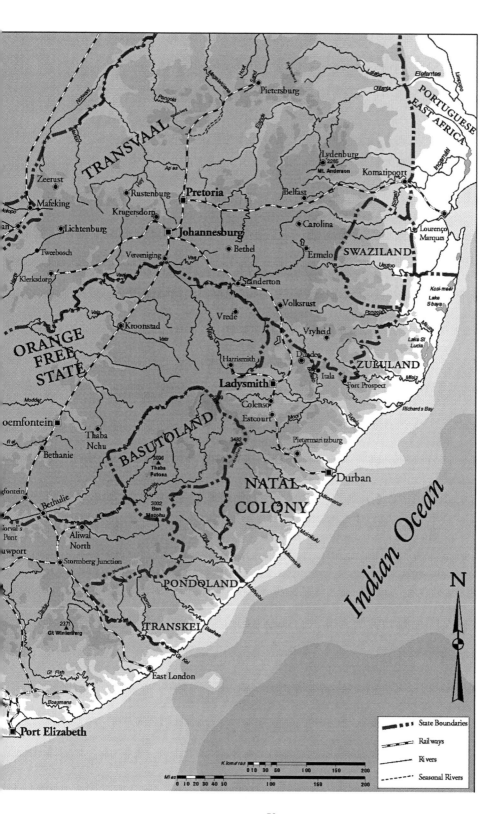

The application was successful and Mellish was officially re-engaged for two years on 11 February 1903, backdated to 9 January 1903. At the same he was granted three months leave on full pay, starting 22 February. A return passage to South Africa was booked for him on the SS *Nubia* sailing from Southampton on 21 April and he reported back to his unit at Fauresmith on 21 May 1903. In fact the three months leave really only amounted to one month at home.

In August 1903, Mellish applied for discharge by purchase. This required the backing of a written offer of employment for at least six months, and he was able to produce such an offer of work on the Springfontein and Jagersfontein railway, then under construction, at the rate of £8.10.0 per month plus board and lodging free. The purchase was completed for the sum of £10 and No.505 Tpr Mellish was formally discharged at Bethulia on 10 October 1903, with an exemplary conduct sheet and the Queen's Medal with two clasps.

Such are the bare facts from the record sheets of service in South Africa for two years, 270 days. Fortunately the account that follows gives a fuller picture of the campaign from the point of view of a 20-year-old trooper. The adventures, perils and hardships which he endured with his comrades are as vivid and real as they were at the time, but they are recalled some fifty years later by a man who, like his father, had a gift for words and lively description, and the country is seen through the eyes of a man who was later to prove himself a useful artist. The account is completely unedited as it was for family eyes only and was never intended for publication.

This second instalment begins with the voyage out to the Cape.

It was quite uneventful. We slept in hammocks, hung closely to each other on a lower deck. During the voyage we were all inoculated against enteric. The treatment was in an elementary stage and made us feel very ill. The inoculation was done in the side of the stomach, induced a high temperature and a good deal of discomfort. It was very painful to move at all, lying in a hammock. However we got over it and as far as I was concerned it did no good at all, for I nearly died of enteric later on. We stopped at St Vincent to coal, but we were not allowed to land as it was a very dirty place, but we were able to buy oranges and one chap ate so many that he got such bad colic that he was very ill.

At last on 9th January we got to Table Bay, a beautiful sight with its white table cloth spread over the great plateau. We marched straight to the train for up country. They brought us dixies of terrible tea which at once made me very sick. We took several days to get to Bloemfontein as the train didn't move at night for fear of attack by the Boers. When we got to the Orange River, looking very lovely in the moonlight, we were allowed to bathe. As I was swimming across the river one of our men, an ex-sailor, suddenly let out a terrified yell and swam for the shore as fast as he could. He had seen an iguana, a great lizard, and thought it was a crocodile. They are perfectly harmless but look formidable – rather prehistoric with great crests on their backs. We detrained at Bloemfontein and marched for the night to barracks. On the following day we were served out with khaki uniforms, rifles, bandoliers and horses. They had been captured from the Boers and were in poor condition and some of them had dreadful sore backs and one had a dreadfully cut mouth from being ridden with a horrible bit. Mine was a quiet old grey without much character. We were given Mexican saddles with bucket stirrups, difficult to fit to horses with bad backs.

Then we started off for our destination, a town called Winburgh about 20 or 30 miles away. I was sent out as a connecting file and soon after a violent thunder storm came on. The horse wouldn't face it and I lost my direction, so, as it got dark, I got down behind a sheltering kopje, fed my horse and ate what food I had, tied the horse up to a bush, which of course was quite wrong and went to sleep. When I woke the horse was gone and I saw him in the distance with a herd of Boer horses who all galloped off. I ran after them but of course couldn't catch mine and then found I couldn't find my rifle, hat and saddle. Soon the sun grew hot and I got thirsty and wandered about vainly trying to catch my horse. At last I saw a farm house in the distance and staggered up to it, no doubt looking the picture of woe. A lot of fat women in sun bonnets came out and laughed at me, but they saw I was spent and when I asked for water gave me many cups of coffee. One girl could understand English and I explained things and they sent a native boy who caught my horse and found the saddle. They put me on the road to Winburg and I arrived at my troop and got well ticked off for losing myself. It was remarkable how kind those women were for I was their enemy and to our shame, later on, we had to burn down those farm houses as they were used by the Boers as depots for food supply, and indeed from some of them our men were shot at. At that particular time the Boers had surrendered under Lord Robert's proclamation, but for the most part after a short interval the war went on under determined leaders like Smuts and Botha and De La Rey, and it continued as a bitter guerilla war for two and a half years longer.

We lived at Winburg for a while and a section of us were housed in a small corrugated iron church of what denomination I don't know, but it was probably belonging to our church. While we were there the troop was increased in number to about 200 and we were commanded by a Captain Dawson who had been a subaltern in the Northumberland Fusiliers but had got into trouble in India through the wife of another officer. She had been divorced and later married Dawson, but she was a worthless though attractive woman and eventually drank herself to death, but that was later; I didn't know anything of her until the war was over. He was a splendid troop commander – tall, quiet, extremely brave and capable, with a quiet voice and I never saw him lose his temper or get flustered. About the same time we got a very good troop sergeant major, ex-Canadian Mounties, a fine horseman and a very good disciplinarian, but fair to all and good in the field.

Our troop was composed of all sorts. One old fellow belonged to a titled family, Villiers by name; he didn't last very long as he was sent down with dysentery. There were one or two Canadians, one Danish ex-seaman, two or three ex-sailors and a few soldiers who had signed on to finish their service. Others were clerks, farm boys, one a Scottish ghilly, and one who had lived in Texas, ranching. My squad leader was an Australian bushman, a most capable man with a violent temper and a rich flow of language, but I liked him and we got on well together as a happy troop.

Kitchener's plan to conquer the Boers was to cut up that vast country with barbed wire fences, with concrete blockhouses at inter-vals, which also guarded the lines of communication and protected the railways. The blockhouses were garrisoned by infantry and we, in common with thousands of mounted infantry, had to drive the Boers and corner them if possible. This is where De Wet and Smuts were so brilliant. We worked column by column to split them up and wear them down. So the whole country was scoured by small mobile columns. There was then no wireless, no telephone and only along the railways telegraphic communication, and that was of course constantly cut. Signals then had only helio for any distance. We were never in blockhouses but constantly moving in conjunction with other small columns. It was a vast open country and the Boers were the most mobile troops in the world. Each commando had hidden sources of supply in farmhouses. The Boers were well mounted on small horses, native bred, who lived on the veld, and they carried their scanty supplies, a bag of buck meat, called biltong, and a bag of meal attached to their saddles, and perhaps a kettle and a blanket or two on spare horses. Where it was safe they had their ox wagons and their women folk. As the war went on the women were taken away to large camps where the children were taught in schools and the rudiments of sanitation were taught to the women, and where there were doctors and nurses to look after the sick. It was inevitable, and though there were violent attacks by people in the home press against what they called the concentration camps, it was prejudiced by political bias. If the women and children had not been taken away they would have starved.

We and other troops had to destroy the farms and to drive the stock to collection areas or slaughter them if they could not be moved. It was the only way by which the war could be brought to an end. But it was a very hard way.

Usually when we halted for any time we took the opportunity to wash our shirts and other things, as we carried nothing but a spare pair of socks in our saddle wallets and our overcoats, as the total weight of man, rifle and 200 rounds of ammunition was quite as much as the horses could carry. It was usual to see men with their shirts off, hunting for lice when we off saddled for a rest; there was no DDT in those days and officers as well as men were always verminous. We rarely came anywhere near a canteen except when we struck the railway. Only three times did I get into Bloemfontein but

I found a good friend there in Mr Hilliard, a curate at the cathedral, who gave me the luxury of a real bath, and once when I went in for remounts I was able to make my communion. We had no chaplains, there were very few then in the regular army and none at all for us.

For some weeks we were at a place called Poplar Grove, a stark hill standing alone in the veld. We had there a few tents but they were so crowded that some of us preferred to build up little shacks for ourselves. I chose a spot on the side of the hill and dug out a hole and built the sides with the iron-stone boulders which lay around, making a nice soft bed with bush, and roofing it with the same and some old sacks. It was very comfortable and I got some mutton fat, which with a wick made it possible to read at night.

We were a disreputable looking crowd as we had had no issue of uniform for a long time. My clothes were in rags and most of us had patched our breeches with pieces of sacking. One day I was driving some sheep back to camp when a young officer, whom I didn't know, called out to me and told me to go up to his tent and he gave me a good pair of breeches. I was the best dressed man in the troop after that. One chap had broken his false teeth on the biscuits and as he grew a beard he looked exactly like a Boer, who all had beards. While we were there in that column we had with us half a battery of RHA Being regulars, they had good uniforms and their horses were plump and lovely. I got to know two of them and they were very good to me, giving me soap of which we had none, and black cake tobacco. Before long we went off and I never saw them again but I shall never forget the kindness of those men.

Our only cover at nights were our ragged and sweaty horse blankets which we used under the saddle by day. Some of our men collected some lean goats while we were there and used to milk them and sell the milk to such as had money to buy it. These temporary abiding places didn't last long and we were soon off on trek. One day as we were on the march Captain Dawson suddenly stopped and, jumping off his pony, picked up a great water melon and very soon the whole troop had their faces buried in the rich cool sweetness of those welcome delights. Another day we came across a shallow pit scooped out by ostriches in which were about 20 great eggs. By luck that evening we halted by the railway and there was a hotel at the station where they made them into filling and delicious omelettes. It was an amusing sight to see our fellows riding along with very distended stomachs apparently, for we put the ostrich eggs inside our shirts until we were able to halt for the night and eat them. Another time I was by myself and found another nest. I had no means of cooking it until I found in a deserted farmhouse an old enamelled jerry which made a very convenient cooking pot in which I boiled the egg for half an hour and found it excellent. Sometimes we saw great herds of springbok, they looked so lovely dancing in the sunshine of the early morning, and once we saw at a distance what appeared to be a Boer Commando, but when we got nearer we found them to be a herd of wildebeest, an antelope which has a head like a small bull with curly horns, and gallops like a horse in a clumsy way, but covers the ground surprisingly fast. Sometimes we got a shot and springbok venison makes a very welcome change after a long diet of bully or McConachie. I only once saw a snake, a black mamba, very poisonous. They are said to spit at your eyes. The one I saw wriggled under my horse's hooves as I rode and I tried to get her near the hole into which he went, but she refused to go near. We saw and heard many baboons in the kopjes. They are savage dog-faced creatures with tremendous teeth and bark at you as you go near. They live on scorpions which they find under the rocks and roots, but they became quite a menace to the farmers when they settled back after the war was over. They get very fearless unless they know there is a gun about. They are too strong for dogs to tackle alone, but the farmers used to organise baboon shoots, as they raided their crops and orchards and in dry weather would come down and take the lambs, tearing out the stomach and drinking the milk. One farmer had a lovely greyhound bitch of which he was very proud. She went after a marauding baboon but the animal tackled her and completely disembowelled her with his terrible teeth and strong arms. The baboons are said by the farmers to be able to count up to two. This man was much bothered by a raider but it always cleared off when he had a gun. One day two of his friends went down with him to the orchard. Two of them left and went back to the farmhouse, but the third hid and the old baboon came back for another feed on his peaches and he shot it. There were lots of scorpions and it was always well to shake one's boots before one put them on, as they like such hiding places, and though the sting is not deadly, it is poisonous.

The old Queen died in January 1901 but the war went on and on. Under Kitchener there was a great combing out of officers who had found soft places in Cape Town and elsewhere and were enjoying the war. But K. changed all that and he sent home all the old generals and such like who hadn't learned that this war was different from the Crimea and Majuba. We learned to take cover and not to advance in column. We became mobile and to look round the other side of a kopje before we went up it. We also learned that Brother Boer could shoot to kill at 1000 yards, for they had been accustomed to use a rifle since they were about five years old and could bring down a springbok from the saddle; the finest mounted infantry the world has ever seen, and they knew every inch of their own country and how to live on it without the heavy and slow moving transport of ox wagons which our columns had, to carry our kit and fodder. They were better teachers of war than any Aldershot text books; we learned our lessons, but expensively.

Kipling draws a true picture of us in those days:

> I wish my mother could see me now with a fence post under my
> > arm,
> And a knife and a spoon in my puttees that I found on a Boer
> > farm,
> Atop of a sore-backed Argentine, with a thirst that you couldn't
> > buy,
>
> I used to be in the Yorkshires once,
> Sussex, Lincolns and Rifles once,
> Hampshires, Scottish and Glosters once,
> But now I am MI.
>
> Our sergeant-major's a subaltern, our captain's a Fusilier,
> Our adjutant's late of Somebody's horse and a Melbourne
> > auctioneer,
> But you couldn't spot us at half a mile from the crackest cavalry,
>
> They used to talk about Lancers once,
> Hussars, Dragoons and Lancers once,

helmets, pistols and carbines once,
But now we are MI.

I wish my mother could see me now agathering news on my own,
When I ride like a general up to the scrub and ride back like Tod
Sloan,
Remarkable close to my horse's neck to let the shots go by.

We used to fancy it risky once,
Called it a reconnaissance once,
Under the charge of an officer once,
But now I am MI.

My hands are spotty with weld sores, my shirt is a button and frill,
And the things I've used my bayonet for would make a tinker ill.
I don't know whose damn colum I'm in, nor where we're trekking,
nor why,

I've trekked from the Vaal to the Orange once,
From the Vaal to the greasy Pongolo once,
For now I am MI.

We never got out of the Orange Free State, though once we trekked
up to the Vaal river. If we had crossed, it would have given us another
bar to our medals, for what they were worth. The Government or
WO served us rather a dirty trick in the matter of Medals. We enlisted
in London and took the shilling, but they didn't uniform us until
we were in the country, though we were practising rifle shooting on
the ship going out. However, being colonial troops we were signed
on again at Bloemfontein in January 1901 and they were mean enough
to count our service from January 9th when we landed, and not from
December 1900 when we enlisted, so they wouldn't give us the Kings
SA medal, so we got only the Queen's. Not that it matters, but it
was a bit of sharp practice.

And because we were colonial troops we didn't get the equipment
we ought to have had but they gave us the stuff that nobody else
would touch. The first draft of us got good cavalry cloaks, but those
who came out in the next draft had no overcoats, though it was
bitterly cold in the winter at night. Then they sent bales of ulsters

with capes, commandeered from a train for the Boers. We did look a funny mob, for a long time some of our troop had civvy caps, one had a black bowler. We, the first lot, got good stetson hats with a badge, which I have still, but what we got next would have made a cow laugh. Some crank had invented a hat which we called block-houses. They had an irregular brim, with a kind of perforated dome on that surmounted by a flat top, furnished with a broad chinstrap.

At the same time they dished us out with leggings with lace loops down the side. We all came on parade in this comical rig. The leggings were so big that they would have fitted elephants and the hats were simply a joke. One very big Irishman named MacMahon was so comical in vast leggings and an outsize hat that the whole troop roared with laughter on parade and the Skipper gave orders to take them all off. We cut the hats down to some sort of reasonable slouch shape and some who were clever turned the leggings into gun buckets. But that was consistent with the way we were equipped, until the WO woke up to the fact that we were really part of an army. In time we got decent saddlery and looked less like stagey cowboys.

The Free State is a wonderful country for horse and cattle breeding and very good for sheep also. In the spring it is green and lovely, lots of flowers on the kopjes, but for 9 months it was brown and dry, an unending expanse of plain, alternating with ranges of rock-covered hills and patches of scrub giving wonderful cover for Boer Commandos. There are few rivers; the Orange, the Modder and the Reit were very low for most of the year but when the rains came they became raging torrents as the water swept through the dongas, deep water cuts through the sandy soil. Once we had to cross the Modder in flood, driving a large herd of horses which had been collected from the country round. Our own horses were barely able to get through and many of the mares and foals got stuck in the mud and were not able to get out and had to be shot. But half swimming and floundering we all got through safely.

Water was often a difficulty, as in the dry part of the year the dams on the farms dried up and there were few springs. We had orders to boil our drinking water, but that good advice was useless as there was usually no time to stop and boil water until the day's march was over and we could get our dixies and make tea. Chloride of lime had not been discovered; if it had, it would have saved tens of thousands of lives. We were not supplied with filters and if we had them much of the water we had to drink wouldn't go through a filter. We had the ordinary service water bottle, and when possible we carried water in our horses' nose bags, if we were lucky enough to have one without holes, but you can imagine the dirt and slobber in the nosebags so it was not the best for drinking.

I remember one day on column seeing a few soldiers using a Berkefeld powerful filter with which one of them had got half a pint of dirty looking liquid. I said "Got a drink to spare?" "Give you a drink chum? It's took me 'alf an hour to get this for an officer." Sometimes when we halted I remember seeing groups of officers sitting round with syphons of soda water, but these things were not for the likes of us. In those days the private soldier had his bare ration and often he had to go on half rations, which meant 2½ biscuits and half a tin of bully. Canteens were things that belonged to the bases, and if we did by luck on our treks get to the railway and there was a canteen we had to pay 5/- for a tin of Nestlés milk and 5/- for a cake of chocolate.

But we mounted troops were much better off than the poor old foot slogger, for we did have the chance to pick up a sheep sometimes when we halted for the night. My squad leader, Wheatley, the Australian bushman, was the quickest man to kill, skin and cut up a sheep that ever I knew. It was of course strictly against orders, but lots of things were done that were not officially laid down in orders, and as we were irregular troops, we were not exposed to the nosy-parkers of Military Police. They belonged to the base those days, and didn't exist for us. We had to keep a good eye on our horses for there were some shocking horse thieves about. I lost my mare once when there was a concentration of troops but I kept my eyes open, at watering time, and a day or two after I saw her with her mane hogged, her tail cut and the numbers on her hooves filed out. But I knew her and took hold of her headrope. The fellow who had her said, "What are you doing?" I said, "It's my mare." He denied it, but she had a little trick. When you touched her chin, she squealed and kicked. I went up and touched her chin and she went through her usual protest and I took her off without further discussion. She was a good mare, very good over the veld in the dark and never let me down. Before I got her I had a good many, for the work was hard and horses didn't last. One poor little mare I rode for a bit, but she couldn't stand my weight and spreadeagled under me. I had another, an Argentine, who was for ever going into holes. We usually rode in line spaced out and often came across large colonies of holes made by a pretty little animal, called a meerkat. They used to pop up their heads and scold and chatter as we came near and then disappear into their holes. It was very difficult in the early morning or evening light to see these holes: country bred horses would dodge or jump the holes but this one had no sense and would go down on his head times without number. The skipper would turn round and in his quiet voice call out "Is the horse all right?" The unfortunate rider didn't count so much.

I was lucky when I got this mare. Her name was "Pretty Gal", and she was very ugly, but she had lots of sense and courage and I rode her right to the end and after the war was over. While I was in hospital with enteric, the troop was in action one day and she got a bullet right through her back behind the saddle. The skipper said she was to be shot, but the man told off to shoot her found that she wasn't vitally hurt and so he gave her another chance. She followed the troop back, or rather led it back to camp, and made as usual for the quartermaster's store and proceeded to gnaw the corner of a sack of oats. It was a habit of hers, that. If she could free herself from the horselines at night, and she was very clever at doing this, she would steal off and find the store and help herself and get a good deal more oats than she should. She often got cursed by the horse guard and so did I, but it served me well as she always kept fit and plump.

There was an amusing sequel to her rifle bullet wound. One day, long after the war was over, I was on patrol and stopped to speak to a Boer who was back on his farm. He admired my mare and I was just showing him the mark on her back which you could see, as the hair went white, when he came close and touched it with his finger. Back went her ears, and she gave a squeal and landing him in the chest good and proper, knocked him flying, but he was more surprised than hurt as we didn't then shoe on the hind feet as we used no roads, always travelling over the veld.

The animals I was sorry for were the poor patient trek oxen. They were spanned in couples on each side of the yoke which lay on their necks, and fastened under the throat with a twisted rein between two wooden skeys which ran through the yoke. The chain ran between each span of oxen fastened to the yokes in the centre and attached to the wagon. These great wooden wagons with huge wooden wheels were the only means of transport. They travelled about two miles an hour, and moved under escort from place to place to supply the troops who were mobile, and only came to the wagons when camps were arranged. Rations and blankets were carried with the troop in a GS wagon drawn by mules, but often we just carried our rations on our horses, going as light as possible, and sometimes didn't see our kit bags for a long spell. It was terrible going for the oxen in wet weather, especially when they had to cross a deep spruit or water way, usually down a deep decline when the wagons were braked with great block brakes which locked the back wheels and were wound on with a great iron handle. Then the crossing of the river through thick mud or sand and a dreadful pull up the other side. Sometimes they would take the whole span of oxen off the wagon that had gone over and hitch it on to the one to cross. It was cruel work for the oxen as they got so poor from overwork and insufficient food. An ox when he is done, will lie down and have to be thrashed up with that cruel whip, sometimes even lighting a fire under his belly to get him up. So, exhausted by overwork, they died in thousands and the last stage was the gathering of the vultures who appeared like specks in the sky, where a few minutes before there was nothing visible. They planed down, obscene and disgusting with their hideous bald heads and their great beaks and tore the ox to pieces almost before it was dead. The whole country was littered with the white bones of horses and oxen. But there was no other means of transport and it was a merciful day for the poor beasts, when after many years, petrol was discovered; but that was long after my time.

During our part of the war we had very little real fighting, only occasions of mainly long-range shooting. One rather exciting thing happened when some of us, with Doris the SM, were reconnoitring a farm and found ourselves under heavy fire from a range of hills. We took cover in a kraal which had low stone walls; the kraal was full of dead sheep and I shall not forget the stink as we returned fire behind the walls. As it looked as if we might be surrounded the SM told me to get back to Dawson the Captain to get orders. I had some little difficulty in getting the mare to leave cover, but when we got into the open she fairly flew. Johnny Boer did his best but we got to the kopje where I found Dawson and Major Pack Beresford who commanded our division. He was a wonderful soldier and I had a great admiration for him, though I hadn't often come into contact with him, but he was a fine leader and very good looking. When I reached them he told me to point out the place where we were and being flustered I couldn't at first see the kraal as it was hidden from the point of view and I got the wrong direction. However I found my mistake and pointed it out and he gave me the order to get back and tell the SM to retire. The old mare and I got a good deal of attention again from the Boers on the ridge but we got back to the kraal safe and sound. Then we made a bolt for it, well strung out and the horses went like the wind. Half way back, the black mare of a dear old Scotsman was hit in the body. There was no time to lose, so she was shot through the head and Webster jumped on the back of another man's horse and they got safely away. Poor old Webster was crying when they got back, for he was very fond of his mare, Biddy.

Next day when we were back again at our camp there was a parade, and Dawson complimented the troop and told me that if I hadn't been such a fool as to miss and muddle my direction I should have been recommended for the DCM. It would have been kinder to say nothing about it, and though I didn't care for myself, I know it would have been a tremendous joy to mother and Margaret. However I never did have much of a sense of direction. My father was like that too, whereas mother, and later Richard, my brother, like Elizabeth, all had photographic minds. Still it was disappointing for them though they knew nothing about it.

The last Christmas of the war we had to ride all night, mostly at a canter, to round up a party of Boers near the Vaal river. We found a laager of wagons with many women and children with their men folk gathered together for Christmas. At dawn we surrounded them. There was a good deal of indiscriminate shooting and we got 7 prisoners.

Nobody was hurt as it was very sudden. We had to get the women loaded up into the wagons with the children, and the women were very vicious and spat at us and called us everything they had. We got the oxen spanned in and delivered them to a convoy and its escort, and we needed a rest after sixty miles hard riding. There was no ration wagon to meet us so it looked like being a hungry Christmas Day. But we found some thin wild pigs and after running them down on our horses, we shot a couple and fried the meat on bits of iron we found about. I had in my wallet a 1lb. Christmas pudding which mother had sent me, so we had after all a very good Christmas dinner.

The nights on the high veld were very cold and we usually marched at night to make surprise attacks at dawn. In the winter months there was usually ice on the water and when we halted we were very glad to off-saddle and make some coffee. I used to carry a little kettle tied on to my saddle. I remember one day Doris the SM: "Ah, Mellish, I heard you coming with your trinkets rattling." The usual rations being McConachie, beef and vegetable ration and a pot of Ticklers inevitable plum and apple jam. The sergeants, we said, used to get all the strawberry. Sometimes we had a rum ration, but it was extremely well watered down before it left the Quartermaster's store. There was no issue of milk in those days: that didn't come in or any ration of butter until the 14/18 war. We never got bread on the veld but sometimes they issued flour and we made it into a sort of chupatee. One crafty sergeant who had been a regular and was finishing his time, used always to be complaining of his headaches and borrowing Eno's fruit salt, but we found that Eno was a very good substitute for baking powder, so we lost any sympathy we had for Sgt. Smith and his headaches.

Ours was a good troop. We took pride in our horses which were much better kept than those of other troops. Dawson and Doris were keen horse masters. Early in the first year I got jaundice, a disgusting disease, which makes you feel foul. We had no doctor or even medical corporal or medicines so we just had to stick these things. Riding day and night in pouring rain doesn't make you feel very fit with jaundice but I got over it.

Some of the men got frightful boils and poor old Villiers nearly died of them and we never saw him again. A friend of mine called

Hanlon got them terribly and when we halted for the night he used to search for an empty glass pickle jar and fill it with boiling water to draw his boils; it was agony, but he never gave in. Others got dysentery, and Dawson at the end of the war had it very badly and only existed on crumbs of biscuit and condensed milk until he became too ill to ride any more and was sent to hospital.

Towards the last year I got enteric. It wasn't good to be ill in those days. When I got too bad to ride I was sent down to Bloemfontein. Lying on straw on the floor of an ox-wagon, which has no springs, at the end of a convoy, in hot weather, breathing the stifling dust raised by a thousand hooves for three days and nights was not pleasant. I was indeed thankful at the end, to be able to have a bath and be put into a bed, the first I had slept in since leaving home.

But No.9 general hospital was crowded out with men like myself. I think my life was saved by a sister who gave me an ice pack when I was just at the end of things with a temperature of 105. I never knew her name but she was wonderful in a place where many of the nurses were bad and the orderlies worse. I had to leave this hospital because I was not a regular soldier and was transferred to what was called a convalescent hospital, but was really a disused leper hospital. I couldn't stand without help when I was moved and the food at this other place was terrible. I think I should have died of dysentery as they gave you fat lumps of meat floating in the dixie, and cocoa, which when it got cold had a thick coat of wax at the top. I believe that what saved me was some money sent to me by my squad leader, Wheatley, the Australian Bushman, who heard from someone I was there, and with the money I was able to buy some milk and biscuits.

When I could walk a bit, I asked to go back to my troop. I had been invited by my cousin Major Hicks to stay with him at Johannesburg where he was on the staff, but I was such a ragged looking creature, I couldn't see myself going into civilization, so I didn't go. I was glad to leave that horrible place but had to walk all the way, 60 miles, with the convoy and they wouldn't let you ride on the wagon. On my way back I met the Skipper and the SM and they hardly recognised me, as I was a bit of a skeleton.

But once back in the troop with my pals and clean food I got on. For some time I had to ask for a push up when I mounted my horse as my legs were not yet much good. But I was fortunate, for many thousands died at Bloemfontein, among them that splendid Major Pack Beresford whom I admired so much, though he did tell me that I had a devilish bad sense of direction, which was very true. But I got better by trying to make my mind into a map. So when the war was over and I had to patrol round that great open veld country with no roads, I got to learn the back and front views of the numerous kopjes and never lost my way again.

But we were never served out with compasses, the Government being very mean in those days in supplying anything more than a bare subsistence ration. And though we got 5/- a day and were much better off than Thomas Atkins with his 1/1 a day, we had no allowances and no luxuries.

Sometimes in our constant trekking about we came into areas which had escaped the damage of war. We had one pleasant glimpse of what a fruitful land the Free State could be with plenty of water, when we came down to the Reit River where there were many oxen left behind when the inhabitants had fled. The oxen were knee deep in luscious grass and because of the soft ground and abundance of water they had grown fantastic hooves all splayed and bent round so that they couldn't be driven and had to be slaughtered for food.

On another farm, well watered, we found enormous crops of fruit, peaches and figs of many sorts and so delicious that our mouths got quite sore from the little hairs on the figs we ate. But such treats were rare in a country which grew more desolate with every month of the war. Broken and destroyed homesteads, which of necessity had been burnt to the ground, left no home for the enemy or any store of food. It was a bitter war with no quarter given. If we approached any farmhouse without care, there might be a hail of bullets and the rapid retreat of a few Boers, whose horses had been under cover, then the usual return fire at the distant galloping figures and another home became a smouldering ruin. Then we rode on with chickens hanging from our saddles and perhaps a few eggs in our pockets for supper when we halted, or we cracked them on our saddle bows and ate them raw as we mounted.

When we took prisoners our captives were gaunt and ragged. Sometimes it was the other way round. The Boers could no longer send prisoners to Pretoria gaol as they had earlier on, so if they captured any of our men, they had little food to give them and they stripped them of their clothes and boots and turned them loose in their shirts to be picked up by any column that came along. I remember one man from another troop who came out in the same ship with me. He was not popular, as he put on a good deal of side. He became sergeant in another troop but the last time I saw him, he was a pathetic deflated figure looking very miserable and half naked; returned empty by Brother Boer.

But at last the war was over. The Boers could hold out no longer and after great losses on both sides, an armistice was arranged and at length peace was declared. Prisoners were released, those of our forces sent home and the Boers who had been deported to India, Ceylon or Bermuda came back, wiser for the things that they had seen in countries that then owed allegiance to the little island which was the heart of a world-wide Empire.

A new phase of work for us then began. Instead of destruction we were sent out to build up the foundation of a new fellowship. Instead of trying to kill our enemies, we became the messengers of a new partnership, which in time bore fruit by the wisdom and courage of two great statesmen, Jan Smuts and Louis Botha. The war was over and the regulars gladly went home but we stayed on at five bob a day and I think we earned it.

Somewhere in 1903, as I had saved a bit of money, I got three months' leave and I got a passage, 3rd class in the Union Castle "Norman", for fifteen guineas and got home for a month, which was good.

My father had aged quite a lot, mother always the same, wonderful. Margaret always an invalid but always bright and sweet. Richard at school at St Bees, Mary and Walter married and living in a tiny house on the hill leading up to Blackheath.

The leave went all too soon and I got back to find the troop settled in a little town in the Free State called Fauresmith and beginning to recover from the effects of the war. We had smartened up a lot, no longer a disreputable mob of ragged ruffians but doing patrol work round a large area, living in houses and making friends with the people.

I was sent out to a small, rather derelict village called Luckhoff with my squad, ten of us, under a corporal named Hanlon, a good chap with whom I was very friendly. The Australian, Wheatley, had been given his discharge as he had a row with the Troop Sgt. Major some time before. Wheatley had got hold of a beautiful bay mare which we rounded up with some other wild horses. She had a vile temper and one day at stables she bit Wheatley and he gave her a whacking which she well deserved, but Doris the TSM happened to be there and went for Wheatley and he, still very angry, gave him as good as he got with the result that Wheatley was discharged. I was sorry, for he had been a good friend, and I liked him, in spite of his temper, for he was straight and generous.

We were very happy in this village and patrolled round the country in pairs, usually going out for three days with a lead horse to carry corn for the horses and our own blankets and food. I had a near escape one evening. We had arrived at dusk at the place where we were going to sleep and I took my horse down to a dam to water, but when I came to dismount at the farm house my stirrup was stuck by mud to my boot and I lost my balance and fell. The horse, always a rather uncertain animal, though a good one, bolted off dragging me in the dark over the rocky ground. Fortunately the stirrup leather gave way and I was unhurt, but the horse went off into the dark and got hung up in a wire fence. However, he was caught after a while, and suffered no real harm and I was quite unhurt.

The account breaks off at this point, but various newspapers subsequently published a slightly different version of the events Mellish describes on page 26 under the following heading:

A Daring Deed in the South African War

Once a number of Baden-Powell's police were surrounded by Boers in a farmhouse and there was practically no chance for them. Mr Mellish was sent on what seemed a forlorn hope for assistance. He got safely through and delivered his despatches. But though his duty ended there he made his way back to his comrades in the besieged farmhouse to tell them that relief was on the way and to do what he could to help them to hold out.

There is one further chapter called by Mellish 'Christmas Reminiscences'. This includes memories of Christmas on the veldt, and in the trenches of France, and by a curious coincidence the two are connected by the near presence of Brigadier, formerly Captain S. Dawson of No.5 Troop SAC, now commanding a South African brigade. So here I am on this Christmas Day, like a cow, chewing the cud of my reflections. Christmas Day in war time to some seems the paradox of Truth and Reason. Yet we hold on for God is True. I remember a strange Christmas just fifty years ago. All through the night we moved, cantering and walking for sixty miles. The horses were nearly done. As the dawn began to break we reached our objectives, a Boer laager, the wagons drawn up in a ring, the oxen out-spanned and grazing. Suddenly rifle shots, men's shouts, and women's screams, as we rushed the wagons. We took a few prisoners, men who had come in off commando to join their wives and children. The women were furious; we had to search the wagons. It wasn't pleasant work, for naturally the women hated us and they clawed and spat in our faces. The oxen were spanned in, the prisoners taken off by another troop, and the long column of wagons lumbered off in a cloud of dust to the sound of the shouts of the drivers and the crack of their great whips.

But the sound that I remember most on that Christmas morning was the sad wailing of the Volkslied as the women were taken off to the camps while their simple farmhouses, won in many battles from wild beasts and not less savage men, not much more than half a century before, were burnt to the ground. We were soldiers and obeyed orders, but we were gentle with those women and courteous, for all their curses.

One is glad to remember that now. Hitler's way was not our way. Then we mounted our tired horses and rode off to find the wagons which were due to meet us with food. But something had gone wrong and they hadn't come. But we found water, off-saddled and turned the horses out to graze. Then we pooled our assets. The total wasn't great, some bits of biscuit and a 1lb Christmas pudding which we divided between the squad, one pound between ten men. But our luck was in. Someone went scouting round and came in with the welcome news that there were some pigs not far away. Horses were caught and there was a wonderful exhibition of pig-sticking with bayonets. The pigs were long, lean, half wild things and they made good hunting. And they made a good Christmas dinner.

My squad leader was an Australian Bushman. He could kill and skin and cut up an animal while most men were looking at it. That pig was good, we fried it on bits of iron and washed it down with coffee. I had a little kettle that hung always on my saddle. Our Troop sergeant-major, Doris, an ex-Royal Canadian "Mountie" used to laugh at it; he said he could always hear me by the rattle of my "trinkets". Doris was a brave man, an expert horseman, with a fiery but controlled temper. He was a good and just sergeant-major without favourites and without fear. Not long after the end of the war, he met his death by accident. He was taking a short cut back to camp at night over the base of a kopje strewn with the usual lumps of iron stone. His mare must have stumbled and fallen. He was found lying there dead, but the mare never left him, she was standing there on guard.

It was a good Troop, No.5. Our CO had been a subaltern in a famous Infantry Regiment. He was tall, thin and fair with a soft and gentle voice. He was a fine leader, he knew the country and made no mistakes. The troop would follow him anywhere. He suffered badly from dysentery, but he wouldn't leave the troop. For weeks he lived on nothing but scraps of army biscuit and tinned milk.

MOs were very scarce in those days. You had to be nearly dying before you saw one and then there wasn't much he could do. No one had yet discovered chloride of lime. We filled our dixies from half dry dams or rivers in which thousands of thirsty oxen and horses had been watered, or what was worse, had stuck in the mud, too weak to get out, and died. For those rivers, sometimes attenuated trickles, became at certain periods roaring torrents, sweeping down things that are not good to drink. Not much wonder then that though the Mauser slew his thousands, enteric and dysentery killed their tens of thousands.

But some of us survived. Long years after, we shared a ruined village named Longueval with some Germans from whom we were separated by a few strands of rusty barbed wire. In a shattered wood to the right was all that remained of a South African Brigade which had fought almost to extinction under the command of Brigadier Stewart Dawson, once of the 5th Fusiliers and No.5 Troop, SAC.

This seems to have led me away from Christmas, but not really very far in thought, for many strange Christmases belonged to war time. In the Ypres Salient, without orders from command on either side, the Truce of Christmas came in 1914.

No-man's land, there, only twenty yards wide, became the scene of great activity. Corporal Max and his men, in broken English, shouted across the messages of good will, souvenirs of cigarettes and badges were exchanged, photographs were shown and to complete the scene, in the opposite line a little Christmas tree was set up on which were lighted candles; while round the tree danced Corporal Max and his merry men and sang carols. All very unofficial, of course, but all spontaneous, for it was the true spirit of Christmas and was not to be denied.

Chapter Three

London University and Ordination

HOW LONG MELLISH worked on the new railway after leaving the army we do not know, but for most of the next seven years he held a responsible post as supervisor in the De Beers Diamond Mines at Jagersfontein in the Orange Free State.

The same newspaper quoted earlier subsequently wrote:

> There was no man more esteemed and honoured all over the mine. During the years he was in Jagersfontein he assisted in the church and native mission, reading the lessons at the mission in the somewhat fearsome language understood by the natives. Despite long and arduous days in the mine, he made light of sitting up all night by the bedside of a sick friend, and his life generally was such as to justify the remark of one of its inhabitants that 'It is men such as Mr Mellish who restore one's faith in mankind'.

Another report stated that he studied hard at nights to learn both Afrikaans and the native language so that he could communicate with the people he was working with. This was essential as he became ever more involved with work in the church and local mission.

Mellish had been brought up with a sound religious education and a firm faith which stood him in good stead through the hard years of the Boer War. Despite this, however, his first impressions of the type of missionaries he met in South Africa were anything but favourable, and he had no sympathy with the hellfire and brimstone militant Christianity which was commonly preached.

But now, settled into the mining community at Jagersfontein, he found himself increasingly interested in caring for the people, both black and white, with whom he came in contact. During the war he had already shown qualities of natural leadership and now he found that his advice and help was ever more eagerly sought. The priest at the local mission encouraged him in this pastoral work and on his recommendation Mellish was formally licensed as a lay reader by the Bishop of Bloemfontein in March 1907.

At some time during these busy years at the mine Mellish was involved in an accident in the heavy crushing plant which left him with a distorted and flattened index finger for life, and must have been incredibly painful. Helped by the mission priest with whom he now worked closely, Mellish gradually came to recognise that he himself was being called to the priesthood. He must have considered this very seriously for some long time, but finally in 1907 he returned on leave and went to discuss his future with the then Vicar of Lewisham where his mother lived, Canon R. P. Roseveare. Roseveare actively encouraged him to follow the call, but, not to make it too easy, he lent him a number of books and worked out for him a course of reading. He then told Mellish to go back to his work in South Africa and if he still felt the same way to return in two years' time for formal training for ordination.

It could not have been easy for a man aged 28 to settle down to learning again after ten years of independence as a soldier and mine supervisor. Apart from this he worked for fourteen hours a day at the mine and in caring for people in the area, before he could get on with his own studies at night. But he settled down and crammed into his spare time the reading for a year's full-time course at home. In August 1909 Mellish passed the Central Entrance Examination with grade As in seven subjects out of eight and a B in that one.

One of the examiners, Rev. C. B. Drake of Wisbech, wrote to Canon Roseveare on August 1909:

> I only wish we had a few more candidates like your friend Mellish. Euclid was his weakest subject, but that was respectable compared with much with which we have to be satisfied. We passed him without difficulty: it was not a matter of mercy, but of justice. I am much interested in all that you tell me about him. As to CEE in general, out of 133 candidates in July, only 53 passed.

With the entrance exam behind him and with the way ahead

becoming clear, Mellish resigned his job at the mine and left South Africa in 1910. He must have wished many times in the years ahead to return there even for a visit, as he loved the country and got on well with both whites and Africans, but sadly the opportunity never arose. However, he had no doubts about the future when he enrolled at King's College, London University, in the autumn of 1910.

Canon Roseveare had written on 4 February 1910:

Dear Noel,

For many weeks this has been due: I don't think I have written since you sent word of your exam success. Everything in your life is quite familiar to me from your letters to me and some forwarded by your good mother – and I am deeply interested and was particularly mindful of you and your surroundings on Wednesday last when we interceded definitely for God's guidance for you, also for Winifred Cooper, sister of one of our workers at Theba Nebu.

But absolutely no time have I now for writing anything more than this, which is of the nature of business – supposing you begin at Kings next September and do two years there, you will be ready for a title (God willing) in September 1912 – my Deacon Hambidge is to be here until Xmas 1912 (possibly longer) and Johnson until Lady Day 1912 – if all goes in something like the way one expects it to now, I will gladly offer you a title for September 1912 – and £120 a year during your diaconate, to rise to £150 when you take Priests Orders. I shall require you to live in the parish of St Paul, and of course work will be very heavy. I put this to you not that I want you to be in a hurry about pledging yourself – but that you may have some definite scheme before you. I know your mother would wish you to live at home – but I am afraid I do not think this is possible for work in St Paul's, unless "home" moved to Deptford. By that time I hope to be living in my parish myself – and certainly all my curates must continue to live there.

While you are studying at Kings and living at Lewisham Hill, I should be glad to give you insight into parish work, but on no account ought you to take up any responsibility – your mind must be quite free for your studies.

It would be a tremendous satisfaction to have you: you know that difficulties abound: but you cannot know yet, though I do, how much more joys abound.

Forgive this brevity – confirmation classes, poor relief, plus the ordinary work of a parish, are a heavy weight just now. My own mother and sister must have letters posted today, and my children are wondering if daddy is still alive.

God bless you –

I was so very glad your Xmas birthday was made so happy, and that Pratt and everyone so approve your move.

I am afraid 8 Lew-Hill has had more than its share of sickness lately; but I have no immediate news – you will receive it by this mail from Mrs Mellish I doubt not.

Yours ever
R. P. Roseveare.

For the next two years Mellish worked very hard, living at home with his mother and his father, who was by now a permanent invalid and doubtless very difficult. Probably he never really forgave Noel for failing to follow in his business and was little interested in his experiences in South Africa or his ambitions for the future.

In these two years Mellish also spent as much time as possible in the parish helping and learning from Canon Roseveare. He was an officer in the Boys' Brigade, led hop-picking parties to Kent for summer holidays and joined in every church activity, so that the people of Deptford and Lewisham were his friends and people even before he was ordained. But there was no let-up in his studies and when the final results were published in the autumn of 1912, Mellish was one of only six first-class passes out of forty-one who became Associates of King's College, the equivalent of a first-class honours degree at other universities.

In June 1912, Mellish came down from King's College, London, and after a brief holiday he was ordained deacon in Southwark Cathedral on 29 September of that year. He immediately took up his appointment as curate in the parish of St Paul's, Deptford under Canon Roseveare, who combined this with his parish of Lewisham. A year later Mellish became a priest at Advent 1913. Now he was able to devote himself and all his boundless energy full time to the parish and people he loved.

In those years from 1912 to 1915 he set the pattern he was to follow throughout his ministry for the next forty-eight years. There is no written record of the early years at St Paul's, but plenty of hearsay and subsequent events make it easy to build a picture of his life there. This consisted of services on Sundays and six days a week of visiting, until there was not a house or a corner of his parish where he was not known and loved or respected. In those days there was much poverty in South London and life was very hard for many of his parishioners. Mellish's time was fully occupied in comforting the sick, encouraging the able, at times dealing severely with drunks and bullies, and always visiting and caring for his people. The greatest satisfaction of those years came from his association with the Church Lads Brigade, of which he was Captain. Every available evening was spent with the boys, drilling, teaching, helping, and when an old pub became available he took it over and set up a club there for the boys. It was the boys themselves who insisted on naming it the Noel Club in honour of their Captain, and in the next few years no fewer than forty of them joined the armed forces. For relaxation Mellish still went with his own people hop-picking in Kent and shared with them the hard work and the evening sing-songs. He loved these holidays and often referred to them afterwards and could hold his own in any concert of cockney singing.

The *Kentish Mercury* wrote of these years in an article dated 28 April 1916:

> Popular is much too cheap a word to use of him, beloved and admired as he is by all who knew him. The patients at the Miller

General Hospital, Greenwich Road, and the nurses there knew his tenderness with the suffering, the poor, the sad. The tempted knew his real friendship for them; if a man is cruel to his wife, or a mother culpably negligent of her child, or if boys shirk duty and do not 'play the game', they know the sternness of a strong character. His colleagues at St Pauls, his fellow officers in the Church Lads Brigade, and all who have served with him in the activities of life know that one of his fellow Army officers speaks a simple truth 'There is only one man whom he never spares, that is himself'.

It would be unfair to the Faith which Mr Mellish confesses with absolute steadfastness and childlike sincerity not to add that he lives the true life of a Christian Churchman and draws power from the living Christ and the Sacraments of His Church. One who had good reason to know spoke of him once as the man of his experience who lived most sincerely the life in Christ.

When war was declared in 1914, Mellish immediately volunteered to join up, not as an officer, but as a soldier-priest in the ranks, after the fashion of the French priests. To this end he searched for and bought the lightest possible vestments and the smallest possible Communion set so that he could readily carry them in his pack with his other equipment, and be instantly ready to minister to his fellow soldiers. But his Bishop had other ideas and would not release him from his curacy as he felt he had an important job to do at home. So Mellish swallowed his disappointment and carried on with his work at St Paul's.

At Easter 1915 the Bishop of London came back from a visit to the front and spoke of the need for more chaplains in France. Mellish at once volunteered again and this time he was accepted readily, and received an official commission as Chaplain to the Forces, 4th class, with the honorary rank of Captain, as from 12 May 1915. Without waiting for the formal commission however, he was off to France on 5 May.

It can only be guesswork on the part of his family but it seems likely that the account was written a few years after the war while the memory was still very fresh but disillusion had set in at home and England was no longer the land fit for heroes to live in. The victorious armies of wartime were disbanded and soldiers were no longer heroes but very often pathetic beggars or match-sellers, forgotten and ignored by the country they had served and saved.

This is the story of one man's war, but far more than that, it is a song of admiration for the British soldier and Mellish's defence of the men he knew so well and now believed to be poorly appreciated. If it was to serve its purpose, however, the book would have to be offered for publication. That would inevitably mean publicity for his own particular part in the war and his exploits at St Eloi, and so we believe that quite typically Mellish decided to say nothing rather than draw attention to himself, and locked the story away. Fortunately it survived and can now be published. Quite apart from the historical interest, it contains delightful flashes of humour, the serious reflections of a dedicated priest, and descriptions of the country seen with the eye of an artist, but most of all it contains constant and repeated tributes to the British soldier and in particular to his friends of all ranks with whom he lived and marched and fought through four long years of war. These years of danger and hardship formed lasting bonds of friendship and admiration which Mellish wanted to put into words.

The dedication at the end of his account suggests a title which we believe Noel Mellish might have chosen had he decided to publish his story – A Gallant Comradeship. In order to fill in more detail the straightforward account is interspersed with extracts from letters written at the time, from the trenches or in odd rest periods. In the early days these are mainly from his regular monthly newsletter to the St Paul's parish magazine, and there are extracts from newspaper reports where appropriate. From early in 1918 the letters home become more frequent and give a fuller account of his daily life.

Chapter Four

Ypres Salient

MY EXPERIENCE OF THE WAR started in May 1915 and it ended in Germany in February 1919, yet, though many years have passed, I feel that those years were the most real of my whole life and even today, I should hardly feel it strange if I were to get off the train at Poperinghe or Arras, find my way back to the Battalion and a place waiting for me and friends giving me a welcome back from leave.

Those long gone years do not seem a nightmare, for with all that was horrid and fearful there was much that was wonderful and many that were loveable, and as their needs then called me back to them from home, so they call now.

If, then, there are any who read these pages, let them know that I write because it seems to me a duty to tell what I know of the splendour of those men with whom I lived. I have no skill to tell it, but this I know, that the men of whom I write are real. The years between have not changed them in my mind. They cannot change, for their characters were moulded of such stuff as death cannot change, nor time alter.

There are many who still live, fortunately for the Nation, and though their names are here written, they will forgive if anything perhaps offends their modesty.

I started at an Infantry base depot at Rouen. The Commandant of the Camp where I lived was an old Colonel and a more incompetent officer to have charge of such a Camp it would have been hard to find. His chief idea in life seemed to be to give entertainment to travelling theatrical parties who came to provide edification for the troops at the base. The Colonel's entertainment, which of course included champagne and liqueurs, was paid for by the Officers' Mess. The unfortunate subalterns, who passed through in great numbers at this time – for the average infantry officer's life in the line was calculated to be about fifteen days – paid for it largely by heavy mess subscriptions. In the ordinary way, the messing was done by a French contractor, who looked like Mephistopheles and charged us 7 francs a day for using our rations, or as much as he allowed us, with artichokes (which I hate) thrown in on every possible occasion.

The Company Sergeant-Major was an old soldier of the Devons, perfectly inefficient and usually the worse for drink. The men who returned from hospital after wounds were in charge of a huge ranker Lieutenant with the voice of a bull of Bashan and the ideas of a Victorian drill manual. The men were completely fed up and very often almost on the point of mutiny. The redeeming feature of the Camp was the adjutant, a regular soldier who had been wounded or crippled by an accident and was forbidden further active service. His mind was keenly sensitive to the unfairness of much of the treatment to which the men were subjected and he was sickened by the mismanagement of the man in command.

Night after night drafts would fall in for the station, and young subalterns, often only boys from school, would have to take them down the 3 miles through the town. The streets were lined with estaminets and more often than not men would fall out from the drafts to have a last drink and never arrive at the station at all, miss the draft and be for punishment when found. I found it was desirable to go down with the drafts and help men out of the estaminets and shepherd them to the train and at least save them from the women and men who fattened on the British soldier and robbed him of his money, health and honour.

The rationing of these drafts was very bad. Great 7lb. tins of meat were issued at the camp and it was hardly likely that men loaded up as they were would carry this extra weight, so most of the meat was given away to French gamins who cried incessantly "Souvenir, souvenir". The men in the drafts really depended for food on the ladies, who, at all hours of the night, kept open a buffet at Rouen station, to supply them with that last meal which seemed to have any relation to home and civilization, and to give them their last sound of the voice of the women of their own land. So through the night lumbered the train, the men lying in all attitudes of discomfort in horse boxes on dirty straw until they detrained for their destination.

Usually I got back to Camp at 1 a.m. after seeing the train off, sometimes catching a tram part of the way. Later I got a bicycle through the stores, but this help did not last very long, for one night as I was going down with the draft I found the bicycle an inconvenience to push, and as it needed a fairly watchful eye to keep men from dropping out, I asked a passing corporal to take my bicycle down with him and leave it at the station. I never saw that bicycle again; perhaps he sold it for a few francs to a Frenchman – at any rate I had to pay for it.

We chaplains at the base had as our leader an experienced chaplain who had been in the army before and was one of the regulars who knew his men and his work. It was a privilege to have one's first few months of preparation under such a man and when we left we went with a real gratitude to him for his leadership. There were many opportunities a chaplain had in a base camp of establishing points of contact with the men. Passing through the camp one day, I came face to face with a man whom I had not seen since the end of the Boer War. He was just down from Ypres, a private in the DCLI, aged and worn. In the years before, we had been troopers together in the same force. It was good to see him again.

One night I was standing in a tent talking to the men as they lay wrapped in their blankets and in the general conversation none of us heard "Lights Out" sounded. Suddenly a harsh voice rapped out: "What's all this noise about? Put the light out! What'yer doin'?" and I felt the cane of the Orderly Corporal come down with no little emphasis on that part of my anatomy which was most exposed as I bent down with my head through the flap. When I jumped up and pulled my head out, the Corporal's jaw fell in astonishment when he saw my collar and a roar of laughter came from the occupants of the tent as I rubbed myself to remove the effects of his disciplinary action.

The canteen was not as it is today in the modern army, but a place of beer swilling only, and I found in it small chance of use. The YMCA huts in that camp were mainly run by men who quite clearly had a bias against the Church of England and regarded me as poaching on their preserves. The Church Army hut contained the chapel and a quiet room for reading and writing and was useful, though not fully used, for the YMCA huts provided entertainments and were better staffed. I found the chapel of great value and many of the officers and men who passed through received their Communion there. I was also fortunate in getting to know a good number of the men and of the Notts & Derby Territorial Battalion and found them keen and thoroughly in earnest in preparing for Confirmation. Later they went up and were for the most part killed at Loos.

Usually on fine Sundays we had our service in the forest. It was like a glorious cathedral, the great pillars of the trees supporting a roof of green leaves and I with many others felt the reality of our worship in this natural glory. One splendid day the Adjutant allowed some of us to go off for the day, taking our rations with us and we spent it by the river like children at a picnic.

One day a YMCA worker and I were going for a walk through the forest, when we came upon an out of the way cottage, from the roof of which an obvious aerial was suspended. We reported it and the sequel was amusing. Next day the APM arrived, a young officer dressed to a nicety, a pattern of the military tailor's art. I acted as guide and brought him to the place. When he came in view of the cottage, he produced a revolver and, in a stage whisper, bade me keep still and with a few men, rushed the place. The greatness of his position forbade him giving me any information. The only amusement I had was in the extreme disarrangement of the gentleman's immaculate toilet, as I had led him through high and prickly undergrowth, which crumpled his collar and spoilt the mirror-like surface of his leggings. I heard no more, but I daresay he was mentioned in despatches for gallantry in action.

Letter to St Paul's, Deptford – 16 July 1915

Dear People at home,

Nearly three months have gone since you sent me out here, and I need not say that I am very happy. I have had many letters, messages, papers, and magazines which I haven't thanked you for. Let me do

so now. I always look forward to the parish news in the Magazine; it is like a letter from home.

I am trying to do the work of a parish priest here. My parish contains no houses of bricks and mortar, and there are no block buildings or flats in it. The public-houses close at half-past eight and there are no fried-fish shops here. There are no babies playing on the doorsteps, and you can't get winkles even on Sundays, so you see it isn't much like Deptford.

My parish is a large camp. Bordering the road which runs right through it are rows of long wooden huts, roofed with iron. Some of them are offices, others are dining huts, drying rooms, washhouses, or storerooms. In front of many of them are little gardens bright with flowers. Behind the huts are lines of tents where the soldiers live. At the head of the lines are the badges and crests of each regiment, cunningly worked in all kinds of material, such as broken glass, brick, coal and chalk. Many of these crests are very elaborate and the amount of skill and work bestowed on them is amazing. Tommy is an artist of no mean order, and he loves beautiful surroundings. On the other side of the road is the parade and recreation ground, the admiration of every other camp. Football is off now, but cricket is in full swing, and we have many excellent players. Soldiers play as they fight, with all their might, and we have keen matches with other departments and hospitals.

At each end of the camp is a hut provided by the YMCA and staffed by capable men and energetic ladies who by their zeal and sympathy are doing very much to help and brighten the lives of our men. The managers of both these huts have invited me to come in whenever I wish and our relations are very friendly. The YMCA is an undenominational organisation, but the church is represented in both huts and the evening prayers and Sunday services held in them are a real "uplift" to the men who throng them every day.

Midway between the two divisions stands the Church Army hut, definitely standing for the church. Here each morning the Holy Eucharist is offered at 7 o'clock and you and we are knit together in one communion and fellowship. At one end stands the altar, consecrated by the Bishop of London. The ornaments and frontal were given by friends of the Chaplain who was here before me. The hut is furnished with tables and forms where the men play games, write letters to you, or read the magazines you send them. We have a piano which is serving its country well; a notice on it pleads with the intending performer, "Don't hit me hard, I'm really quite tame".

At the other end of the hut is a bar where one can purchase anything from a boiled egg to a boot-lace. My room is at the end of this hut and here I expect to remain for some time.

I had a great surprise last night. I went into one of the YMCA huts just as they were going to have prayers and we sang our dear old "hopping" hymn, "God be with you till we meet again" and when prayers were over I found that I was standing next to five Deptford men, one of whom comes from Crossfield Street, another from Baildon Street, another from Albury Street, and another from Evelyn Street. It was so good to meet them and they all look so fit and happy; I am sure they are a credit to the "Buffs". I have also met other Deptford men in the Middlesex Regiment and the West Kents. Dear old Deptford! Roll on the time when the war is over and the righteous peace that we pray for shall be granted us.

Now the Editor's face appears before me forbidding me to add another word, so I will obey orders.

Always yours affectionately,
Noel Mellish, C. F.

Letter to St Paul's, Deptford – 19 August 1915

Dear People at home,

Since writing last month I have had many letters, papers and cards to thank you for. I expect you will like to know something of our surroundings and of the people here.

Rouen is a city full of history. Everywhere one is reminded of Jeanne d'Arc, the maiden champion of freedom and liberty who gave her life for her country in Rouen market square. In the cathedral there is a chapel dedicated to her. On the morning after my arrival I went into the cathedral while mass was being said and found this chapel filled with worshippers praying for the safety of their dear ones in France's long battle line.

There are many stately churches in the town, rich in beautiful glass and the carved ornaments of past centuries, but much of the fine work which adorns the churches was damaged in the dark days when France first disowned her religion. We hope that in happier days to come, when the sacrilegious invader has been beaten to his knees, a new-born France will once again restore the Church to her place of honour as the mother of nation and State. There are many signs which lead one to think that it will be so. One such sign was a procession which took place not very long ago.

Last August when the Germans were rushing forward to Paris and an advance party of Uhlans had even reached the hills not more than twenty miles east of Rouen, the archbishop made a vow that if God in His mercy would spare the city from the horrors of siege and invasion he, with clergy and people, would go in solemn pilgrimage every year for twenty years to the chapel dedicated to our Lady of Good Help, and make an act of prayer and thanksgiving, and would raise a fitting memorial to Jeanne the warrior-maiden. As we know God answered by a wonderful deliverance; the invading army was driven back by our splendid men and their French brothers and Paris was saved. In fulfilment of the vow, a procession composed of military and state officials and thousands of people marched to the high hill on which stands the beautiful chapel of Notre Dame de Bon Secours, and there made a great act of witness, thanksgiving and prayer.

The streets of Rouen are more full of colour than our own; everywhere you meet French soldiers in their smart new sky-blue uniforms which look so conspicuous in town, but harmonise and blend well with natural surroundings. Here comes an Algerian in his scarlet fez, short yellow tunic, and wide baggy breeches. Groups of older soldiers stand about chatting, wearing the familiar dark blue tunic and red trousers of the infantry.

Many women in black give quiet evidence of the toll France is paying in the struggle for existence. A couple of nurses dressed in grey with scarlet capes are going into a shop; a group of young officers can be seen in that café – they are having their last comfortable meal before starting for the trenches tonight. A small boy has marked you down and runs up to ask you to buy a "Deely Meel to-dees". Huge grey motor lorries laden with army supplies rumble past, familiar ASC wagons drawn by great English horses, rattle over the cobbles and you wonder whether those were the horses that used to clatter up and down Evelyn Street a few months ago.

Trams run through the city and the suburbs; those later in the evening will swarm with soldiers returning to camp on pass, crowding every available inch in a fashion that would drive an LCC inspector into hysterics.

There is much variety of sound: the rude, peremptory screech of the impatient motor, the incessant clang of the tram gong, or the jingling of bells attached to the gaily painted collars of huge grey Norman horses that draw the ponderous two-wheeled farm wagons or long narrow carts loaded with barrels of wine.

Another sound causes the bystander to turn round. It is the marching song of English soldiers. Here they come, drafts of different regiments for the front, a compact body of hard, bronzed, fighting men. Each man carries a heavy load – pack, ammunition, entrenching tool, and rifle. His ration-bag is tied at the back and swings backwards and forwards with his stride. His hat is pushed back on his head, he is sweating under the heavy load and a three mile march from camp but he cheers the French people who shout farewell on the pavement. He turns to wave to the white-capped old granny who says goodbye at the window. Little children run alongside reaching out eager hands for souvenir or "bisket" and what is the song he sings? Its constantly repeated refrain is "We are not down-hearted yet".

After twelve months of frost and cold, heat and rain; after wounds and sickness, bullets and shrapnel; after having been stunned and shaken, even buried alive by high explosive shells, after poison gas and liquid fire, they are not down-hearted yet.

Oh we are proud of our soldier men – generous, kindhearted, unselfish and brave, giving themselves so readily with such unsparing sacrifice for home and freedom. Pray for them, that they may be helped to go on and that their lives may be noble and pure.

> I mustn't write any more.
> I am always yours affectionately,
> Noel Mellish, C. F.

In September came orders for me to go up the line. I reported at HQ at St Omer with instructions to go to the 27th Division which pleased me very much as there were many officers and men in that Division whom I had met in the previous months. However, the Bishop's staff chaplain had other designs for me and to my disappointment I found myself en route for the 3rd Division, to report to the 1st Northumberland Fusiliers. I got to a dreary looking detail camp at Ouderdom and found the Quartermaster in his tent and reported my arrival. Quite obviously he didn't want me. The battalion was up the

line, they had never had a padre, there was no room, they were short
of tents and my place was at the Field Ambulance. However, I pointed
out that my orders were to go to the Northumberland Fusiliers, so
I was allotted a tent until the CO should decide what was to be done
with me.

Next day the Battalion came out and after giving the CO time to
wash and refresh I reported. He was at one with the QM that there
was no place for me. The colonel was haggard and worn, and such
officers and men as I saw seemed to be tired out and certainly had
no interest in me, which was not to be wondered at. So I was packed
off to the Field Ambulance. I found myself in an environment which
had no welcome for me. The officers were friendly but detached.
They had already a very popular Roman Catholic padre there and
they clearly did not want me. The CO was a rigid kind of man,
quiet in manner, having no kind of use for padres as such, but treating
me with a distant tolerance, which was cooling to enthusiasm. However, I made the best of things and found the men, a good number
of whom were Church of England, friendly and kind. I now became
acquainted with the other padre of the brigade. My predecessor having
gone sick, I was part of the establishment of the 9th Brigade, which
contained four regular battalions and one territorial, the 142nd Field
Ambulance and the 56th Field Company RE. Curiously my fellow
padre seemed to resent my being sent to this brigade and allocated
to me a very small part of it, namely the Church of England members
of the Scots Fusiliers, numbering perhaps 100, and the men of the
Field Ambulance. So I was not exactly cheered by my first introduction
as a padre to the Army at the front. The best thing seemed to be
to get to know people and find my surroundings, but the Field
Ambulance and detail camp were not at first wide enough ground
for my ministry.

However, soon things began to brighten up. A servant and a horse
had been arranged for the padre whose place I took and I found the
finest mate a man could ever have in Pte. Robins, of the Worcester
Regiment, who had been sent back from hospital with a steel plate
over his wounded ankle and recommended for a soft job, such as an
officer's servant might provide. He wore the ribbon of the DCM,
won in the famous charge of the 3rd Worcesters at Gheluvelt. He

was a heavy-weight regimental boxer, had a great fund of humour and a clean, wholesome mind and body. Jim was a cavalry charger with the scar of a wound on his near fore leg, a bright chestnut with good manners. One day I found that there was an advance dressing station of the Field Ambulance, located in a dug-out on the road from Ypres to Vierstraat. This discovery seemed to open up possibilities and the CO gave me leave to draw my rations from the advanced post, so Robins, Jim and I took up our residence in part of a house with a good roof over our heads. The cooking range consisted of a farm-yard fork without a handle and we possessed a few plates and cups from neighbouring rubbish heaps, a teapot from Ypres and a tub for a bath. There was also a chair in a state of senile decay. Here we lived very happily, Robins and I. There was a cellar, but we preferred shells to the cellar, as it smelt like sudden death; I never knew what was in it – we kept it closed and hoped for the best. Perhaps our choice of residence was not altogether what could be called a desirable villa, but there was little else to choose. Our next door neighbours were a couple of our own 60 pounder guns – I did not know what a noise they made or what a flash when fired, but we had to live somewhere, so tried to be useful where we were. Jim the horse was quite happy in the kitchen next door, which had a door and a sink from which he had his meals.

This position was convenient, for I used to go on a round of visits to dug-outs round Zillebeke Lake, not the palatial dug-outs of later days, but shelters which might keep out a coconut if not thrown too hard. One day, finding that many voices hailed me in familiar accents I discovered that they belonged to the Royal Fusiliers and the 4th Middlesex, so we had liaison at once and some of them came from Deptford.

What a marvellously cheery person the infantryman was. He went up the line slipping through slime, falling into holes, loaded up with pack, over-coat and gas bag, 2 bandoliers, 200 rounds of ammunition, haversack, clothes, rations and water and very often a bundle of firewood or a bag of coke, a few funny home-made looking bombs or rifle grenades and often the whole lot surmounted by a huge round Belgian loaf. The gas mask of those days was a bag made of flannel, steeped in some chemical, provided with windows and a rubber mouthpiece, and the ends of the bag tucked inside the collar. This was a great advance on the earlier protection, which was a piece of gauze furnished with tapes, which was later replaced by a black gauze veil, with a chemically treated pad inside. It was a marvel indeed that these men, dressed like a jumble sale, were able in those conditions to carry their loads, but they had to carry it all, otherwise they had nothing, for no one knew how long they were going to be "up" at a time, nor where they were going next.

We soon discovered that we were on the highway for those men of the Brigade who passed down, after having been relieved from the trenches at Hooge or Sanctuary Wood. Every night parties of tired men used to drop in for a rest and lie on the floor while Robins and I made tea for them, for we "scrounged" all we could of milk, sugar and tea from our Field Ambulance friends and collected a Woolworth-looking assortment of china. And when our visitors went on their way they left behind any dry sugar and tea they happened to have, to carry on the work with.

Then the comparative quiet changed into preparation for the great offensive at Loos. No advance was planned in the Salient, but a demonstration was ordered to keep the German troops in their place round Ypres. Zero hour 4 a.m. and the Gordons went over, to the accompaniment of a tremendous gun fire – or so it seemed then, though it was nothing to what our artillery put up later. Then the wounded began to come down, excited, laughing Gordons, with pickelhaubers and field glasses slung round their necks, glad to be out of it with an easy "blighty" wound. Afterwards came rain and it was a hard matter to get the more seriously wounded down the track to Kruisstraat on wheeled stretchers.

I found a man wounded in the leg and, as the track was being shelled I took him over to the Lille Gate, where there was another aid post, and coming back, had my first painful experience of shell fire. My direct way back lay past some guns and apparently they were attracting some attention from the Hun batteries and I got there just at the wrong time; finding nothing better to do I lay still, while the ground seemed to shake all 'round me with the force of the explosions. One feels so infinitely small and lonely when one is under shell fire by oneself; however, the "strafe" cleared off and I found my way back again.

A day or two after this the Division went out for the first rest it had had for many months and we found ourselves at Godwaersvelde, a Belgian village some miles back from the line, in pleasant surroundings. I was billeted with a very old man and woman, who had a mentally defective daughter. I had a comfortable room with another leading from it, which Robins appropriated for himself. He also succeeded in persuading the old man, after a good deal of remonstrance, to stack up his potatoes and other belongings, and fix up a comfortable sleeping place for Jim. The old lady and her daughter were very devout, but the old man was an unpleasant person and quite clearly resented our presence, but we soon moved to Winninzeele where we were made comfortable. Robins was a good interpreter, for in a language which was a mixture of English, French and a little Hindustani thrown in, he always managed to smooth troubled waters and we were very happy, and the mothers and daughters wept when Robins departed.

On the first Sunday, after service with the Royal Fusiliers, I was invited by the CO to join the Battalion and take up my residence with the HQ Mess ... and I had a home at last.

This was a great joy to me and I attributed it to the impromptu tea parties on the Kruisstraat Road and to certain efforts at persuading unappropriated motor buses to carry down tired parties of men to the detail camp. Whether the buses were really for them did not much matter, at any rate we got them, for "scrounging" was a fine art – and the Boer War was not forgotten in this.

Letter to St Paul's, December 1915

I have felt the loving sympathy of St Paul's folk, and have had many kind letters and tokens of affection. I am attached to the 142nd Field Ambulance, the headquarters of which is near a town about ten miles from the firing line.

My work lies with these men and with the staff of the Ambulance, the majority of whom are of our communion. I have at present a promising class of keen ambulance men who are preparing for confirmation. The men are all of the new army, and are a most useful lot as nearly every trade and profession imaginable is represented. We had a sergeant, a priest of the Church of England, who has just gone home to get his commission as chaplain. He will be much missed by his comrades in the RAMC. A corporal carpenter who is doing excellent work in building huts is a candidate for the Welsh Nonconformist ministry. We have a good tailor, a bootmaker, a surveyor's clerk who is employed in map-making for the time, a hairdresser, and a baker. I haven't met a candlestick maker yet but no doubt we should find one if we needed him. Most of our doctors are Canadians, splendidly resourceful and useful men.

In this village I have now taken up my abode, as it is much more convenient to be nearer to the regiments of the brigade to which I am attached. So here I am sitting in a basket chair, which has seen its best days and requires to be propped up on one side against the wall. The table at which I am sitting is composed of ration boxes. My soldier servant, a splendid fellow who won the DCM for gallantry in the famous charge of the Worcesters at Gheluvelt, is cooking the dinner on a home-made grate which used to be a farmyard fork in days of peace. We have a miscellaneous collection of pots and pans, including a teapot which came from Ypres, given me with two odd plates, a cup and a tub for my morning bath, by a friendly MT driver. Alas the stock of plates has been reduced by 50 percent as I dropped one, and my horse who has an inquisitive disposition, put his head through the window which hasn't known much glass for many a day and knocked the cup down and broke its handle off. The horse, a beautiful chestnut with four white socks, is a dear intelligent animal and as gentle as a kitten. I call him "Sunshine" but my servant calls him "Jim" so I suppose we must compromise and call him "Sunny Jim". He lives in a kitchen two doors away, the sink makes a very convenient manger and Jim is quite comfortable.

When I last wrote we had settled down in a little village in Belgium not very far from the firing line. Now I am writing in the homely kitchen of a French farmhouse far away from the noise of guns and the sights of the ravages of war. Our division has been resting for three weeks. The officers live in farmhouses near their men and the men live in barns and outhouses, sleeping on piles of hay and straw. We are all having a real rest.

Resting doesn't mean idleness, for each company does several hours training every day, but it is a real rest for war-worn men to have a complete change of scene, beautiful country, good sleep at nights and quiet and calm after the incessant noise and strain of the front.

This is a beautiful country; when we came here first the trees were clothed in their autumn dress of many-coloured leaves and each little garden was gay with flowers; the trees are bare now and the flowers have been blackened by frost, but the houses with their red-tiled roofs and gaily painted shutters, the barns with their picturesque thatched roofs often covered with brilliant green moss and the windmills with their red sails, form a cheery contrast to the ruined towns and damp dull country we left behind. The people are very kind and hospitable and in every farm kitchen Thomas Atkins learns French and teaches English to the great satisfaction and merriment of both parties.

We have been fortunate in obtaining through the kindness of the dear old curé of this village a schoolroom for services and recreation. Here each morning we have the Eucharist, every afternoon the room is open for reading and writing, and each evening a different regiment of the brigade gives a concert. The room is too small for a regimental service, so we still have our Sunday parade services in the open air. Yesterday I had three open air services; the wind was very cold, so they didn't last long but I know the men are glad to have services in spite of the cold.

I have a partner now in the brigade who shares the work with me which enables each of us to give more individual attention to our charges. I am attached to the 4th Royal Fusiliers now and live with the regiment so if you write to me please address to 4th Royal Fusiliers, BEF.

I want you to pray for the men whom I am preparing for confirmation, the date of which is fixed for December 2nd, so you will remember us all especially on that day. I have about thirty-five candidates and may have more. I had a class of thirteen very keen fellows but their regiment was moved out of this division to another so I have handed them on to their new chaplain.

Now I mustn't take up more room in the Magazine. I have many letters and papers to thank you for and do so now, and I know you will forgive me when I don't answer you all with personal letters.

Noel Mellish C. F.

Chapter Five

The War 1915–16

So now I began a new page in my life with the Army. I ceased to be a piece of flotsam which had been cast by the fortunes of war into an infantry division, but had a part in the life of a Division which from the very beginning to the end of the Great War bore an honourable name and carried it unblemished through its course.

When after a rest of three weeks we returned to the line I found myself a recognised member of HQ in the battalion, going up with them to the trenches and sharing the fairly uneventful life of that particular period. Since the CO had been appointed to a Brigade there was much speculation at HQ as to who would come to take command. When the news came through that Colonel Ottley was appointed, the Second in Command was emphatic in his disgust. "It's a damned insult to the Regiment," he said, for the new CO was a Major of the KOYLI and neither knew the history of the Regiment nor had any association with it. He was a spare, dark man with shrewd twinkling brown eyes. He had served in India, with the King's African Rifles, and in South Africa in the MI.

Almost at once he became at home in the battalion, having the wonderful gift of knowing every man and remembering his name. He treated men as individuals and they knew it. Full of joie-de-vivre, he loved every minute of life. He never seemed tired, was always thinking of the men he commanded, and identified himself with the whole life of the Regiment. Every day he went round the line, accompanied by his redoubtable couple of orderlies, "Darky" Bounds and "Dutchy" Sewell, the former a taciturn man always shrouded in a mysterious reserve – I never knew what lay behind that sphinx-like face – the other of commoner mould, but both gallant and unswerving in their loyalty to duty and, like most cockneys, most humorous when the danger was greatest. At night too, the thin wiry figure of the Colonel, face still tanned by the West African sun, eyeglass screwed in under the peak of his cap, with long ash staff in hand, was very familiar to each man on the look-out as he passed. Often he stopped to encourage a timid sentry, probably a lad straight out from home, always inspiring officers and men with the magnetic personality of his friendship.

At this period we had four days in the line and four days out at Poperinghe which was a pleasant place for officers and men, with restaurants where you could have good dinners with plenty of champagne. There were also many eating houses where decent bread could be bought and above all, "eiks and chips" as one notice had it, could be obtained as a change from the bully of the trenches and the stew of the camp. At one restaurant, popular with the officers, was a small pert red-headed girl called "Ginger"; she never asked questions, but I imagine that what she did not know as to what was happening in the British Army in the Salient was not worth knowing.

The Belgian people were amazing. They seemed so detached from the war and at that time apparently short of nothing in the way of food though so close to the line. I went down to Dickebusch one day to bury some men and after that was over, seeing a notice in the window of a house, I went in and ordered coffee and chips. A great steaming bowl of coffee and a huge plate of chips with a heap of good bread and butter were produced at a cost of under a franc ... Going back to the line with an officer one day, we saw some lace hanging in the window of a house which looked far from safe to live in. We crossed to have a look and there in the room sat three wizened old women, their thin hands going for all they were worth as the bobbins flew in and out. War seemed to have lost its terrors for these poor folk.

Poperinghe afforded a very welcome change from the trenches. It had a cinema and a theatre run by the 6th Division and Toc H, lately born out of the agony of Hooge. "The Fancies", the 6th Division Theatrical Party, was a wonderful success, its chief artist being a

George Robeyesque person, who always brought down the house with "Rogerum". This kind of relaxation, with baths and clean clothes, made it possible for men to carry on and keep their splendid cheerfulness.

In spite of modern war books, I do not think anybody thought things out much, the work had to be done and officers and men deliberately kept themselves from thinking much. No one was morbid and few introspective. The letters the men wrote were perfectly natural; they suppressed the horrible and expressed their love for home. Those letters really conveyed the characters of the writers, who in those days looked at the inevitable through the medium of humour, which was made splendid by the utter self-giving, which in the trenches or at rest was the Grace of God working in the heart of the common man.

Their language was limited, punctuated by words emphasised out of all proportion in many of the so-called realistic war novels; they became as commas are to sentences, only they meant less. One thing I will state with emphasis: that the soldiers I knew never used swear words in the presence of a lady, never except at times of tense excitement before an officer and never before a chaplain. In all my experience, I never had a rude word flung at me by officer or man, for the chivalry and courtesy of the man in khaki was of as high a grade as that of the fighting man in Knight errant days. The dirty-mouthed and dirty-minded man was an exception. One sergeant in the Fusiliers, later an officer, never lost the nickname given him in pre-war days: "Foul-mouthed – –", which goes to prove my case.

The normal man in the Army was the normal man in the street of today, only he was disciplined and trained by a loyalty and half-conscious self-offering, in war expressed in deeds, latent in peace, but still ready to respond when need should call in mine or railway disaster. There was very little drunkenness; certainly there was little opportunity, but when out of the line the majority of men would rather sit round the fire in a French farmhouse or billet, drinking coffee and chipping Madame, than waste money on the stuff that went by the name of beer and aroused the sarcasm of the private soldier.

Our battalion HQ was in a line of dug-outs built of timber and sandbags on the bank of a little stream, which ran past the shattered remains of Voormezeele a few miles South of Ypres. We were pretty comfortable there, until one day we returned after four days out to find the whole place blown to pieces. The people who took our place had not been careful about smoke, so the German gunners, spotting the place, got busy and as one shell had hit the gum boot store the trees around were decorated by strange fruit – hung about with gum boots and looking like distorted Christmas trees.

Each day we had casualties. I suppose that at any time the German guns could have blown us out of our front line, for they could practically enfilade it from Wytschaete, Messines and Pilckem. Their advanced posts and ours were only 10 yards from each other and they had the advantage of the rising ground.

At the end of the year the Division lost several of its regular regiments, their place being taken by battalions from the New Army. I lost sight of a small detachment of the Bermuda Rifles who had been serving with the 1st Lincolns. When I knew them there were only about twenty left under a Sergeant-Major; I heard no more of them and missed them for they were a gallant party and keen churchmen.

Letter to St Paul's, Deptford, 19 January 1916

Dear People at home,

You will expect a line from me. I am writing this in a most luxurious dug-out made of strong iron in the form of an arch, protected from shells by layers of sandbags. It is furnished with a bed, two tables, two chairs and other home comforts, such as a fireplace and door, and even a glazed window. It has been recently built; the drains are sound and there is no rent to pay. This is my home for a week; then for another week we go back to live in tents.

At first sight you would think no one could live in such a very ruined village as this, but on closer inspection you find that inside the broken houses are many of these iron-framed cottages, some of them capable of holding twenty men. The firing line is about three quarters of a mile away. Don't imagine that everybody lives in these hidden palaces; the dear fellows up in the front line have very little shelter from showers of rain or of shells. They live in narrow alleys hemmed in between thick walls of sandbags. Here and there are dug-outs, but there are not enough to provide shelter for all. The trenches wind about with constant bends, so that no part may be exposed to fire from either side.

An hour before daylight and an hour before dark, every man stands ready for a possible attack, and all the day and night men are constantly on the look-out, for the enemy is in places only 40 yards away, and he may attack by a sudden rush or by using gas or by an underground mine at any moment. Yet in spite of cold and strain, our splendid men are always cheery. I've told you nothing new.

It's a mud-coloured world here; the country is flat and adorned by rows of stumpy willow trees and broken by streets of winding trenches, and here and there, savage ugly mantraps in the form of mazes of barbed wire. There isn't much left of the village church, part of the tower stands, and the clock hands point to five minutes past twelve. The bell lies on its side at the foot of the steeple; I wonder if it will ever call the village folk to worship again. Away in the distance is the unceasing thunder of a heavy bombardment. Here the occasional scream of a shell as it passes over the village, hoping in its evil black heart it will find the battery which has been worrying those who sent it on its errand. Up in the air there is no peace, for man is fighting in wonderful machines, and little white puffs of smoke show where shells are bursting near the bird-like aircraft which are always on the look-out to locate guns, skilfully hidden under innocent green mounds or in woods far below.

But God's good gift of hope fills our hearts – hope that soon all this will be over; "Hoping all things, enduring all things", so these gallant officers and men go on unwavering.

A man who had been sent out on a very dangerous job said to me when I congratulated him on his safe return to the trench, "That was because we prayed, sir, before we went out." He did his difficult job well and an hour later was badly wounded in trying to save his mate under fearful shell fire. He was recommended to the General for his bravery and promoted to sergeant, but God had a greater reward than the DCM and sergeant's stripes, and called him to higher duty on the day after the comrade for whom he gave his life. Now I must stop.

> Always yours affectionately,
> Noel Mellish, C. F.

Letter to St Paul's, Deptford, 18 February 1916

Dear People at home,

The time flies so quickly that the date for posting my letter to you generally goes by and finds it unwritten. We are now resting once more in Sunny France and much enjoying the change to beautiful country, kindly people, green fields, new-laid eggs and other delights. The battalions I look after are very much scattered and my good horse, Jim, is kept busy but he enjoys the country as much as I do, and the good roads have a nice strip of soft sand at the side which makes a good canter possible.

The centre of our life here is our club called Hounslow House, an estaminet once, but now a dry canteen and recreation room. Behind the canteen is a tiny chapel, large enough for daily Eucharist and confirmation classes which I am holding here. Every afternoon and evening the room is crowded and we have sing-songs; the chorus of one of the most popular songs goes thus:

"Goodbye mother, sister, brother,
Dry away those ready tears,
England's not in danger when there's bomb-throwers
In the Fourth Royal Fusiliers."

This is the bombers' chorus composed by one of them. Well, the post corporal has just arrived, so I mustn't write more. I hope to see you again before very long. I have many letters and papers to thank you for and must do so now.

Always yours affectionately,
Noel Mellish C. F.

Chapter Six

The War 1916

THE SECOND CHRISTMAS of the war passed quickly. We had Saxons in front of us; they made many attempts to repeat the "fraternisation" which had characterised the first Christmas, but orders had gone out that this was forbidden. But there was a complete silence and we saw that the Saxons had a lighted Christmas tree in their trench opposite our advanced post.

At St Eloi the front line lay low and we were constantly harassed by "whiz-bangs", small low-velocity guns, or by snipers, equipped with highly efficient telescopic sights, who let few opportunities go. Steel helmets were not introduced until early in 1916, so head wounds were common. I often wonder whether the Germans held their line as fully as we did. They certainly learned to make their troops more comfortable than we in later days, yet I doubt whether the fact of spending a long time in deep dug-outs and concrete "pill-boxes" helped their morale. For my part, to stay for any while in a deep dug-out made me much more "windy" when I came up again.

In that sector our company officers and men slept in crazy shelters, wet and over-run with rats. More loathsome things than those rats I can scarcely conceive; they used hardly to get out of your way; great mangy bald-faced things that looked at you from the parados with red cruel eyes and as you walked along the duck-boards you sometimes trod on them, when they squealed with a hateful scream which made you sick.

The wonder was that the men kept so fit as they did in the conditions of the trenches in 1915 and 1916 in the Salient. It was always wet and muddy; gum boots kept the water from coming in, but the feet grew soft and the men suffered from frostbite during times of attack, when there was no chance of taking off the boots and rubbing the feet. Marching back to Poperinghe down the cobbled roads was misery, for the feet had got soft and inflamed. During those four days in Poperinghe we enjoyed such comfort and gaiety as it provided, but the Fusiliers had a bad spot chosen for their billet. It was too close to the Railway – about four o'clock each morning a HV gun used to disturb our rest.

People used to bet on the number of duds it sent over in the daily ration, for you could almost count on seven out of ten not exploding, but one morning our poor transport men got badly caught. I heard the first shell come over, and finding it closer than usual, woke those who were with me, but the next one exploded in the yard below and wounded several men and killed one of the drivers and his little dog, which had been with him since the beginning. Afterwards, I looked for Robins and couldn't find him; but found that Jim was so terrified when the shells came over that Robins, hearing him scream, had gone to him and lain down in the straw by his side and the poor old horse was perfectly quiet until the shelling stopped. After this, the battalion billets were more scattered, but a company commander had a wonderful escape one morning when the same gun fired. The shell burst on the house and pieces came through the roof and the ceiling of the room where he slept, making nine holes in his 'flea-bag' as he lay on the floor, and passed through the floor beneath him; and he was untouched.

One Sunday after dinner I planned to go up to the 4th South Lancs., who were our pioneers, and told Robins to get Jim saddled up and bring him along. I waited some time and was rather vexed when Robins arrived making excuse that Jim had run away and that he had had difficulty in catching him. I thought this was unusual but said no more. Next day Robins came up and said: "What I said yesterday was not true, Sir. What happened was that we were talking down the lines about football and I said that our battalion had the Army record, so Simmons said theirs had. Then we had a bit of an argument and one of the school who'd had a drop of beer, came up and gave me a tap on the head, and I had to drop him. Then yesterday two or three of his pals came up to me together and I called out and told them I'd take 'em all on one at a time, so they did and when the three had had enough I was a bit late, but it's all right now, Sir."

In February we went out again and we had only been at rest a few days when the news came that the Germans had broken through at the Bluff, south of Hill 60, so back we had to go. It was a long march back and the pavé roads were terrible to march on, so we were all pretty tired. One lately joined youngster was completely done and almost on the point of falling out, when a giant named Davis in his platoon, a Billingsgate fish porter in "civvy" life, caught hold of him, unbuckled his belt and lifting the whole pack and all his equipment on to his own head and shoulders, marched on with as much unconcern as if he was carrying boxes of fish in the market at home.

The 2nd Suffolks, in the 76th Brigade, retook the line, but suffered heavily, and before they had established the line the Germans blew a mine, and half a company of the Suffolks was wiped out, but the remainder hung on desperately and prevented any further advance. When we took over, the ground was white with snow, the shattered trees along the ravine looking very strange and eerie in the quiet that succeeded the counter-attack. The trenches were blown to pieces of course, hardly any parapet being left and the MO and I found some sort of cover in a shelter, but there was a foot or so of water underneath, so we sat on a stretcher laid over the pool and waited for daylight.

It was bitterly cold and the men were nearly frozen; the Germans had no heart for any further attack I suppose, so both sides made the best of the calm by that eternal re-building which was the lot of the infantryman. Further down, at Bedford House, in a great barn, the scene was terrible – dozens of men with their legs swollen to double the normal size by the cruel cold, writhed in agony as the returning circulation burst the skin. Our own supply column had gone out so we were dependent upon that of the disordered division we had relieved.

The cold was so intense that the RSM and I set to work to make an oven to make charcoal, as the supply was very small. It was fairly successful too and we got a certain amount to the front line, for our men were so close to the enemy that no smoke must show. We found hay boxes very useful for carrying hot cocoa up, but it was a very slippery track and hard to keep one's feet, for the trenches ran through a wood in which every tree was stripped by the furious shelling when our division won back that few hundred yards of muddy ditch, which meant so much to those who were behind. In a day or two we were relieved.

A corporal of the Northumberland Fusiliers with his squad had orders to leave an advanced bombing post. The half-frozen men crawled out, but the corporal, coming out last, got stuck in the mud. His pal went back to help him and he, too, got stuck fast. There they remained until they were rescued twenty hours later. No one can realise that mud could be so like glue: I saw some Highlanders come down with no boots on at all – they had been sucked off and left behind.

Chapter Seven

St Eloi

FIRST CAME RUMOURS and then orders that we were to take part in an attack on the objectionable spot called the Mound, from which the Germans had observation for their artillery and could whiz-bang us at will. We were short of officers for at that period of the war they were very scarce. There had been that awful wastage at Loos and the organisation of the new armies was far from complete. What a difference it would have made if we could have conserved the magnificent supply of potential officers in the first line Territorial regiments. In our division we had the HAC, the Liverpool Scottish and the London Rifle Brigade. The majority of the rank and file of any of these would have been invaluable as officers. The only battalion which was then serving as an OTC was the Artists Rifles and hundreds had already been supplied as officers to all regiments.

The original plan of this attack was that the Northumberland Fusiliers and the Royal Fusiliers were to attack and destroy the Mound. Then the scheme was expanded – a large artillery preparation was added and five mines were to be blown up. All was practised carefully in country only a few miles behind the attack. I wonder if any leakage of information took place. There was, I suppose, always the readiness to suspect espionage. The station-master at Poperinghe must have had more lives than a cat for we were constantly hearing that he had been shot as a spy. I myself was taken for a spy in Ypres early one Sunday morning, by a zealous policeman, but they apparently had no difficulty in discovering my harmlessness.

On Sunday afternoon we went up to the support line. The Royal Fusiliers were even shorter of officers, for two had now gone sick. In the afternoon the young transport officer, Guy Boddy, came up to see the Colonel and asked if he might take over the bombing party. The Colonel said "No, you are wanted as Transport Officer," but he pleaded and Colonel Ottley knew that it was of so great importance that the party should be well led, that he gave in, and Boddy got ready for his work and left the comparative safety of the transport lines.

26th March

Four a.m. zero hour. The whole heavens rent by an awful roar as the five mines went up and our artillery burst out, blasting down the German defences. The Colonel, the Adjutant, the RSM and I waited in a shelter in the support trench. Then the whole earth shook as the German artillery was turned on to the counter-attack. How long it lasted I cannot say, but it was as though we were in the centre of an earthquake, yet our frail shelter was never hit.

At last a runner managed to get through to tell the CO that our men had gone over, but there was no officer left so far as he knew, to take charge. Only three were left unwounded – seven were killed, Guy Boddy amongst them. By the end of the day two of those three were so shaken by the terrible shelling that they were unfit for anything. The Colonel and Adjutant each in turn went to take charge of the line. In the afternoon, heavy gunfire broke out again, but the Germans made no attempt to attack and the line was held. The remains of our weakened battalion held on and as darkness fell, the enemy artillery plastered us with ceaseless fury. Along the edge of the mine craters and that which had once been a trench, but now was a sea of churned up mud, our men were subjected to a continuous volume of fire. In the dark it was a hell of white flares, red flashes and screaming shells, while dead and dying men lay with those who still kept their sanity.

I shall never forget Corporal Webb, an elderly man, holding his Lewis gun always ready, greeting me with a cheery hail in that place of torment, when I was almost ready to collapse. His was the only gun left in action – all the others had been smashed or clogged with mud. As I walked my foot struck something white; it was a skull, while towards me, supported by another man walked one whose face was gone, flayed, featureless, an awful thing, yet living and trying to speak his need of help.

On the right the Northumberland Fusiliers had gone right through and gallantly held on to their objective; they had suffered less severely, losing but few officers and not so many men. Early in the morning the 89th Brigade relieved us and what was left of our battalion moved out, the only officers fit for duty being the Colonel, the Adjutant and one other. The Mound had been destroyed but at what a cost.

This was the first time I remember meeting our Brigadier. He was wonderful, always the same, calm and cool in any battle, always cheerful, never flustered. He was constantly round the line and knew everybody. Unsparing of himself – he never seemed to think of self at all – and everything at Brigade HQ spoke of the same simplicity which marked his life.

The 9th Brigade was truly fortunate, for from the beginning of 1916 until I was demobilized in Germany in 1919 we had no other Brigadier than General Potter. His life seemed charmed; twice he was blown up and never wounded. However great the strain he was unbeaten, inspiring all with utter confidence. His whole being was in his work, yet he was always ready to advise and help with sympathy. The secret of his wonderful calm and courage was I believe a real and deep religion which consecrated his whole life and work.

The task of getting the wounded out would have been impossible but for the gallant volunteers of the 142nd Field Ambulance, who worked throughout the night bringing them out; one of their number, Sergeant Grimmett, being wounded in this work. For the next night's work sixty officers' servants, grooms and duty men of the Royal Fusiliers volunteered to go up and they carried up canvas mats to lay over the mud, thereby making it possible to move the wounded men. Of this party, Pte. Webb was killed and Pte. Cherry wounded, but at last all were taken away, except one, a very tall man who was lying with a broken leg in an exposed position. As daylight dawned they got him out and then the German Gunners saw and opened fire, but just as they had "bracketed" them a fall of snow came and hid them from view and so they were protected.

On each of those two dreadful nights my groom, Robins, insisted on accompanying me and indeed I think that on one occasion I should never have extricated myself from the unthinkably clinging mud of a crater's edge, if he had not come back and hauled me out by his great strength.

Chapter Eight

Award of the Victoria Cross

Letter from Lieutenant Colonel Ottley, 1 April 1916

Dear Mrs Mellish,

I think it simply my duty to write and tell you what I think of your son, Capt. Rev. Noel Mellish, and my opinion is held by over 400 officers and men of my battalion. Four days ago I could have given the number as 650. Capt. Mellish, although Chaplain to the Brigade, has attached himself to the Battalion under my command and it has been my privilege to mess with him for the last four months.

My battalion was chosen to attack a certain section of the enemy trenches on 27th March in conjunction with another battalion of the Brigade. Capt. Mellish's place should have been at the rear with the Ambulance, and fairly safe, but he chose to remain with the Battalion up in the front. We had a bad time and our casualties were heavy in officers and men – six officers killed and four wounded out of 14 who took part in the attack, and 251 NCO's and men were killed, wounded, or missing. The Padre as we call him, treated most murderous and incessant machine gun and shell fire simply as if it was not happening and, absolutely callous to all bullets and shells, and regardless of danger, rescued any number of my poor wounded men, who but for him, would have probably died. For fear of being accused of exaggerating I will not tell you how many he tended. Not content with carrying on his glorious work from about 5 a.m. on 27th until 6 a.m. on 28th, he went back to the trenches on the night of the 29th and with a party of volunteers rescued some more again on the night of the 29th. His pluck, his absolute disregard of personal danger, his resourcefulness and energy are a byeword through the Brigade. I am writing to you on behalf of myself and my whole Battalion because we want you to know what we think of "The padre" which, put plainly, is that he is one of the grandest men in the world; there is only one person he never spares, or thinks of, and that is himself.

Sincerely yours,
Glendower Ottley, Lt Colonel
Commanding 4th Royal Fusiliers.

Letter from Captain Bell (2 April 1916)

Dear Mrs Mellish,

I feel I cannot let this opportunity pass of telling you what a splendid man your son Noel is. During the recent operations at St Eloi, in which my Battalion unfortunately lost heavily, he did the work of ten men in dressing and helping wounded men. He is a most modest and unassuming man, and would probably say "he was only doing his little job", but I was there and know the splendid work he did. Many a man owes his life to your son and we are proud of him.

The men of the Battalion love him and swear by "our padre". I hope Mr Mellish is much better in health than when Noel went home.

My best wishes to both, please excuse the hurried scrawl.

Very sincerely yours,
W. Bell, Captain
Adjutant 4th Bn. R. Fusiliers

Extract from the *London Gazette* of Thursday, 20 April 1916

His Majesty the King has been pleased to award the Victoria Cross to the Reverend Edward Noel Mellish, temporary Chaplain to the Forces, for most conspicuous bravery.

During heavy fighting on three consecutive days he repeatedly went backwards and forwards under continuous and heavy shell and machine-gun fire, between our original trenches and those captured from the enemy, in order to tend and rescue wounded men. He brought in ten badly wounded men on the first day from ground swept by machine-gun fire and three were actually killed while he was dressing their wounds.

The battalion to which he was attached was relieved on the second day but he went back and brought in twelve more wounded men. On the night of the third day he took charge of a party of volunteers and once more returned to rescue the remaining wounded.

This splendid work was quite voluntary on his part and outside the scope of his ordinary duties.

Letter to St Paul's Parish Magazine

My dear friends,

What an honour is ours. I can neither say nor write what I think about it. One's words and thoughts, one's very life seem so petty, and one is not worthy of the friendship of so great a man: great not because the world is applauding and the King is honouring him, but because he is capable of doing and enduring such things. How near indeed Christ must have been to him. How pleased the angels must be. It was not a mere rush of heroism but a long sustained effort; we can well understand the joy of that party of volunteers on that third day as they went forth nobly to be led by him. Of course, we knew that if any man was equal to it, he was; because we know the life and its inspiration, but in our faithlessness we had not dreamed of any human agent being spared on such a field to live so long on so high a plane. It is marvellous. It is miraculous. Apart from Divine Grace it is impossible.

We hope to have our hero with us in a week or two. We shan't be able to tell him what we think of him, but we will do our best. Meanwhile, let us thank God from the bottom of our hearts for what he has done for, in and through Edward Noel Mellish, His Priest, and let us take courage and rouse our faith and resolve that we will be better and truer men, women and children and believe as we have never believed before the truths of Good Friday and Easter Day.

Yours humbly and very happily,
R. P. Roseveare, 25th April 1916.

22 April 1916.

Dear Mrs Mellish,

I am enclosing a document which I know will interest you deeply and

I am certain you will like to keep it among your most treasured possessions. The first part will interest you, but I am inclined to think that your son will value it most for the information contained in the last part because I am sure that he was more pleased at the success of the Battalion in the Divisional Sports than he was to learn that he had gained the VC. The copy of Battalion Orders I am enclosing is one of eight special copies I have had made. The remaining seven are for Capt. Bell, Robins, myself and one or two others who are particularly interested. The result of the Sports appeared in last night's Orders, but I have had them repeated on to the same sheet with the VC announcement in tonight's Orders because our Padre was mighty keen on the Sports and was so pleased that the Battalion walked away with such a large share of the prizes.

I was on leave last week and intended to ask you to let me call on you, but unfortunately was recalled from leave and I had to leave home on Sunday instead of on the following Thursday. I saw your present to Diney while I was at home. It was really too nice of you to send her such a charming and useful present. I was going to say that it was too good for her, but that would be wrong because she is old enough and sensible enough to thoroughly appreciate your present. It was paraded for my inspection very soon after arrival and every detail of its composition minutely explained to me because of course, being only a Daddy or man, I must be profoundly ignorant of such matters. You will see your son in the flesh pretty soon I hope, but please send him back because we are only lending him to you. In the language of the West coast of Africa, "he belong of us".

Sincerely yours,
Glendower Ottley.

Extract from a letter dated 24 April 1916 from Rev. Pat Leonard (later Bishop of Thetford) to his parents.

Today I have been present at a most gallant and thrilling ceremony. Mellish, one of the chaplains of our Division, has been awarded the Victoria Cross for an unequalled act of gallantry at St Eloi. Seventeen times he went out into the crater and brought in wounded men under a constant hail of shells and bullets. You can judge of its severity, for three men were killed as he was bandaging their wounds out there. Today he was presented with his ribbon by General Haldane and no man deserved the honour more, for he is a perfectly charming man – a real white man and a saint. There is no chaplain and very few men whom I would rather see decorated. The whole division was represented by detachments from each unit, drawn up in a hollow square to do honour, as the General said, to a very brave man and a very gallant gentleman. By the way do you remember I told you once about a chaplain who lived in a cottage in a shelled out village and kept open house for wearied Tommies coming back from the trenches – well, this is the man who has earned the Victoria Cross.

Luckily nature was kind this morning and a brilliant sun looked down upon the scene and caught and reflected the glittering bayonets of the assembled troops. The fourth side of the square was occupied by a line of some twenty officers and men who were to receive DSO, MC, DCM or MM ribbons, while in front in solitary grandeur and visible discomfort stood Mellish. In front again stood a group of generals and staff officers resplendent in their red and brass fixings.

Before each man in turn the General took his stand, read out the deed which had earned the decoration, pinned on the ribbon and perfunctorily shook hands; then repeated the process with the officers until all had received their ribbons except Mellish. He, poor man, stood stiffly at attention, as one hearing his death sentence, while the General made a speech and eulogised his courage and his deed and then while all the world stood still, silent and expectant, pinned on the red ribbon and called for three cheers which were given "con amore". Then came the general salute, followed by the royal salute and the King, and as a grand finale, three cheers for his Majesty.

Extract from a letter by Captain Guy Stubbs to Rev. Harry Freeman

The Church of England runs its show about as badly as the Army used to. Wrong men in the wrong places – we have got out here Chaplains, quite useless, who carry out funerals, "burial fatigue men". I call them, and do very little else. Others, perfectly splendid, know all the men, talk to them, smile at them, make them cheery, arrange concerts etc. etc., and are worth their weight in gold just to look at. Did you see the account of Rev. N. Mellish's VC? I met him coming from the trenches after three days continuous work in a perfect turmoil. He looked like the last survivor from Jellalabad, (do you know the picture?) I did not know then who he was or what he had done –

*Beautifully illuminated scroll from the congregation
and parishioners of St Paul's*

the saving of many lives was nothing to the life he gave to all who saw him working quite undisturbed.

Telegram to: Rev. N. Mellish, VC Att. 4th Royal Fusiliers, BEF, France.

Sir, congratulations.

RSM Savill

During all this time of trench warfare we padres were able to carry on our spiritual work more or less regularly. If on Sundays our battalions were out of the line we had services wherever opportunity offered. At Reningheist we had them in the YMCA hut and in Poperinghe at the Cinema or, sometimes, in the beautiful chapel at Toc H. I tried to have Holy Communion at least once for each of my battalions when we were out of the line and there was always a response amongst officers and men. Treated by all with a freedom and confidence which allowed us to go anywhere, we found a welcome from all.

It was my custom at the time we were holding the trenches at St Eloi to have short prayers and benediction with each company before they started up to the front line. I believe the men appreciated this. I gave it up, however, for the following reason. One night a section was to make a raid. The Colonel was waiting for news in the support trench. Some hitch occurred, or the enemy discovered it, so the raid never came off, and in the tense anxiety of waiting and uncertainty the Colonel turned on me and said: "Padre, you must stop this prayer business of yours, it makes the men windy." I said nothing at the time, for I knew how he felt, but afterwards, like the sahib he was, he told me he was sorry for what he had said and gave me leave to do as I thought fit.

Early in April the division was withdrawn and we had a splendid rest at Meteren. It was the nicest village I had yet seen; clean and tidy and the people were so kind and hospitable. The HQ of the Royal Fusiliers was in a farm house; the men of the family, of course, were all away fighting, the eldest a priest serving as Sergeant-Major in his regiment. Madame and the household were up each morning with the lark, the girls singing at their work.

There were plenty of eggs and chips for the men to buy and our Colonel and the Colonel of the West Yorks, each pitted his battalion against the other in every kind of sport; there was a splendid comradeship between the two. By this time we had an entirely fresh lot of officers and large drafts of men. Colonel Ottley set himself to train his officers and men to the high standard he required. All the other battalions were doing the same and in the freshness of that lovely spring in a part of the country which had quite recovered from the damage of war caused in 1914 everyone enjoyed himself.

However, the best things do not last long and we soon marched up to take over the line at Kemmel. Here a new phase of trench fighting now began. We took over from a division sadly reduced by heavy casualties. They had taken over a line which had been allowed to get into a state of decay as far as defence was concerned and apparently all had been neglected.

Meanwhile, the enemy took advantage of a quiet time and completed a new system of attack. Along this sector he had built in trench-mortars and from the cover of Petit Bois, about 40 yards from us, he was creating havoc with a form of artillery new to our experience. With morning light he began a ceaseless bombardment with trench-mortars on the front line and shells on the support.

Unfortunately our 3rd Division artillery was otherwise occupied and for the first four days we had a terrible time from dawn until after dark. A new factor was introduced by the cooperation of aeroplanes. Each morning a plane used to sail up and down over our lines, just out of rifle range, and mark for the trench-mortars, for the new shining steel helmets only lately issued made excellent targets from above. These mortars were fired with great precision: the particular feature of these things was that you could watch the shells come up, lobbing about in the air, but you could never tell exactly where they would fall. The men, as usual, treated them as a joke and called them "sausages" or "rum-jars" according to their shape, but it was a dreadful strain and sometimes men went mad.

Sentries were posted all along the line to blow a whistle for warning and the call went up "sausage right" or "rum-jar left" or "right over". But often it was not over and from a volcano of earth, pieces of wood and debris, a few mud-coloured figures would crawl, shaken and shocked, bleeding and maimed, and sometimes there were figures that lay still. Gently they were lifted and carried down the trench and later a little procession would wend its way across the green meadows, through a sweet smelling wood, rich with spring flowers, while the birds would sing as the body was lowered to rest and the gallant soul committed to the care of Him who gave it. And the sun would sink in a haze of amber and crimson and Nature would speak of the peace that is given to tired soldiers, whose work for peace was done. The men had to spend most of the night in repairing the neglected defences of this line. The strain of waiting for the bombs to drop was almost unbearable and we had no trench mortars yet with which to retaliate; moreover, the aeroplanes directing the German mortars in the wood made their fire most accurate.

The plan of holding the front line thinly and keeping a large number in the support trenches was the alternative, but since by aerial observation the enemy knew our disposition, his bombardment of the support led to large numbers of men being killed or wounded there also. Either the artillery in position was lacking in ammunition or ineffective, I do not know, but our casualty list in those days was dreadful. The Colonel asked me to go down and find an anti-aircraft gun and get their help. I found a Naval anti-aircraft gun but the officer in charge said he could not help because he was out of range and we were not in his sector. I told him that we were being murdered for want of help and begged him to move up so that he could prevent the German plane from observing the movements and disposition of our men.

He did not do so that day and a second time I went; his complaint was that the ground was too wet for the heavy car on which the gun was mounted, to be moved. At this I felt almost in despair, and using every argument at length he was persuaded and moved into range and the offensive aeroplane ceased to worry us. On the fourth day, to our great joy, our own magnificent artillery came in and the Colonel explained the position. Warning us that they would have to fire so low that their shells would almost skim our parapets, the gunners got busy. It was a joyful relief from the terrors of the day before. For every one trench-mortar that came over 10 shells went back, until either the mortars were knocked out or the enemy gunners were terrorised, but we established an ascendancy which remained as long as we were in the sector. I never realised so keenly how utterly dependent in trench warfare of that sort we were upon our artillery, and how ready they always were to help to the utmost their brothers in the trenches.

Kemmel Hill to all outward appearances was an ordinary hill, but its westward side was honeycombed with gun emplacements. No movement by day was ever visible from above but the whole hill was a hive of industry. From narrow slits carefully concealed by gauze the enemy positions for miles could be observed. I suppose the enemy were short of artillery, for though they constantly shelled Kemmel Hill they rarely succeeded in doing much damage to our guns. Our battalion HQ was in a little estaminet called Le Rossignol, in a clearing in the wood about half a mile from the front line; the communication trench going forward was a dark tunnel through the trees, and this wood and Kemmel wood behind us were thronged with nightingales and the louder the gunfire the more they seemed to sing.

In the village the Church, like most others near the line, was a broken ruin standing by the crossroads, but not a safe place to linger by. At the dressing station I met a dear old Roman Catholic padre, with whom I became very friendly, and we agreed on a joint ministry to the wounded, so that when either of us was away the other would be ready if needed.

Below Kemmel on the road to Locre were several innocent looking hayricks, but occasionally from one or the other the end would be lowered and the long black snout of a 15 inch naval gun would protrude and when she fired the earth would bump and hit your head if you happened to be resting in the lines, to which we occasionally withdrew in reserve.

After each tour in the trenches at Kemmel we used to go out to Locre. This was a pleasant little place and the billets were comfortable. Our HQ was in a convent school and a dear old Mother Superior with her attendant nuns used to cater for our needs by supplying us with hot water for baths, getting our washing done and showing us all much kindness. Here, year in, year out, those devoted women remained, always within range of German guns, never out of the sound of the firing line. Even in 1918 they could hardly be persuaded to retire until the Germans were almost on the skyline.

One day I found myself in a strange position. I was riding back to Locre with the Colonel when a lorry met us. Jim objected to lorries; I rather fancy he must have been struck across the face at one time by a passing wagon flap; so he suddenly swerved round and came backwards with me into the ditch, which was deep though dry. Fortunately for me, the sides shelved down so that although I lay underneath the horse I was unhurt. Jim lay with his head on my chest, my arms round his neck to keep him from trampling on me and his legs pointing to the skies. I was stuck fast as the stirrup leathers had gripped me tight. At once the Colonel dismounted and ungirthing the saddle set me free and I crawled out none the worse. Jim, with a snort heaved himself out and we resumed our journey.

It was strange to see the Belgian farming folk going about their usual life, apparently unheeding the war. One farmer was pretty closely watched as it was thought that some of his movements with the plough might convey messages and the location of our batteries to the observant Hun airman, for several of our batteries were shelled at that time. Whether this was so or not I do not know, but Nemesis came very horribly to the poor old man, for in their efforts to locate our batteries the enemy pitched a shell right into his homestead and converted it into a flaming mass of ruin, and though he and his wife were unhurt they saw their home no more.

At the end of March a man who had deserted was caught, tried by Court Martial and sentenced to be shot. It was a bright spring morning when the battalion was drawn up for his sentence to be promulgated. I had to prepare him for his tragic end which he seemed not to realise himself. Whether his mind was deficient I do not know, but he seemed benumbed, showing no signs of fear or any emotion. Early in the morning I went with him and the escort and there at one side of a field the firing party stood. The man's eyes were blindfolded and as I turned away and went apart the volley rang out and the poor lad passed to his account.

I felt that he was certainly not so much to blame as Hartley, the leader of the little gang of men who had deserted and hidden themselves at Poperinghe. He was the man who ought to have been shot, for he gave this boy away and escaped himself. In 1918 Hartley himself was captured and sentenced to death, but was released and given another chance on the ground that at some other time he had acquitted himself gallantly in action. Yet I fear the leniency was misplaced, for at the first opportunity he escaped again and gave himself up to the Germans and after the Armistice was returned as a prisoner of war.

In June my leave arrived, but some days before it was over I had a letter from Colonel Ottley saying "Back in the same place again, come back". I left early in the morning and found them the next day at Locre; they had been rushed over to St Eliol to help a sudden attack and had suffered a great many casualties.

On Saturday, 3 June Mellish was sent home on leave, arriving late and without fuss at Lewisham where his parents lived. The following day he celebrated Communion at his own beloved church of St Paul's and took part in the other services, notably a special thanksgiving in the evening. In the next few days he was honoured at a civic reception by the Mayor and Council, signed the Roll of Honour and was presented with an illuminated address. He also received a beautifully illuminated scroll from the congregation and parishioners of St Paul's. There was a guard of honour from his own troop of the Church Lads' Brigade, a drive with the Mayor in an open landau and a new Honours Board was unveiled with his name the first to be inscribed. Lewisham Borough also claimed him as one of their own and there was a similar civic ceremony there.

Mellish was thrilled by the welcome from his people, delighted with the guards of honour and escorts from his boys, and thoroughly embarrassed by all the publicity. When he had to speak he simply stated that he was lucky and said how splendid the British soldier was and that the honour was really theirs. He could not escape this publicity however, and every town and organisation with which he had a connection joined to claim a share in the glory. Launceston Town where he had lived as a child, King's School, Saffron Walden, the mining community at Jagersfontein, South Africa, even the Guernsey press where Alice, his half-sister was headmistress of the Ladies' College, and the Jamaica press where Cecil, his half-brother was chief Resident Magistrate.

King's College, London elected him an Honorary Fellow and

presented him with a long Latin address, the *Daily Mail* presented him with an award of £100 which he promptly gave to the St Paul's Church Lads' Brigade, and telegrams of congratulation poured in from many regiments and units of the army with which he had been connected. A number of artists' impressions of the action at St Eloi appeared, together with some very bad photographs and a very good colour postcard and cigarette card. And on Monday, 11 June Mellish went with his mother and sister, Mary Hodson, to Buckingham Palace where King George V presented him with the Victoria Cross and listened eagerly to an account of his deeds at St Eloi. It was a hot June day when the little party returned from Buckingham Palace on a bus and Mrs Mellish noticed with surprise that her son was wearing his trenchcoat although he was sweating profusely in the heat. She was about to ask him why, when she realised that underneath it he was wearing the cross and ribbon King George had recently pinned on his chest and this was an attempt to hide it and avoid further publicity.

Then came the telegram from Colonel Ottley – 'Back in the same place again, come back'.

Chapter Nine

The War 1916–17

ON THE 17TH JUNE the Division went out to a delightful part near the Forest of Eperlecques, not for rest but for intensive training for the great Somme offensive, and there we remained hard at it until the second of July.

One day on a round of visiting companies, I came across a crown and anchor school belonging to the Welsh Fusiliers, and as crown and anchor is a game which always pays the banker too well, I told the owners to clear out to their own billets. Some hours afterwards I found the same gang at our Lewis gunners' billets. I made them pack up, which they did with bad grace, and I thought no more of it. However, there was a sequel, which I heard from the RSM months afterwards. The Welshmen, when I passed on, used strong abusive language about me, but Davis, the Billingsgate lad, interrupted and told one of them to "shut his face" and as he didn't do it quickly enough proceeded to shut it for him; after a short round the Welshman retired hurt. Next evening a crowd of Welsh Fusiliers came up to get their own back and there was a royal fight, the result of which was that all the enemy went into the pond.

The 12th West Yorks, under Colonel Oswald, and the Royal Fusiliers under Colonel Ottley, were great friends. Each battalion had been trained to perfection under its own CO for many months and Ottley and Oswald were alike in many ways, each having the wonderful gift of knowing every officer and man in his command, so that the whole had become in each case a family, strict in its discipline, but with an intense pride in its corporate life. A competitive programme lasting throughout this training resulted in the two regiments coming out level.

Then a great blow fell on us. One night while we were at Mess a strange officer came in saying: "I have come to take command of the Royal Fusiliers." We stared at him and Ottley said quietly: "I have the honour to command this battalion." No orders had been sent; neither Division nor Corps HQ knew anything about it. Col Hely-Hutchinson was sent from the War Office. It was a great shock to Ottley and indeed to all of us a grievous loss.

The rest of us dumbly left the Mess Room and these two talked out the position, with the result that it was agreed that Ottley should remain in command until orders were forthcoming; but the decision was upheld. Hely-Hutchinson himself had no option in the matter. He had been at home since he was wounded early in 1915 and he felt keenly for Ottley and invited him to stay on as second-in-command, but Ottley felt that it would make things very difficult for the new CO; he could not but know that every officer and man in the battalion loved him, for it was his own work.

He told me afterwards: "I wanted to stop, but I couldn't decide, padre, so I tossed a coin and I lost." So he made the great renunciation because he was such a sportsman, but his heart was in the regiment. As he went off it chanced that the battalion was on parade and he had to pass, but he could not say goodbye and his eyes were filled with tears.

Just after we left this place an enormous ammunition store at Audruicq Station, prepared for the Somme offensive, was exploded by a German plane and literally acres of shells stored in large dumps exploded in countless numbers, scattering fragments of steel over miles of the countryside, yet though much damage was done to houses only seven people were killed.

We had an uneventful march down. At nights we billeted in dirty, dilapidated French villages, or in the open. This Picardy country is dull, uninteresting, chalky and dirty. The inhabitants were dull and surly. We skirted Amiens and marched through Bray, past Albert, where the Virgin hung over the roadway from the steeple, and on to Carnoy, where we made our HQ for a while. It was at Bray that I first saw the French army. They were what our own men called a "rough old lot", the men unshaven and dirty, their horses ungroomed, with harness patched and tied with rope. Even the famous 75's looked like dingy old iron besides our spotless guns.

Colonel Hely-Hutchinson found the battalion in splendid order and, though we naturally missed our former CO, we were fortunate in having such a man to succeed him. Just before we started down for the Somme he paid me the high honour of offering me the command of a Company, but it seemed to me my work lay where I had been sent, so I declined; for though opinion is divided I am sure there is room for a priest's work even in war. Much that we found to do could have been done better by others, and nobody knew that better than we, but we had our orders and work, which being spiritual, none who were not priests could do. We wore Army uniforms and badges of rank, yet officers and men in my experience treated us, not as officers, but in a kind of sacramental way, as though we supplied something which was their right and privilege to have and use; and never in all my relations with the Army, from the highest to the lowest ranks, did I experience anything but the most ready help, generous comradeship and perfect courtesy.

The "Push" like a new piece at the theatre, had to have its "properties" and the green room, from which we made our entry on to the new stage, had to be prepared. Each night several hundred men went up to the "Happy Valley" carrying rations, water and tools. This valley had been recently taken from the enemy and, though they couldn't see us, they shelled it carefully and systematically from end to end.

For four nights, parties of men in single file, all heavily loaded, filed over the crest down into the valley; each man carefully piled his load and then returned for another; but every night many of those men never came back, for the shells were accurately placed by those who knew each yard of ground. At last the job was done.

It was a dark night when we moved and we reached the valley without loss. It is a test of discipline to march steadily and very slowly into a place when every minute you expect the scream of shells. The valley before the attack was a mass of guns; never before had I seen so many. I think it was Mr Lloyd George who predicted that we should have our guns standing wheel to wheel and here in this valley on that morning in July his words came true. Close to where I was a tragic thing happened. A splendid boy from my parish enlisted before the war began in the Horse Artillery. He was much under age but being so tall and strong had no difficulty in getting into the army. On the outbreak of war his father, an ex-sergeant-major of the Gunners, rejoined and claimed his son and his battery, and there in that valley, father and son were killed by the same shell.

On Wednesday 14th July at daybreak the attack began. Our aid post was a large German dug-out built into the side of the wood, bordering the valley. It faced, of course the wrong way for us. It was well built and deep and possessed a piano brought there by its former German tenants, who had made themselves very comfortable. We could have done without the piano, but couldn't get it out. About an hour before dawn, along the bank of the valley there burst a continuous wall of flame as hundreds of guns crashed out in a long drawn out roar. The air was filled with the noise of huge masses of metal sweeping overhead to their destination and the hills took up the thundering echo.

It was an awful exhibition of concentrated power set free in a moment of time. Then the troops went over and soon the first wounded came back. We had four doctors in our dug-out and each had two orderlies with him. Very soon all of us were hard at work dressing. The stretcher bearers brought their loads down and hurried off for others, and as fast as the wounded were dressed the RAMC men carried them up the hill through the wood back to the next post, where relays of bearers met them. The Kings and the West Yorks took Bazentin-le-Petit with the Northumberland and Royal Fusiliers in support. By a sad disaster, due I suppose to the wear of the gun, Col Oswald was hit by a blow-back from one of our own guns. He was just conscious when I saw him, proud of his regiment for the splendid way in which they had done their duty, but sad at the thought that he would have to leave it. We could not have cleared the wounded but for the help of German prisoners, who came down escorted by a few tired men with fixed bayonets. We used the prisoners as stretcher bearers and very glad they were to get away from the terror out of which they had come.

A sergeant I knew, badly wounded and waiting, pulled a little book out of his pocket and turned over to a quotation for the day. "I was reading that," he said, "before we went over." I read it. "My presence shall go with you and I will give thee rest." "I knew that was true all through," he said and he smiled as they carried his broken body away. I asked another boy if he had any message for his mother. "Tell her I've done my duty, I couldn't do any more." All day he lay in terrible pain, but he smiled through it all and in the afternoon his brave soul passed.

Amongst the German wounded was a young officer. I had not noticed he was an officer, and I took his heavy coat and put it over another worse wounded than he, because he complained of the cold. Then another squad of stretcher bearers came and I sent this man off with the cloak over him. The German called out: "That is my coat. But it doesn't matter, let him have it." I then saw he was an officer and could speak a little English. He offered me cigarettes but I declined as I was smoking a pipe, so he said: "Take them and give them to your men."

During the morning the Indian Cavalry went through. The attack by our brigade had made a gap through which they hoped to get at the enemy. It was a fine sight when the bearded Lancers, their faces glowing with excitement, each dressed in khaki relieved with a blue sash and a scarlet and khaki turban, cantered through the valley, the long manes and tails of their beautiful horses flowing out in the breeze. A cloud of dust and one lay quiet beside his horse, which two or three times tried to rise and then was also still. Later we dug a grave beside the graves of some of the Indian's white fellow soldiers and two of his mates stood by while I committed his body to the earth and his soul to the God of all Nations.

On Sunday Oswald died. We had first met some months before in a trench under a tremendous counter-attack, near Ypres. I shall never forget his perfect calmness. He might have been at home having tea, though the whole place was rocking. He was a Cavalry officer at first, was wounded early in the war and then appointed APM, but his heart was with the men, so as soon as his wound was healed he came to an Infantry battalion and made what was an indifferent crowd into a splendid regiment. On the same day Oswald was wounded, the officer commanding the 13th Kings, another regiment in the 9th Brigade, was killed. He was a gallant man, an old Boer War irregular, but somehow his battalion lacked unity. My impression was that the CO was remote from his men. It used to make one almost weep to see this battalion; their billets were filthy, their line of march was a rabble and the men looked dirty, uncared-for and miserable.

Then General Deverell found the man for the job. He chose a sergeant of the Greys and promoted him to the command of the Kings. The mob became a regiment, gallant enough before, but the officers and men had never found themselves. From that moment the Kings was one of the smartest battalions in the Division and it was happy, keen and full of that esprit-de-corps which grew under the leadership of Colonel Cranston. It spoke well for the General's discernment that when Cranston was moved to command a machine-gun battalion, the appointment was given to another from the ranks, a sergeant of the Gordons, Colonel Lawrence, who carried on the same tradition.

On 19th July our Brigade was withdrawn and we hoped for a rest. The following day I celebrated the Holy Eucharist, the first chance for about a fortnight. We were out at Carnoy, camping on the site of a previous battle, torn with countless shell holes, with every sort of battle waste lying round. The only thing of beauty was a great clump of scarlet poppies, so there on some empty ammunition boxes over which was spread a cloth, I offered the great memorial of the Crucified, with the glowing mass of scarlet behind the altar, while 40 communicant officers and men knelt round. That evening after a service with the machine-gun company we set off for the unknown. We didn't know quite where we were going but our immediate destination was the village Lonqueral on the edge of Delville Wood.

The companies went up with a long interval between each, Head Quarters following; the Doctor and I brought up the rear with stretcher bearers and a supply of water in petrol tins, which we always had to carry as we never knew where we should get water. On coming to a sunken road just past Bernafay Wood we got into a terrible blast of shells and our stretcher bearers were scattered in the darkness. Many of them were wounded and some of the stretchers were broken, so we got the wounded back to the dressing station at Bernafay, and leaving the rest of the bearers in the trench, the Doctor and I walked up to find the battalion. It was very dark and as we reached the top of a rise we saw sparks of light and thought they were cigarette ends glowing in the dark; we found however that they were the charred remains of a burning house.

We met a few men coming down but they were men of another Division and no one knew where the Fusiliers were, so we moved on until we came to a few strands of barbed wire across the road. Fortunately, we halted there; if we had not done so we should have walked right into the Germans' hands, for they were in the village at the time; our troops holding one part of it and they the rest. We got back again to the men and waited for orders; at daylight a runner arrived and we got up safely to the village of Lonqueral, on the edge of Delville Wood. Our aid post was a shallow cellar only a few feet down, about 3 yards square with but one layer of bricks above and a layer of rubbish to cover it.

The battalion held the line of shallow trenches on the edge of the wood from Friday till Tuesday, getting more and more reduced in numbers of officers and men every day. Sometimes the shelling was desultory and at others a furious storm, and as the whole advance was so confused it was very difficult for our artillery to know exactly the position of our infantry. Constantly shells were bursting in the trees above the trenches and our position was such that when I study the map now it is clear that the Germans were nearly round us, and were shelling us from the West at Martinpuich, from Flers and Bapaume on the North and Ginchy and Guillemont on the East, and from Trones Wood almost behind us. If they had pushed on they must have surrounded us. On Tuesday we expected them and the shells came in unceasing streams, but the counter attack faded away, blotted out by our massed artillery. The Regimental runners managed to keep communications open, for telephone wires were impossible; sweating at every pore they ran through the stream of iron fragments, staggering into HQ with a grin on their faces, or through the shattered village down that dreadful sunken road to Brigade HQ.

This road was the only exit from our position and it was strewn with bodies and broken stretchers, yet the whole time during that awful five days our regimental stretcher bearers, now sadly reduced in numbers, worked with the bearers of the 142nd Field Ambulance, carrying the wounded down to the dressing station, in the side of a bank at Bernafay Wood. Our MO, Captain Hunter, had hardly time to rest. The frail cellar was more like a shambles than an aid post; Hunter would dress the men as they staggered or were carried in, then exhausted for want of sleep, would fall over asleep. So we went on.

On the march down to the Somme, Basil Umney, a young subaltern who had joined us straight from Harrow in April, strained a tendon and after enduring the pain for two days, reluctantly went to the clearing station at Corbie. Early one morning I met him in the village of Lonqueral as he was coming across to report to the Colonel. He was still very lame and I said to him: "You ought not to be here." But he replied: "I couldn't stick it any longer down there when the Company was here, so I left." A few hours after, he was killed; he would have been safe where he was, but he would not save himself.

Every night, in spite of the incessant shelling of the roads behind, our transport never failed us, the sergeant and his men risking their lives every mile of the way, and never did we go short of food or water. I had given strict orders to my servant to stay behind, but several times he turned up and when I abused him for risking his life unnecessarily, he only said: "Oh, I just wanted to see how you were getting on."

In June my former groom, Robins, left me. When we were preparing to come down to the Somme he came one day and said: "I'm quite fit now and I feel I ought to go back to my battalion. I've had a soft job long enough," so I answered: "I'm very sorry to lose you, but if you think you ought to go, you are right."

So he returned to the Worcesters, was wounded slightly, returned and was promoted to corporal, was wounded again, but not severely, and on his next return (as sergeant) was severely wounded and that ended his splendid career in the army. Never was a man better served than I by those gallant men who through the War years looked after my personal comforts. Often they risked their lives without orders or asking and they would not be refused.

On Wednesday morning, 26th July, we were relieved and filed out, grimy, unwashed and exhausted. At Carnoy, consistent with the amazing efficiency of the Army, breakfast was ready, after which we tumbled over and slept for two hours.

I found my friend Davis, the fish porter, with a nasty wound in his chest and I asked him why he hadn't come to the MO to have it dressed. "Oh," he said, "I wasn't going to leave the company." I sent him to the Doctor, who sent him down to the clearing station and as he had a badly swollen knee, due to a former wound, he was operated on and sent home; so we lost the cheery giant from the gallant company, for his wounds necessitated his discharge from the Army.

On the following Sunday we had a solemn eucharist of thanksgiving and memorial for those who had so nobly answered the last great call – about a hundred made their Communion. Now we were at rest again in a dirty little town called Ville sous Corbie, refitting and refreshing. Our Division was much reduced in numbers and was made up with drafts from home. Mosquitoes were very troublesome and the doctor ordered a perpetual warfare on the swarms which infested every stagnant pool, distributing liberal largesse of paraffin and trying to get the place into a decent state of sanitation. I began to feel very slack and the MO sent me off with a temperature to the CCS. And thus ended the first stage of my partnership with the 3rd Division.

The regimental Medical Officers in our Division did noble service. Up to the end of 1915 the Liverpool Scottish were attached to our Brigade. Captain Noel Chavasse, who twice won the highest distinction for personal bravery, was their MO. In billets and in the line he devoted himself completely to the care of his men and was loved by all.

Other medical officers, Glynn with the Northumberland Fusiliers, Mann, Hunter and McGreehin with the Royal Fusiliers, by their splendid service earned always the highest gratitude from all ranks in these regiments, while Sugars, MO of the West Yorks, with utter devotion, lost his leg and nearly his life in repeated efforts to attend the wounded at Bazentin in July 1916. The doctors and sisters in No.5 CCS were all most kind and attentive. I was not really ill and in these strenuous times there might have been reason for inattention to such a minor complaint as trench fever, but even the GOC himself could not have been better treated than I.

The RAMC of the old order amongst the rank and file had no

very great reputation, but certainly in the 9th Brigade the 142nd Field Ambulance, one and all, did their work as from a high vocation. In places of the greatest danger the doctors, dressers and stretcher bearers were always constant and unfailing in their efforts to help the wounded, risking their lives day after day, offering them freely for the sake of those whose work was in the fighting line. Moreover, they were tender and thoughtful for those who were sick.

What a different spirit from those in the same department in the South African War. It was understaffed and overworked. As a trooper in 1901 I was ill with jaundice: on duty all the time I was not given a pill, and stayed with my troop. Just before the end of the war I got enteric, and was sent down to the railway in a bullock wagon, jolting for three days on the springless floor, with a tin of condensed milk and some dirty water to live on, shrouded and choked with dust at the end of the ox convoy. No.9 Hospital at Bloemfontein to which I was sent, was overcrowded and inadequately staffed. My only pleasant remembrance of that awful place was the loving sympathy of one nursing sister, whose tender care during the short time I was under her charge I shall never forget.

The roof of the marquee in which we lay was so black with flies that you could scarcely see the canvas. I got a relapse and nearly died. After being out of bed for three days, too weak to stand alone, I was sent to a so-called Convalescent Camp where the food was so bad – lumps of meat boiled in a dixey, and cocoa coated with hard wax being the chief items – that we all got violent dysentery and if it had not been for the kindness of a squad leader in my troop, who sent me money to buy chocolate, Quaker oats and milk, I think that I should have died, for we had no attention of any sort. At length I asked to go back to my troop and had to walk sixty miles, not even being allowed to put my rifle on the wagon; when I returned to duty I had to have help to mount my horse, for I was still too weak to do it alone.

But now, from the fighting line to the base, everything possible was done for all, and I was soon sent home in a hospital boat and found myself in a delightful hospital in Grosvenor Square.

Through the kindness of the Countess of Grosvenor, my mother and I were invited to spend my sick leave at Saighton Grange, near

Chester. At Euston Station I met our Brigadier, now on leave recovering from a shell burst which had injured his ear drum. He hailed me with a splendid piece of news, "Ottley is coming back to you again." Colonel Hely-Hutchinson's horse had slipped with him and he had broken his leg. However, the return of our CO never took place, for on September 3rd that gallant gentleman, G. C. Ottley fell in action leading his battalion at Guillemont.

For a while I was ill with concussion after a fall in the dark and was unfit for service for some months. At the end of November I had a letter from Neville Talbot, ACG of the 5th Army, telling me that he had a place for me as Chaplain to the Heavy Artillery of the XIII Corps. My acquaintance with him dated back to the days at Poperinghe, when he was senior padre of the 6th Division. One used to see his giant figure coming down the streets of Poperinghe, mounted on a truly colossal chestnut. He and Tubby Clayton, by their genius for fellowship, have done what no words of mine can ever express for the spiritual welfare of the nation in arms and after.

Letter to St Paul's, September 1916

My dear People at home,

I didn't write last month because of the "push". A "push" keeps everybody busy. Our preparation for it began before we got to it. It began when we left the muddy trenches of Belgium and found ourselves scattered about in French villages, where everybody was kind and hospitable and there was no mud. Every day my brigade used to practise making attacks on an imaginary enemy or marching on hard roads, and the two things, combined with good nights and quiet surroundings, made the brigade very fit and hard and ready for that often longed-for thing – open warfare. This means that instead of sitting or standing about in damp ditches waiting for people you never see to drop large bombs on top of you or to knock down your parapet with shells, you will really be able to see real Germans in real helmets (one of which will you hope one day decorate your happy home) and that you will really run after those Germans and have the pleasure of seeing their hands go up above their heads in token that they have had enough. So we got fit, and when we were fit we had to get to where the "push" was to take place. That meant a long train journey packed in trucks labelled "40 hommes, 8 chevaux" and it was hot work being one of the "40 hommes". However we got there.

At one station on the way we arranged to have tea on leaving the train. It was a big business getting tea made for nearly 2000 men and it was owing to the kindness of the RE's who were stationed there, and especially of a certain corporal of RE who came from Deptford, that we did start off from the station full of tea and buns and gratitude.

The march down wasn't eventful. At nights we billeted in rather dirty dilapidated French villages or out in the open, and eventually we reached a part of the country which is well known by this time to those who read newspapers. It is dull, chalky, dusty country and quite uninteresting. We settled down in a valley near a ruined village and the Huns dropped shells occasionally near us but didn't do much harm. Then we had to get ready for our particular push. I must tell you how we continued in the "push" next month, for I think I have used up enough of the Magazine; but I must tell you that our bit of the "push" was completely successful and our objective was gained entirely but it was bought with a price.

In August 1916, Mellish was invalided home with trench fever. As he states in his own account, he was invited by the Countess Grosvenor to convalesce at her home, Saighton Grange in Cheshire. While there, he went out one night to fetch some coal and in the dark fell down a flight of stone steps. For two weeks he was unconscious and hovered between life and death, but finally he came to and slowly recovered. Even then he was very badly concussed and for months afterwards he would suddenly find himself unable to produce the words he wanted if he went to a shop or had to speak to strangers.

When he was recovered enough to return to France in December 1916, Mellish was posted by the ACG to a heavy artillery unit. Presumably this was in order to keep him away from the trenches for a spell, but it seems an odd posting for a man who had been severely concussed and indeed, as he explains in his account, the injury recurred about six months later and he was once again sent back to base hospital and then home to England.

Chapter Ten

The War 1917–18

I FOUND BRIGADE HQ rather far from the centre of things, so Major Bullough, commanding the 117th Siege Battery, invited me to go and live with them. It was a 9.2 Howitzer Battery and every member of it was keen and efficient. The Captain was a young west country business man, the subalterns a school master, a solicitor, a master gunner, a young Scottish student and the last a public school boy.

They were a delightful company. All were devoted to their Major and he was a splendid representative of the old Army, cultured, efficient and lovable. I was very happy there. The winter passed fairly quietly and we had not many casualties from shell fire, but the cold was intense and there was much illness. The ground was frozen so hard that the firing of the guns often broke or bent the trails, while the cooling chambers had to be filled with glycerine to keep them from bursting.

I shall not quickly forget the surroundings of one service held at a Battery on the outskirts of Hébuterne, the nearest we had to the front line. There was no shelter beyond a half ruined barn, so there on shell boxes I offered the Blessed Sacrament with a dead horse in each corner of the area frozen fast into the ground. There was a great reality in the words "that we should at all times and in all places give thanks unto Thee." On Hébuterne plain a remarkable number of hares could be seen and stoats, which also abounded, had snow white fur with jet black tips to their tails.

For months serial photographs had shown that the enemy was constructing a new line, four or five miles behind his present position and our artillery was kept busy hindering his operation. It was easy to see the immense width of the barbed wire defences, showing like a grey ribbon on the airmen's photographs.

In the middle of March patrols found that the enemy had retired on his Hindenburg line, boasted by him to be impregnable. We had long suspected it, for he had for some time before been firing only long range guns while he removed his lighter artillery. He waited until the thaw came and then left us four miles of mud and complete destruction. Every road and railway was destroyed and he brought in a new kind of frightfulness in the form of mines in the roads. Not only were all crossroads blown up, but everywhere, in expected and unexpected places, he laid mines, which in some cases remained inactive for weeks before exploding. They were apparently so constructed that the wire which released the percussion was gradually dissolved by acid until it gave way. He also left traps such as bombs shaped exactly like oval briquettes and mixed with them so that when fires were lit with apparently innocent fuel, explosions took place whereby many of our men were injured. Perhaps all these abominations were fair in a war where nothing was fair and where all the sanctions of civilization had been thrown to the winds by an enemy who had no scruples about using any form of hideous invention. But it was a fresh revelation to find that every well in the destroyed area was poisoned and it taxed the resources of our engineers to keep the advance supplied with water.

It was a noble sight to see the first of our batteries move forward. The roads were impossible rivers of mud, so the Major commanding the 60-pounder guns hitched up his first team of 18 horses and 16 for the second and it was thrilling to see the magnificent "hairies" with a heave, swing the guns through mud thick to the axles and in two hours they were in action, hammering at the Germans' new line.

The area which was abandoned by the retiring enemy was that which had been attacked by us in July 1916, at the beginning of the Battle of the Somme. Just in front of us was Gommecourt Wood, where the gallant London Division had been held up. Now we saw why, for the wire was still unbroken and after all those months, our dead were lying in hundreds on the wire, which all our artillery preparation had left untouched. Yet nine months of heat, rain and snow had not altogether prevented the identification of their bodies.

There I came across Edward Campbell, who had been senior padré of our Division, now promoted to a Corps, doing a piece of work which most would shrink from undertaking. Day after day, with careful system, he searched the dead for identification. Because of long exposure many of the identity discs, being made of paper or wood pulp, seemed at first quite obliterated, but with wonderful patience he collected them and, taking them to his hut, washed them carefully in petrol, and when they were dry was able, in most cases, to read the name, number and regiment on each. For six weeks he continued that noble work, labelling those identified and directing the burial of them all. Through his devoted work over 600 before marked "missing" were certified as "killed in action". Imagine how dreadful and repulsive this work must have been to a sensitive man, yet he never shrank from it till at last, having nearly finished his task, he was taken ill and had to leave it to be completed by others. There is more true devotion in such work as this than much that is spectacular and applauded by the public.

The advance over the devastated area was an enormous tax on the resources of every department of the Army. The destruction was so thorough that nothing was left. There was not a house, bridge, culvert, embankment or crossroads that was not completely destroyed; not even a tree was left, except a very few for the German guns to range on. They even broke down the fruit trees in the orchards. Now we understood the reason for all the explosions we had heard in the last few weeks.

Every pound of food for horse and man had to be carried over five miles of destruction, without a road or rail to carry it on. Tens of thousands of men were urgently needing food, water and shelter. It was a marvellous achievement that in a few days heavy guns with hundreds of tons of shells were in new positions firing far into the enemy's lines. There was no confusion or chaos; everywhere was order and method and with amazing rapidity railway banks were rebuilt and lines laid, roads reconstructed and wells cleaned and huts carried up and erected by the genius of the Royal Engineers.

I remained behind for a few days to get the contents of my hut moved and the mice and rats grew so ravenous that it was almost impossible to sleep, for they ate the straw on which I lay and swarmed round when I tried to eat. As I could get no transport to clear the hut, at last I locked it up and went up to the batteries and when I returned with an MT lorry to get the piano I found the chain marks of an MT lorry outside and the piano vanished. I never saw it again.

When we had settled into our positions we had more snow and the only moderately dry approach to the battery was by using a succession of mounds that were really dead horses. Horses died by the hundreds of exposure. Two new second-line Territorial Divisions had lately arrived on our front and it was pitiful to see their splendid horses with clipped coats standing in mud up to their hocks in that bitter weather. There was no cover for horses, hardly enough for me.

One big house was left in the village of Gommecourt, which was taken for a Brigade HQ but it was found to be mined and fortunately a particularly brutal trick of the Hun revealed it. In the courtyard was a heap of rubbish and when a party of men was detailed to clear it away, one of the men took hold of a shovel sticking out from the heap and pulled it out, exploding a mine which blew him to pieces. Without delay the house was vacated and in due course went up without doing any further harm.

On Maundy Thursday I borrowed a lantern and slides from Neville Talbot, who was ACG of the Army. Coming back at night from a Brigade where I had been holding a lantern service, I found the weight of lantern and gas container rather too heavy, so I hailed a passing car driver, who kindly gave me a lift. A moment after we had passed the crossroads the whole road went up skyhigh in a great spout of earth and rubbish. We ran back, to find that many men who had been sleeping in dugouts at the side of the road were killed or wounded.

Neville Talbot gave into my charge a Church Army motor coffee van. This was a splendid acquisition and the officer in charge of the MT workshops fitted it up and put on new tyres. When I went on leave I took some canteen money to spend on anything useful for the men and I found a portable disinfector which greatly took my fancy, so I took it out with me. I was able to carry it about on the motor van and rid the men of those most unwelcome visitors, of which both officers and men had too full an acquaintance.

Early in June, much to my grief and disappointment, I was

pronounced unfit for further service at the Front by reason of a recurrence of head trouble due to my accident in 1916, so I was bundled off ignominiously to the Base. Fortunately I found a friend whom I had known in the 3rd Division, now Staff Officer to the Base Commandant, and with all kindness they arranged for me to be sent home from No.7 General Hospital at Boulogne.

Thus ended my service with the Gunners, and no man could ever have had more happy associations than I. Often I must have been in the way, another mouth to fill when rations were short, my kit to move when transport was scarce, but never in word, nor I think in thought, was anything shown me but the perfect courtesy of gentlemen, whether it came from Generals or Bombardiers.

A padre to Gunners had not perhaps the same opportunity of identifying himself with a unit as he had with an Infantry Brigade, because of the great number of batteries and the area over which they were distributed. Moreover, the conditions were never suitable for parade services, whatever they are worth, but I always felt that the officers and men, by their very real friendship showed their appreciation and helped me more than I can say to do the best I could, while their ready response proved that their religion was a true ennobling of their splendid service.

Letters to St Paul's, June 1917

Dear People at home,

I am going to try and tell you how a night in a battery of heavy artillery is spent. In the canvas hut it was dark and very quiet. The only sound to be heard was the breathing of the tired owners of the hut. Steps outside – a knock at the door. "Half past two," said the gunner: paused for a moment, then repeated it and got his answer, "Alright". Silence once more for a few moments then my hosts wearily turned out of the blankets and pulled on coats, boots and gas helmets. In a little while a gunner came in with a teapot and cups. By this time everyone was dressed and ready, for dressing is not a long business for artillery officers, who have to turn out at any time of night. Then after a cup of tea and a bit of bread and butter, everyone went out to the work in hand. Nearby was a line of massive howitzers, between and around which lay the trunks of great trees felled a few weeks ago by the spoiling Boche, and a little distance away were the skeletons of broken houses. Behind each gun was a group of large yellow-coloured shells each placed on its base, ready for use. Beside them were clumps of cartridge boxes containing curious white bundles tied together with tapes. Nearby were many round tin cases of fuses, of different shapes and sizes. Each sub-section was busy around its gun. Some men were drawing off the tarpaulin cover, others uncasing fuses and screwing them into the noses of the shells.

It was dark, for the moon was not yet at the full. All was quiet, except for the occasional rattle of machine guns and the burst of an odd shell or two in the distance. A little to the left of the guns was the battery commander's post, a shelter made of sand-bags and iron. Nearby was another dug-out in which two telephonists kept constant touch within the battery and received messages to send to those who, miles away, control and order the work of many batteries.

"Stand by. Load." Behind the guns the subalterns gave orders to their sections and saw that all was right. Each gun was loaded and, by a perfect balance gear, the great muzzles were lifted, pointing over the crest of the bank. The layer of each gun, taking orders from his officer, with a clever arrangement of lenses and prisms, laid his aim, while others regulated the exact position of the gun, so that within a few moments the great howitzer stood loaded, laid and ready.

Each "Number 1", the sergeant of his gun, stood on the left of his gun and as it was loaded and laid reported to his officer: "Number 2 ready sir", and so on until all had reported. On the right of each gun stood a gunner with a cord in his hand hooked to the detonator which fired the charge. The major and the captain were standing together. The last quiet words had been given. Each officer stood watch in hand marking by the light of a torch the flight of the few seconds which were left before zero time. All was tense and still. "Fire". With a crash and roar from each uplifted muzzle there belched out flames and smoke, while through the torn air rushed out four great masses of steel to their aim far into the German lines. After that tremendous zero, each gun continued at "Gunfire" – that is continuous firing until further orders were given. By a turn of the lever, the breech was thrown open; the sergeant lowered the muzzle by a swiftly revolving wheel, four gunners lifted another shell, by a carrier which gripped the shell, enabling them to place it on the crane, which others swung up until the shell was level with the barrel, then four men with a long pole rammed the shell home with a shout; another threw in the cartridge, a bundle of terrible concentrated energy. With a turn on the lever the breech was closed and the muzzle swung up once more. The layer having set the aim jumped to the ground. Again the order, a tug at the cord, a crash and a roar as each shell flew to its mark. An ear-splitting unending chorus of bellowing sound, not only from this battery, but from others behind and on the right and left. As each shell tore its way through space, one could see, by the blaze, the forms and faces of sweating men as they fired ceaselessly.

In the battery commander's post, the major was bending over his map laid out on a rough table. The dug-out, lit by two guttering candles, was time after time plunged into darkness as the blast from the nearest gun blew out the lights and shook the hut. Now and then one could hear the sharp squeal of answering shells sent from guns way back in the enemy's batteries. What does it all mean?

This. A few thousand yards ahead, line upon line of our men were advancing to the attack behind the terrible paralysing barrage of our artillery. Part of the great Hindenburg line was being attacked. In front of our line, with a horrid roar and volumes of red flame, in smoke and torn-up earth, the shells were pitching in an unthinkable storm of horror. This was how the gunners were helping their brothers in the infantry. Over there, khaki figures and grey were struggling to win or hold a few yards of churned up land or ruined village. Blood and steel and awful explosive are the brush which paints upon the map that little line which seems so small when you open the paper tomorrow. High up one saw a curious red light which flashed for a moment as the rising sun shone on the wings of an aeroplane, as the pilot circled round and round, backward and forwards, watching the fight going on in the plain below.

It is a great co-operative business – the infantryman, the airman and the gunner has each his part to play. If one fails to do his work, there can be no success. But their toil and energy, their splendid bravery and courage, is wasted if they of the front line are not backed up and supplied by their home partners whose object is to supply the shells, the guns, the machines which are being used in such enormous numbers at the front. It is sad reading to see that the strike spirit is about in these days. It seems impossible that men at home, whose lives are protected by their brothers, friends and sons, can refuse to help those who so nobly and ungrudgingly give their lives for us, our nation and our peace. A strike at home means that a certain amount of help is not forthcoming. A strike means death and failure for many who have given their all. I do not think there can be many who would strike for money or for any other cause if they could see, as I see, the agony and sweat of those who fight and die for us.

Today I have been shown over two munitions factories where the shells which my batteries are firing in such huge numbers day and night are made. I was greatly impressed by the work of the women and girls – not that I thought little of the men's work but one is accustomed to see men doing such work, not girls. Yet today I was shown that the vast proportion of this work in making shells was done by women. I remember too that sometimes my gunners find little messages of encouragement slipped into cases of munitions and now I have seen the work of those whose hearts are with the men who use the products of their handiwork.

This is a long letter. I can only tell you how lovely England is, dressed in sweet fresh green of the springtime. Coming from the sad ruin and ugliness of poor France, spoiled and mutilated by the ravaging Hun, England is more beautiful than ever and one cannot feel thankful enough that our homeland has been spared.

Yours sincerely,
Noel Mellish C. F.

Letter to St Paul's, June 1917

Dear People at home,

It's radiant, hot and glorious. The country is covered with delicious long grass and the trees are trying to assert their right to grow. Even the poor blasted stumps of shell-shocked trees are covered with little clumps of leafy twigs. The horses are making up for the bad time of the winter. I have the use of a lovely chestnut mare. Yesterday was Sunday and she took me round to many batteries, standing close by cropping the rich grass.

It was a glorious day. Every service was a "Benedicite" – the green things of the earth, the fowls of the air, the beasts and cattle and the children of men, all blessing and praising and magnifying the Lord. Our church tent is near the hut where I live. It is beautified by the loving gift of the St Perpetua Guild. Here for the first time I have been able to have the altar as beautiful as it should be. In our mess hut a pair of swallows have built on the wall. In the nest, cosily made of mud and warmly lined with feathers, there are now six little fluffy yellow things, which seem all eyes and beak. All day long the happy little couple are busy feeding the family, flashing in and out through the window, sparkling in the sun with their rich dark blue wings, white breasts and red necks. At night, every now and then, the cock pulls his head out from under his wing as he sits on a wire close by the next. Then he asks how the family is getting on and she answers with a clucking noise and under the wing goes the bright little head. There is so much that is beautiful. Many of the gunners have made gardens round their guns in spare moments, they are gay with flowers. I'm just back from visiting my batteries. A warm day has been followed by the cool calm of evening – the sun setting in a globe of red glory and the moon rising silver and beautiful in the East. The West is tinged with spreading splendour. The clear music of the cavalry "first post" is ringing out from a camp where sleek, contented draft horses are peacefully munching their evening hay, placid and calm, as if there were no such thing as ugly war. A kite balloon sinks slowly to its rest, red-coloured by the sun-set. The resting infantry are playing football. A few miles away there is no peace – but they are forging it. Pray for them.

Yours affectionately,
Noel Mellish, C. F.

Letter to St Paul's, August 1917

Dear People at home,

There wasn't much to write about last month. I had to leave the "Heavies" for a while under doctor's orders and after a few days in Boulogne, I was sent to "Blighty" and spent ten days at a hospital up in Town receiving the great kindness and attention one always has at these wonderful places. My mother and I spent three weeks leave in beautiful Surrey and then my orders came to go to another delightful spot. This is the best camp I have ever seen. It is situated in a park about three miles out of the city. A mile away is a mountain, rugged and beautiful, and eastward is the sea, while in the distance are ranges of hills decked in glorious shades of colour.

The regiment to which the camp belongs is the —. The camp

consists of rows of wooden huts, dry and well built. At the east end is a large regimental institute and at the other end of the camp is a YMCA hut. There is a large parade ground and there are several acres of grass land beautified by fine trees and containing golf links. Many flower beds make the place gay and bright, while between the huts are large beds of growing potatoes.

Here are all grades of soldiers. There are many who have been out to the front, have been wounded, and after treatment in hospitals and at convalescent camps, have come back again. Many of these men have three, four or five wound stripes on their left sleeves. How hateful it is to see in the papers of strikes being proposed by men who earn ten times as much money as these splendid fellows and who know nothing of the agony of which those slips of gold braid are the outward and visible sign. Many of these returned soldiers are not yet fit for more than light training. Every day classes are held for those who have injured arms and hands so that by means of gradual exercises they may become fit again to serve once more. Other classes are made up of men with crippled legs and feet. These have to learn to walk and run and this costs pain and time. Each day as one walks round the camp, one sees classes being held for drill, physical exercise, bombing, machine gun, bayonet work and musketry. In one class a batch of recruits is being drilled in marching, alignment, balance and use of arms; a little way off a squad of NCOs is performing, very smartly, the movements which they a few weeks hence will teach others.

A piece of land represents a bit of battlefield and contains trenches, dug-outs and bombing posts. Further on is a section of front line and a No Man's Land, full of imitation shell holes, while a row of straw-stuffed figures is waiting to receive the attentions of the men who are being taught to rush the trenches and make the best use of their bayonets.

The whole camp is a school for those who, starting from the awkward civilian stage, in a few months arrive at the alert and ready condition of the infantry soldier. Besides all this the camp is a study in right economy. Everybody, officer and man, is well fed and well housed. The kitchens are models of good camp cookery. There is a hut in which all the fat which is not necessary for food is rendered down to dripping. This is graded and packed in barrels and sent away to be used for munition work. All waste pieces of fatty food such as bacon rind and scraps of meat are treated so that no fat is wasted. A not inconsiderable amount of grease is saved by means of a tank, in which all the plates used at meals are washed in boiling water. All spare scraps of bread are collected, baked in an oven and ground up with the refuse from the fat-treating process, and the product is, I believe, sold to poultry food and dog biscuit makers. No food is wasted here and much money is saved for other needs.

In the excellent YMCA hut and in the Institute everything is done for the comfort and recreation of the men, while ladies by their kindly work make these places comfortable and attractive. On Sundays we have services at 7 and 9 a.m. for Church of England men in the YMCA huts and at 11.30 on Wednesday I have a Bible class for those charming little ruffians, the band boys in the Institute library. We have three bands – pipe and drum, brass and string. The band plays once a week in the officers' mess, at church services on Sundays, and in fine weather after service the park is open for the townspeople to come and listen to a band for an hour or two.

The Doctor is a very hard-worked man here. He sees the sick at 7 in the morning and from 10 o'clock onwards he is supervising the training of unfit men in their exercises, inoculating those who are going to the front, examining drafts, lecturing to officers and men and seeing that the camp is hygienic and clean. In the evening sick men parade again and those who need attention for slight wounds and sore feet are dressed by the doctor's wife who during the day works with other ladies in the canteen of the Institute. There are many officers in the camp, a large number of whom have been at the front and are on home duty for a while until they are fit for service abroad. A mile away from here is a barracks occupied by a battery of —. Here officers, men and horses are training for active service. At one corner of a square we have a chapel which was once used as a storehouse. Now the colonel has had it fixed up and furnished. I hope that in a little while the walls will be painted and it will be worthy of its purpose. The altar frontal, dossal, and curtains sent by the Guild of St Perpetua which I used in France, are now adorning the alter in this chapel. There is much more I can tell you, but this must go by tonight's post, so I will say goodnight.

> Yours always affectionately,
> Noel Mellish, C. F.

Letter to St Paul's, September 1917

Dear People at home,

There is no news to tell you. It was a great joy to me to be able to spend a Sunday at St Paul's and to see many of the folks during the last few days. Tonight I am on my way back. I cannot give you my address yet. I met a medical officer this evening who is attached to the same battalion of which Father Hambidge is Chaplain. His address is 2nd Batt. The Queen's, BEF. Mr Lloyd is in His Majesty's Hospital Ship "Sudan", GPO London.

I was glad to see Bert Nash, our once hardworking sergeant in the CLB company. He has been badly wounded, but is, I hope, now recovering the use of his right arm. He was in the same battalion of the Queen's of which Father Hambidge is now the padre. Harold Beardow is now expecting corporal's stripes. He is still serving at home after his bad wound. It is good to see that our CLB boys are doing well and are very happy. Claude Pratt is recommended for a commission.

Will somebody at St Paul's kindly undertake to collect news of our boys who are now serving, and to forward that news and any interesting extracts of letters received from them to the Editor of the Parish Magazine each month? I hope the Men's Club will do the same. We want to hear news of each other.

With all greetings and hopes for the safety and happiness of you all.

Yours affectionately,
Noel Mellish, C. F.

The bracing air of Scotland and the hospitality of the KOSB combined to make me fit and as I had little to do I explored the noble city of Edinburgh and the holiday habits of the Glasgow people which amazed me. At Portobello the holiday makers used to take shifts at the numerous lodgings. The first shift would sleep until midnight and then take to the beach and the fresh air. The other lot would then come into possession and the relief would be complete about 1 a.m. It has been said that the English enjoy their pleasures sadly, but the Scots beat them hollow. I learnt a good deal from the MO at Duddington Camp when I accompanied him to medical inspections. There must have been thousands of fit men who were exempt from military service and it made me ill to see some who wore His Majesty's uniform incapable of walking, let alone fighting. One boy was there who had an overhanging deformed knee, this leg being two inches shorter than the other. Yet he had been enlisted, served out with uniform and kept at the expense of the nation for six months at a cost, I suppose of about £100. There was another youth who would only walk on the side of his foot, obviously mentally deficient and unchanged by argument or reason. The Q department of the Army was at this time earnestly reducing waste and there was keen competition as to how much fat could be saved for conversion into high explosive. The Scots are noted for economy; the QM here was so enthusiastic in increasing fat returns that he looked with severity at the corpulence of any in the camp who appeared to be well nourished and made mental notes as to how such matters could be remedied. I often wonder why the whole nation was not conscripted at the outbreak of war. We should have taken to it with enthusiasm and it would have saved the tragedy of men at home striking for more money when their brothers were being blown to pieces in thousands to protect them from the savagery of the Hun. I suppose our leaders were afraid of committing the crime of interfering with the freedom of the subject.

Back to France again, and a visit to Bishop Gwynne, who received me with the unfailing friendship which made him beloved, not only by chaplains, but Generals, with the result that I was posted once more to the 3rd Division. On 27th September the train landed me back again at Poperinghe and I found my way to the detail camp at Vlamertinghe. The Division was in the line, but as it was expected out very soon I remained where I was. The Passchendaele Battle was going on and I found that behind the lines in 1917 was almost as bad as it was in the front line in 1915, for though there was no shelling here, during those moonlit nights activity in the air was unceasing.

There were enormous camps of labour corps, and Chinese, beside prison enclosures and masses of transport. Fighting went on in the air in bright moonlight, while the rays of many searchlights lit the whole heavens. All night long bombs were dropping, causing panic, especially among the Chinese, for there could be no concealment of the tents in such moonlight and there was absolutely no cover of any sort. Here I met Colonel Hely-Hutchinson, who had just returned from home, looking very ill; a bomb had fallen into his tent, killed his servant and shocked him badly.

On the night of 1st October I heard that the Royal Fusiliers were coming out, so I went up with a corporal and nine men, who were sent up to act as guides to the out-coming companies. As we passed through Ypres some bombs were dropped and five of the guides were wounded. The rest of us went on to the Menin Gate, standing stark and tragic, one charred beam alone remaining of the archway. Soon the battalion came along, the men covered with mud, and we got back without further incident.

The next day the General inspected and spoke to the Brigade, telling us what was in store – no rest, but a quiet place further South. Later we got into buses and soon found ourselves in the familiar haunts of Winnegeele. Entraining at St Omer, we got to the ruined city of Bapaume and after a few days at Ypres went up to the line at Bullecourt, from which the Hindenberg line ran North towards Arras. The battalion had changed very much since I left in 1916, there were only one officer, the Regimental Sergeant-Major and a few NCOs and men whom I knew, but the spirit of the regiment was the same.

During the fighting at Passchendaele my predecessor, L. M. Andrews, had been wounded and Bernard Ruck-Keen, a very devoted priest in the division, was killed. I found Alec Fraser with the Royal Fusiliers taking Andrew's place. It seemed almost a shame for me to push him out. He had gone to Passchendaele on a push bike, how he ever got there I don't know. He got away with the battalion, but the push bike was left in a shell hole, which was not surprising for the Passchendaele Ridge seemed to be nothing else but shell holes, and the whole ghastly area was flooded. Bullecourt was a salient and always unpleasant. It had been the scene of terrific fighting when the Australians took it early in 1917 and there was a constant succession of counter attacks from both sides, until the place became a veritable mortuary. The parapet in places seemed to be composed of little else than the bodies of the dead.

Its position was important as it commanded the slope Southwards to Bapaume.

We were now in the same district as I was in before with the Gunners, but nearly all the batteries I knew had gone north and Major Bullough, my old battery Major whose friendship I so valued, had been killed at Ypres. I found some whom I knew and as the old motor van was not being used I got it back with the disinfector and found them both most useful for the battalion.

The division was fortunate in that we had the same General. From July 1916 until the end of the war General Deverell was in command. He was a captain at the outbreak of war, but soon rose by his amazing capacity. I do not know that the Division ever had a black mark. The General certainly expected a high standard of efficiency and he got it. One day he came to one of our chaplains' meetings and told us he was pleased with our work. He said he would help us in any way he could and approved of our living with the battalions and liked us to go into the line with them. This all made a great deal of difference to us as we felt we had his support. Before the Somme Battle a Corps or Army Order came out stating that all chaplains were to go to clearing stations. What a nuisance we should have been. Of course nobody took the slightest notice of it and the order died a natural death and was never repeated.

The 3rd Division was never much mentioned in the papers, though I once saw it called "the Iron Division". It is not an inapt name, for it was very hard to bend and it never broke.

Those October days were more or less uneventful; a good deal of shelling but otherwise fairly quiet. The whole country was devastated and hideous. Our rest camp was wretchedly cold, for the huts at Favreuil where we went out on relief were made of iron and had been stripped of their wood lining some time before; but the dugouts in the reserve line made by the Germans were very deep and well fitted up and the front line was no worse than most front lines. In one of these deep dugouts we found an enormous black Newfoundland; she was suffering badly from shell shock and refused to go up to the daylight. She lived on the food given her down below and had a great capacity for drinking soapy water. We used to hear her at all times of the night lapping up the contents of our basins. We took her down to the transport lines much against her will, and, while there, she was taken for walks on a chain by the Major's servant. He was rather small, so she used to pull him along at a trot; however, at the first opportunity she escaped. I suppose she returned to some dugout, for we never saw her again.

In November came the famous surprise attack by the Tanks and the dash to Cambrai, followed by the struggle for Fourlon Wood and the defeat of that gallant enterprise for lack of reinforcements.

On November 29th we took up a new position, our Division holding an enormous length of line from Bullecourt towards Havrincourt, from which position we were just in view of the fierce fighting going on at Moevres. The line we held was the old French one with no support behind us. I suppose the Germans were so much engaged in beating off the attack that they could give no attention to us, but we held the long line so thinly, with small groups of men at long intervals, that it would have been an easy matter for them to get through.

On December the 6th we went back to the Bullecourt trenches and the following morning the enemy made a very determined attack; for some days we had a lively time and the Germans gained a few yards of our line, but they got no further. On Sunday December the 16th we were relieved and just as the relief was finished, two companies had to go back again to strengthen the defences, which had been weakened by recent attacks. It was a terrible strain on the morale of the men to have to return into a bad and dangerous position just when they thought they had got clear of it, but back we went and did not get out to our rest camp until 7 in the morning. We hoped to spend Christmas at the camp close to the place where I had lived with the gunners in the spring, but Sunday night and Monday night had to be spent on work in the front line. It was disappointing, but had to be done.

Late in October Colonel Hartley was appointed to the command of the 4th Royal Fusiliers. He came from one of the service battalions. There was one member of the 4th who was not pleased to see him and that was the Quartermaster. For a short time the battalion had been commanded by a Colonel who allowed the QM to please himself. Now "Togo" (for we will treat him incognito) was not popular with the men. He was one of those men who live in an atmosphere of suspicion. He had long service and wore the decoration "for 18 years of undetected crime" as the men used to say. I suppose some Quarter-masters are apt to look upon everybody as trying to "do them down" and act accordingly. Togo was in his element. He never by any chance came up to the line, he had no use for Germans or their shells, so he hatched little schemes for making people uncomfortable at the least expense and was very comfortable himself.

Then that CO left. When Colonel Hartley came he requested Togo to come up every evening with the rations and report to Battalion HQ and, more than that, he ordered him to go up to each Company Headquarters and report to the Company Commanders when the rations were up. This was a great shock to Togo, it hurt his feelings. So like the old soldiers he didn't die, but faded away. He found that his services were required at home. How he managed to work it I don't know, but the climax came when he was gazetted as the recipient of the Military Cross. The Army is a strange institution in some ways. But at any rate we scored, for in place of Togo we got a first rate Quartermaster, who really cared more for the men than for himself; so we never mourned the loss of Togo and now I believe he runs a pub somewhere and I expect he waters down the beer.

On Christmas Eve we were working very close to the enemy lines putting out barbed wire but there were no friendly advances, nor any attempt this time. We had in front of us no pacific Saxons, but watchful and determined troops. We finished this work and moved out and had just got clear of the trench at midnight, when the last Christmas Day of the War was ushered in for us by a salvo of shells from the enemy, but they did no harm and we got home to bed safely.

At midday I had the first Christmas service, but everyone was tired and there was a feeling of depression over all of us. I suppose the failure of the attempt to get through at Cambrai accounted for it. I don't know that we thought about it very much, but it damped our spirits and the men were very tired.

On the Sunday after Christmas I had a good many men to the services and a fair number of communicants; we sang some carols in the evening, but without enthusiasm – "See amid the Winter's snow" was too real to sing about it. On Monday we prepared our Christmas dinner and I took the old bus over to Arras to hire plates for the feast. The men had dinner at 6 o'clock and there was a limited supply of beer, Mark II, then we had a concert. After this the sergeants' and officers' messes each had their dinner, for which we procured two noble turkeys, and the Royal Fusiliers Association provided all the battalion with excellent plum puddings to complete the equipment. The officers of the Northumberland Fusiliers came over and joined us and we all enjoyed ourselves.

We had an excellent Concert Troup called the "Elegant Extracts". They first took the stage at Arras under the supervision of a Major Winnington Barnes, who was a soldier of fortune, amazingly good company and very popular. He was popularly known as "The Mate" from having had at some time a connection with the Merchant Service. I first met him swinging down through the Menin Gate on my return to the battalion, his jovial face beaming with a smile which almost engulfed one. He had great histrionic talent and under the tuition of "The Mate" and Padre Andrews the company was very successful.

The star turn was Doris, the girl, (not according to the flesh). He (or she) cultivated the part with such success that even on parade as a Lewis gunner he was sometimes known to blush and pout and when suitably made up he was really charming. Curly was another talented member of the troupe who in "Civvy" days had seen a good deal of life as a boxing partner in the East End, but Miller was to my mind the most valuable of all for he could always make his audience rock with laughter by simply looking at it. He was a little man, with a lean, sad face, a taxi driver by profession (who drove the motor bus when required); his face was his fortune and he would have made a good understudy for Charlie Chaplain. I wish I could hear him sing "Whizz-bang Lane" now.

The Colonel allowed me to have two of the pioneers to work the disinfector and it was most successful in freeing the mens' blankets and clothing from unwanted allies. Of these I had no small experience in the Boer War so was glad to find an effective means of dealing with them.

Miller looked after the bus and in it we were able to get a good deal of stuff from the EF Canteen and French stores at Arras, including sometimes crates of eggs, which were a great luxury. Then overwork and underoil put the poor old thing out of action, but I found some friends in a Balloon section, to whom I used to go from time to time to hold services and they kindly promised in return to fix it up in their repair shops, as Miller had operated on the radiator with a red hot poker with small success.

Letter to St Pauls' Deptford, October 1917

My dear People at home,

On 18th September, I arrived at Boulogne after a good crossing and left for St Omer at midnight. Early in the morning I found an estaminet, where the good lady gave me breakfast, the usual omelette, coffee in a glass and slices of bread cut off a huge flat French loaf. Then I went up to see the Bishop and get my orders. I sometimes wish that in the Church at home, where we so often in prayers and hymns speak of the church as an army, there was more of the army order and discipline. Out here the Bishop is to us chaplains our general. He is truly our father in God, and exercises a real generalship in kindness and wisdom. The Bishop at first wanted me to go to another division but he kindly heard my reasons for wanting to go back to my old division and then promised that he would send me to it. I had to wait a while for a vacancy and during the week I spent in St Omer I had the opportunity of attending a Retreat, at the house where the School for Chaplains is held. Canon B. K. Cunningham took the Retreat – you will remember him, for he spent several days at St Paul's a year ago. The Retreat was most inspiring and the lectures which followed were very good. Then orders came for me to go back to my old brigade and to the same regiments with which I was before. When I got to the railhead, I found that the brigade was in action so went on to the detail camp and had a very kind welcome from all those whom I knew, and indeed from everyone who was in the camp. As the brigade was soon to be relieved, I spent the next two days looking up old friends. Late on Saturday night one of my regiments came back and on Sunday morning I found a good many of my old friends. At 11 o'clock we had the Eucharist in the YMCA hut, the other padre of the brigade and I sharing the service. In the evening an officer took guides up to the post at which the battalion was to be met. On the way an aeroplane dropped a couple of bombs, wounding five of the guides, but to our joy there was no further damage when the companies began to come out. Everyone was very thankful to be out, for they had had a very hard time in some of the hardest fighting during this year. Next evening motor buses came to carry the regiments back to the place where we were to go to rest.

Two days afterwards the Divisional General inspected the brigade and said that he was very well pleased with the steadiness and splendid behaviour of this brigade. He told us that as the operations were to be continued we were not going out for a month's rest, but that we were to move to a quiet part of the line. So after another day we moved away by train and took over a part of the line near the places where I was when I was working with the Heavy Artillery. We had two days in a camp behind the line and then we came up to the old trench life.

For a week I have been living with the Royal Fusiliers in reserve trenches, and now this battalion is in the front line, the others are close by and my other units – Field Ambulance Detachment and Field Company of Royal Engineers – are within easy distance. We are having good weather and our casualties are small in number I am happy to say. We are now looking forward to going out for change and training and cleaning up.

It was a great joy to come back and find that the same colonel is again commanding this battalion and the same General commands this brigade. In both my battalions there are a number of officers, NCOs and men whom I knew fifteen months ago. Everybody is very cheery. I can't say how glad I am to be back in the infantry again. The gunners are splendid people and were all kind and responsive, but one can't help but be glad to come to one's old friends again. My horse "Jim" is still with the regiment. He was very ill with the cold during last winter, but he has quite recovered and is as willing and clever as ever. Here I am writing in a deep dug-out, very safe and rather stuffy but quite comfortable. The people who were here before us left a large black dog. She is a dipsomaniac, her weakness being a craving for soapy water of which she drinks enormous quantities – she seems to prefer soapy to good water. It's a curious taste. The weather is getting colder and anyone who would like to send a pair of socks to a soldier who has to spend many hours in trenches which will become slimy bogs, will do an act of kindness. We also want illustrated papers and magazines; trenches are dull places. Now I must finish up by wishing you the safety and protection of God and His Angels in these present days and nights.

Yours affectionately,
Noel Mellish, C. F.

Letter to St Paul's, December 1917

Dear People at home,

We are in winter again. This letter brings you all my best greetings for Christmastide and the New Year – "Peace on Earth" at home and abroad. What we have to remember is that the good news of God's messenger, His dear Son, was news of peace on earth amongst men of goodwill. We long for peace, but not for peace at any price. Out here today and every day, men are being wounded and killed that there may be peace. They are the peace-bringers and they are paying the price. But at home also you must pay part of the price. Jesus, the peace-bringer, came to be the General of the army of those who are out to win peace. He is not the agent of those who would sacrifice honour and right. Every soldier takes Him for his Hero, whether he knows or not. Jesus is the Hero, the Leader of men – the men who go over the top for the sake of home and all that is good. Home is a sacred thing made holy by the King of homes. Never, never long for a bad peace. We must win – and all of us are trying to be like Him, by paying in blood and courage and fortitude.

He was born at Christmastide in a poor home so that all homes might be right in Him. He suffered the strain and agony of uncertainty that we might all be certain that good is a gift of God. He bore all evil and pain so that all men and women and children might be cleansed from pride and selfishness and love of low things that are hateful to God. He loved men so utterly that He died for them and rose to the new life that we might share it with Him.

The "peace at any price" cry is the work of the devil, who wants men to fight and grab and hate. God hates war, but He still more hates a sham peace. Therefore, whether you suffer poverty or pain or fear from the enemy, look up, lift up your hearts to the Maker and Leader of all who are for right. When you suffer want of food, your men out here suffer more. They are patient and noble and great and they, day by day, are sending you the best Christmas gift that a man can give – peace. They give it to you with all the love of their great hearts.

Dear people of St Paul's, be brave and strong and true to our Master. By your love and your loyalty be true to our Lord. The great General, Jesus Christ is out to win for Deptford, for England and for the world, a new life.

My love to you all. A happy, happier Christmas next year, a better New Year. We hoped for it this year, but not yet. We must go on and hope and work. Pray for us.

Your affectionate friend,
Noel Mellish, C. F.

Chapter Eleven

The War 1918

ON THE 25TH JANUARY 1918 we went up into the Hindenberg line, part of which had been taken from the Germans the year before. There were rumours of a great attack. The trenches were in good order and the dugouts very deep and splendidly built, fitted with bunk beds, tables and chairs. During the next month the enemy was quiet, nothing eventful happened and I went up and down visiting the various units in and out of the line, holding services with all of them.

On February 20th my leave came and I got home the next day. A great change for good had been made in providing comfort for the men going on leave. During the bitter winter of 1916–17 the railway carriages were old French ones with hardly any glass in the windows and I believe it is true that some men died of chill on their homeward journey. Now all was changed. Each truck had a brazier and seats round the sides and every man was issued with two blankets, so we were quite comfortable.

On 7th March I returned and reached Headquarters on the following day. The attack was expected on the 13th and a big barrage was put up by our artillery all night, but nothing happened. During the next week the enemy kept very quiet and it was glorious sunny weather. March 17th was Passion Sunday and we had Holy Communion in a shelter in our reserve trench and later went down for services at the transport lines. The Roman Catholic padre and I arranged to fix up and share the shelter as a chapel for our services; we were very good friends and spent some time getting the place ready and making a rough altar and a notice board.

On Thursday the 21st at 5 a.m. the silence was broken by a terrific outburst of fire, but the fog was so intense that we could see nothing. The enemy came over in massed formation and in the fog broke through the Division on our right. This left our flank exposed, but all attacks were beaten off by our Brigade on the right, while the left of the Division held the Germans on their side towards Arras. Colonel Hartley brought the companies round to face the enemy's attack and in the afternoon the pioneer battalion of the King's Royal Rifles was brought up to face the other way, so that we were fighting outwards from three sides of a square.

During the night constant attacks were beaten back, but under cover of darkness the enemy got his guns up closer and was able to fire right down our support and reserve trenches, but we kept him back by rifle fire and all along our line he never got a foothold, though attacking all day. At nightfall on the second day the Germans ceased, but by their lights we could see that on the following day when they renewed we should have them advancing all round us. At midnight we had orders to evacuate the line. Each battalion moved through the last and each left a covering party to form a rearguard. In perfect order and quiet, without a cigarette alight, or a word spoken, we stole out, leaving in every dugout small pieces of candle and cakes of gun cotton. This retirement was completed by 3 a.m. and the last company had the satisfaction of seeing great flames bursting out of the dugouts. A new line of defence had been prepared and it was manned with good troops. There was not a single casualty in the 9th Brigade during the retirement and we got away all our wounded, but had to leave the dead.

On Saturday we had a rest day. I went up the Arras Road in the afternoon to see how my balloon friends were, and found they had been shelled out and had gone. My poor old coffee bus stood there without an engine, so there I had to leave it.

On Palm Sunday morning at 5.30 all the men went out to dig another reserve trench and at midday after their return I celebrated the Eucharist, out in the open away from the trenches. While I was consecrating, a German plane came over so low that I could see the airman. I expected he would signal for the line to be shelled but nothing happened. Evidently the enemy had had a serious check. From Monday to Wednesday he made tentative attacks on our front, which were all beaten back. One morning before daybreak a German ration party lost its way and we got their rations; brown bread, in large heavy loaves, rather sour but not bad to eat, and biscuits, quite sweet and nice. The tinned meat seemed to be rabbit, though it was possibly cat, and they had some sort of weak coffee to drink, tasting rather like "Instant Postum", possibly made of wheat.

During Wednesday we could plainly see without glasses the enemy bringing his guns into action. We had no guns to fire for all had been withdrawn. In the evening the Northumberlands took our place in the line and we got out to a camp behind at midnight. After some food, I read my letters, of which I found eighteen awaiting me. I was just thinking of getting into my blankets when a shell exploded and soon the whole line was bombarded. We lost no time in clearing out to a trench. My servant Bennett, with his usual smartness, rolled up my valise, and dumped it into the sunken road; thus by his care I lost nothing. Many of the officers lost all the kit they had, for the huts were soon on fire. We had five hours of shelling and at eight in the morning the enemy came over in swarms.

The King's Liverpools and Northumberland Fusiliers kept back the first attack and before they could be over-powered, the Royal Fusiliers went up through the barrage and all day long the Division was fighting hand to hand, firing so fast that their rifles were too hot to hold. At one critical moment a mass of Germans got round, but Captain Lord swung his company round and beat them back by a flank attack. Once more our infantry proved too good for the Germans.

Early on Good Friday morning a Canadian Division came up to relieve us and we were glad to go. The Doctor had been busy dressing the wounded after the attack had ceased, but a German 5.9 gun was searching for a battery behind and his shells came very near our aid post. We sent off Bennett and the last two stretcher bearers who were in the shelter, and moved out to the place where the battalion was assembling. Just as we had gone a shell burst in the dugout and left nothing of it; a short time before it had been full of men.

Our losses were very heavy, but the German attack was broken and, as we learned later, broken for good in their attack on Arras. The Brigade staggered out, officers and men utterly exhausted, but with a few hours' sleep at Ficheux we were able to go on, and after a further match, stopped for the night.

Easter Day we spent in beautiful surroundings in quiet unspoilt country with flowers and trees around and some of us made a very real Thanksgiving at the Eucharist.

The following morning we all got into dear old London motor buses and lorries for a 25 mile ride through the country, the bright green of the early crops springing up in glowing squares like a beautiful chess board. The men were all chaffing as usual in the buses till we came to our destination, near Noeux-les-Mines, where we spent a restful week in good billets. On 9th April we went off in buses to the other side of Bethune into a new battle area. The Germans had made a sudden attack in an attempt to get over the canal. Only a few days before it had been pleasant country with peaceful farms, now the farms were smashed with shells, dead horses and cows lying about and the people had fled for refuge, poor souls. Some of the animals we found still tied and we let them loose. The attack had been so sudden that the French people had scarcely time to get away with their lives. Yet they had not all run. In the morning I saw a grey-haired man and his little daughter go up to their farm and try to get back their few cows. The girl was cool and collected, showing no fear of the shells, which were bursting in and over the village. Another family was harnessing a horse to a cart, on which all the household stuff they could save was packed, a little child of six helping to get them ready. We had been brought up to help a division which had been rushed into the gap near Bethune when the Portuguese bolted. There was Portuguese equipment all over the place and the French people were loud in their curses for leaving it to the Huns.

In this sector the Germans were using a gun which fired an enormous shell. It came along through the air sounding like an omnibus and when it burst it fired the largest shrapnel I have ever seen. We were in support and had few casualties, but Oswin Creighton, padre to the Gunners, was killed by a shell; he had been out in Gallipoli and had been with this Division for 18 months and the gunners were very much attached to him.

We moved up into the line and on April 18th the enemy made a determined attack but our artillery was too much for him and he did not get through. One very gallant German officer brought up a pontoon to bridge the canal in face of heavy fire. He got his bridge over and the infantry attacked, but were simply mown down in heaps. It was a desperately brave thing to do and one could not but admire such courage. Our men cheered the German engineer when, after placing his pontoon across, he got back with only about fifteen men of the two hundred who put it across.

On May the 5th we moved to the Hinges sector, our front line being in Locon, which the Germans had tried hard to take. Before this attack it was Corps HQ, now it was front line, with the enemy in one half of the town and we in the other. The German gunners did their best to smash up all the coal mines they could; day after day they hammered away at Choques mine pithead. But the mine was kept at work by those gallant French people until at last the engines were smashed by a shell. Hinges Church got a liberal amount of shelling and was knocked to pieces.

Our aid post was a cellar not far away, but very comfortable. I discovered a great deal of silver plate belonging to the Church and packed it all in a great linen basket and handed it over to the French mission further down the line; I hope it got back to Hinges Church after the war. I think there must have been a laundry near our post for we found dozens of clean sheets in the cellar; it was strange to sleep in a cellar on sheets, they seemed to belong to a different existence.

It was pitiful to see the country. Since 1916 this part had been delivered from the destruction of war – it was all cultivated and new houses built by those industrious people. But now their nice little villas were smashed into ruins and the land ploughed up by shells again. There were beds of strawberries growing near the front line trenches and lots of asparagus, most unusual luxuries in those days.

At Hinges I met General East again. He used to bring up eight inch howitzers at night to the annoyance of the enemy and run them out again before dawn. I never saw him again for he was killed not long after at Ypres.

Sundays do not count for very much in war, so I held services when I could. I had long given up parade services, but found that the men came pretty well. Certainly there were more communicants than in the old days, very often 200 men came to service, and there were often 40 or 50 men who made their communion. Some people think that religion was a "wind up" but I am certain it was not, for many of the bravest officers and men were regular communicants and they felt the reality of the nearness of God in the Blessed Sacrament.

The Germans used constantly to shell the back lines with gas shells and twice the King's Liverpools were badly affected with mustard gas, which used to hang in dips and hollows and take effect when the sun rose, with the result that the skin was blistered and the eyes became inflamed and swollen, and in the worst cases blind. Twice Colonel Lawrence of the King's was blinded by this horrible stuff, yet on neither occasion would he leave his command and fortunately he soon recovered.

In 1917 the Germans introduced a new type of shell. One night I was sleeping in a small shelter with our Intelligence officer, when they began to send over a little shell which made a peculiar sharp whistling sound. This woke me up and as the next came nearer I woke Honeywell, who was by my side, when the third hit the roof of our shelter. Fortunately for us, the shell was one of the sensitive sort, which had a little stalk at the end of the nose. If it hit anything it would burst upward making no crater at all, but shredding into a thousand pieces with a very wide lateral range. In the morning we looked at the place and a great hole had been blown in the roof, right over our heads, but the burst was upwards and, beyond covering us with dust, did no harm.

One night 200 men had to go up to dig in a cable along the canal bank. It was not a very healthy place and unfortunately the officers in charge were both of a poor type. The men would have gone anywhere and done anything with the right officer. We had other ranker officers, who were simply splendid, but these were not that sort. The men were tired, the ground was as hard as iron and they were goaded on by the signals officer, who swore at them for not digging and then disappeared into a dugout, and when the two came out were much the worse for whisky. It infuriated the men when they were sworn at and they struck work. Then shells began to fall along the bank and some of the men were wounded. At last the job was finished and the men got back to their billets very sore and angry.

I never felt more angry and intended to report the matter, but when I went to see that officer and told him what I thought of him he was so penitent that I did not. I was glad afterwards, for it changed the man; he became a much better company officer and later was seriously wounded, gallantly leading his men in a counter attack.

A June morning, bright sunshine and a gentle breeze blowing the tufts of reed which spring here and there from the grass-covered field; patches of gorse aflame and, on a little rise, backed by a great clump of briar set with pink wild roses, a table spread with a green cloth. On it, a copper cross fashioned by one of the men from a German driving band and on each side sprigs of wild rose. A hundred officers and men kneeling round as the Eucharist is offered. No sound, except for the distant droning of a plane overhead, the croaking of frogs in the neighbouring pond and the singing of birds. Lift up your hearts. We lift them up unto the Lord.

Letter to St Paul's, Deptford, March 1918

Dear People at home,

I had a short visit to Deptford while I was on leave. I didn't see half the people I wanted to, but it was good to see those I did. I was struck by the way in which the rationing difficulty was being faced, and glad that people seemed to be contented with it. It is hard to hear that people at home are grumbling. I was intensely glad to find that there was no grumbling amongst St Paul's people. You will see from the papers that this year has so far been spent in preparation for an attack which may come at any time. I believe that we are quite ready. If people tell you that the officers and men on whom our nation depends are having an easy time because there has been no great amount of fighting, do not believe them. The mere fact that this battalion has been in the trenches for weeks on end will show you more than one can say. We are so used to the current expressions "in the trenches" and "up the line" that we miss the meaning of it sometimes at home. To live in a deep ditch during wintertime, even if there is little shelling, is a painful thing, for nights are very cold and extreme care must be taken to prevent the enemy surprising us. Every night wire has to be repaired and fresh wire put out, for barbed wire is a great defence. The officers and men who put out wire have constantly to run the risk of enemy shells and machine gun fire. Each night patrols must creep out to get what information they can of enemy movements, or to lay wait for a German patrol out for the same purpose.

One thinks that this year the war in the air will be far greater than before. We know our airmen are doing enormous damage behind the enemy line. I was lying out this morning in a shell-hole behind our trench, where there was quiet for prayer and reading. Behind me was a line of observation balloons, watching far away for hostile guns and troops. In front I could see German balloons doing the same thing. Great is the art of camouflage. It is a very old science. I suppose the old woman who lived in a shoe was an inhabitant of a village in a war area. She was wise enough to borrow the shoe of one of the Antediluvian people. In this she and her many children would not be so likely to suffer from the enemy attack. She was also an economist, who saw the value of good vegetable soup, thereby saving her ration of bread. Perhaps her notions of justice were rather Prussian but at all events it was a great saving of light and fuel when she sent the children early to bed. As camouflaged houses saved inconvenience in those days, so do the modern artists disguise guns and roads and trenches from the impertinent gaze of the men who live in balloons or who hum along through the sky like great hawks looking for their prey.

We are having lovely summer weather and are much enjoying it. By the time you get this it will be Easter time. I wish you all the blessing of that season, and that for all of us there may come the call to the new Risen Life by Him whose Cross and Passion won for men the glory of His Resurrection.

> Yours affectionately,
> Noel Mellish, C. F.

Letter to St Paul's, Deptford, April 1918

Dear People at home,

I have several letters to thank you for and a beautiful picture of the chancel, I am very glad to have. It reminds me of so many things that are beautiful and all of them belong to home.

For nearly a month we have been in the thick of this colossal struggle. It started on March 21st early in the morning. We were all ready; for a long time past our men had been working day and night preparing reserve trenches and putting out acres of barbed wire. On January 25th this battalion came into that line and we went out for one short day and night. That evening we heard that there would probably be an attack so were ordered up again. I tell you this that you may know that our men had been holding the line of trenches for eight weeks, with a good deal of enemy activity during that time, and one big raid, constant watchfulness, unceasing work night and day. In all my experience the men had never had so long a period of trench life.

Then with daybreak of March 21st came the great attack. The Germans came in swarms and were driven back along our front, but unfortunately the attack was too heavy for the troops on the right of our division, and they were driven back. This left our right flank exposed and open. So during the day and that night and the next day there were constant attacks while the enemy attempted to get round our right flank. It was a time of great anxiety. The courage of the officers and men of this division was splendid. On the evening of the 22nd I thought that at any moment the enemy might get right in amongst us.

In the aid post the doctor had been busy all day and as the day went on the enemy was shooting well into our trench. From time to time our colonel had to withdraw companies to straighten the line and to keep our front to the enemy as he advanced round our flank. At nightfall the Germans ceased their attack and by their lights we could see that on the following day, when they renewed it, we should have them advancing on three sides. At midnight our brigade had orders to evacuate this line. It was the famous Hindenburg tunnel line which we had to leave. Each regiment of the brigade moved through the last, each leaving a covering party to form a rearguard. In perfect quiet and order we marched out, leaving with regret the tunnel which had been our reserve line, built by the Boche before we took it from him early in 1917. We left it mined with gun-cotton, placing little pieces of lighted candles where they would fire the woodwork. The retirement was completed by about 3 a.m., the last company having the satisfaction of seeing great flames bursting up out of the deep dug-outs. There was not a single casualty in the whole brigade during the march out.

We got away all our wounded but we had to leave our dead.

From Monday until Wednesday the enemy was busy reorganising his front. Meanwhile he made tentative attacks on our front, which were all beaten back by our men, who were holding trenches previously dug and wired. One day an enemy party carrying rations lost their way and our men got the rations, brown bread in large heavy sour loaves, but not bad to eat and their biscuits were sweet and very nice. The meat ration seemed to be tinned rabbit. During the day we could plainly see the German batteries coming into action and they shelled our lines pretty severely but made no big attack, except on the right, where they got a severe cutting up. On the 27th we were relieved by another regiment of our brigade which had been out in a camp two miles away for three days. At midnight we got out to this camp and I found to my delight eighteen letters waiting for me. I didn't go to bed at once, but was sitting over the fire in a hut reading my letters when at 3 o'clock a shell landed close to the camp. This was the start of five hours shelling. Three companies were in the trenches above and HQ company and another company were in the camp. We lost no time but roused up from sleep and bolted to the trench behind. The shells pitched all over the camp and round the trench. In a little while many of the huts were on fire and a good many officers lost all their kit. I lost nothing as my servant, Bennett, packed it up and put it in a safe place in a sunken road where practically no shell hit it. It was a speedy retirement and we only had two men wounded through all that shelling. About 8 o'clock on that morning the battalion moved up to the forward position, going through a very severe barrage to reinforce the front line. Here the Germans attacked in swarms and our men beat them off and relieved one battalion of this brigade which had been holding them back since early morning. Not an inch of our line did the enemy take. One of our companies led by its captain did a splendid piece of work coming up without orders to the rescue of a company which was being hard pressed. All our men were tired out but they fired into the enemy swarms, reeling from want of sleep as they stood.

Maundy Thursday was a day of blood, anguish and conquest, for our splendid brigade held good. Good Friday was the same, and on that night we had the welcome news that the Canadians were coming to relieve us. All day long we had been heavily shelled but mercifully we did not have a heavy roll of wounded and killed, though we lost not a few officers and men whom we can badly spare.

The march out was a wonderful sight of the patience and heroism of utterly exhausted men and it was a 12 mile march. At 6 o'clock we reached a camp where spring flowers were growing and the birds were singing. So we left the Passiontide to reach the beauty of Easter Eve and rest. Not a very long rest, for five hours afterwards we started again on another long march, and reached our destination at 9 in the evening, the men singing on the road as they got to their billets.

Never have I more loved Easter and its beauty of new life and hope than I did on that Easter morning when I offered the Blessed Sacrament.

Since Easter we have had five days rest in a nice little town where the people were kind and hospitable. Then we had to move northward to be near if we were wanted. Another three days in billets and a quick journey to help another division, to which we were in reserve for four days, during which we came in for a good deal of attention from enemy guns. Now we are holding the front line and I write in the cellar which is our aid post, which I share with the doctor and his dressers and some stretcher bearers. We are in a ruined village which a little while ago was full of happy industrious people. Now there are none, for they have been driven from their homes by the enemy. Our brigade is holding a line of very shallow ditches. They can't be dug deeper, for the country is flat and water comes in if over two feet deep. There were numbers of cows, pigs, and calves when we came here, but our men have collected them and must have been driven down to towns behind. The old gentleman who owns this house came up to collect some of his property two days ago. He had only a small cart. He took away most of the bedding and some of the pots and pans. He said he would come for more. It is a risky business, as the village is heavily shelled at any time. It is sad to see these well-cultivated farms being daily destroyed, and the comfortable houses gradually being smashed up. Since 2 o'clock this morning the enemy has been attacking on our right. I do not know if he has had any success. I expect he has been held back.

I have taken up too much room. There is much more I would say, but I won't now. With love to you all.

Yours affectionately,
Noel Mellish, C. F.

Chapter Twelve

Engagement to E. W. M.

IN MARCH 1918 Mellish became engaged to Miss Elizabeth Molesworth and a new future opened up to him. Born in 1894, Elizabeth was the elder daughter of Lawrence Molesworth, one of a large family from Rochdale in Lancashire, who in about 1885 went out with a brother to seek his fortune in Texas. Here he was for a time a Texas Ranger and then became a rancher. About 1890 he married an Irish girl, again one of a large family named Bournes from County Mayo. For some years Lawrence and his little family prospered on the ranch but in the 1900s his wife's ill health forced them to come home to seek treatment for her. While in England, Lawrence received a letter one morning from the partner he had left in charge of his ranch, saying that things had not gone well and that he had sold up, lock, stock and barrel and cleared out, leaving Lawrence almost penniless and with his last twenty years' work dissipated.

Owing to his wife's continuing ill health Lawrence then took a small farm at Babcary in Somerset, where in 1903 a younger daughter, Margaret, was born. Elizabeth was then at school at Blackheath High School, living with her mother's sisters, Aunt Georgie, and Aunt Rita in Blackheath. Here she got to know Canon Roseveare, the vicar of Lewisham who taught her in the early years and knew her aunts well.

In 1910 Elizabeth left school and went home to help her mother but in 1914 when her parents moved to a small cottage near Harwich she returned to London and enrolled in a domestic science course at Clapham High School. Her reports from here speak very highly of her helpful influence and in her second year as senior student she was invited by the head of the domestic training department to accompany her with a party of girls to the Lake District as assistant in charge.

When she left Clapham in June 1916, Elizabeth took with her the lasting affection of some of the students and the head tutor, and received glowing testimonials from the college and Canon Roseveare. These ensured that she very easily found a job as junior domestic science teacher at St Anne's School, Redhill, where she threw herself into the job and was ecstatically happy. Sadly she was forced to leave St Anne's after only one year for a major operation, and when she had recovered the school was closing and Elizabeth had to find another post. Again she took with her from the school the deep affection of a number of the girls and staff and formed friendships there which lasted for life, among others with the headmistress, Miss Young, and the art mistress, Claire Evans, who was an outstanding calligrapher and artist.

At the beginning of 1918 Elizabeth was appointed matron in charge of one of the houses at a large girls' school at Wycombe Abbey, under a somewhat formidable headmistress, Miss Daniels. Here she was in charge of not only the girls at Airlie House, but the domestic staff. This was an altogether more demanding job, in which she was responsible for the welfare of about eighty girls in addition to engaging and dealing with the domestic staff, arranging the catering and dealing with all the problems arising from war-time shortages and casualties and the difficulties and stresses of an autocratic and intolerant head-mistress.

Mellish had of course known Elizabeth for some years, probably meeting her first on one of his leaves from South Africa, and certainly many times between 1910, when he entered King's College, and 1915 when he went to France. He saw in her all the qualities he loved and admired but, as he later admitted, he had always expected to remain single and he probably gave little thought to the possibility of a future until it seemed that the war might come to an end fairly soon. Even then, as admiration deepened into love, his decision to ask Elizabeth to become his wife was not taken without much thought and prayer. He also consulted his friend Canon Roseveare who knew her well, and Roseveare's delighted response must have given him great encouragement. Roseveare subsequently wrote to Mrs Mellish about the engagement: 'They are both beautiful in mind and body.' Months later Elizabeth's beloved Aunt Georgie confided to her that she had always hoped she would marry Noel Mellish. When told this in due course Mellish wrote, 'My love to Aunt Georgie. How funny to think she is Aunt Georgie. I always was very fond of her. I used to see her toddling round Deptford; did I say toddling – it was flying – and every morning rising so early and racing down to St Paul's. I used to trot along by her side out of breath.' From the day in March when Elizabeth wrote accepting his proposal, Mellish wrote almost every day and sometimes twice, on message forms, scraps of paper or whatever was available, a correspondence which, starting a little hesitantly, developed into the outward expression of a passionate love affair which lasted for over forty years. The steady stream of letters to which Elizabeth replied as regularly do much to fill out the picture of life in the trenches or out at rest. Lyrical descriptions of whatever beauty there was to find in the landscape, a burning admiration for the British soldier generally and his own men and fellow officers in particular, and the most wholehearted expression of all his inmost hopes and fears and ambitions. Above all there is his delighted joy in finding someone with whom he could share all his thoughts and plans for the future and who shared his deep and absolute trust in God. By the time his first leave after the engagement came, in June 1918, Mellish had established the complete and total understanding with Elizabeth which was to form the basis of their whole future life and work together, in a lovely and intensely private correspondence, tender, passionate, often delightfully humorous, and sometimes gently teasing of Elizabeth's slightly erratic spelling or grammar.

For her part, Elizabeth looked on Mellish with a shy hero-worship for a man whose name was at the time on everyone's lips, and a diffident unsureness that such a man could find anything of interest in her and her daily tasks. But the sharing of ideas, interests and ideals soon broke down the barriers and it was not long before Elizabeth realised that she had an equal part to play in a lifelong partnership.

Extracts from Letters to E. W. M. Written from the Front Line

Easter Eve 1918

On Good Friday I wrote and it seemed as if the sorrows and the wounds had it all their way. On that day our men had to go up from reserve, tired out as they were, through a terrible barrage of shell fire; through it they went unwavering and gained this line and reinforced the line which was in danger of being broken. Since then our brigade has splendidly held the line through a most critical time and against terrific attacks by swarms of the enemy.

1 April

One letter I wrote was in the early morning of the day we came out of trenches, Good Friday. I had got mixed up when I wrote on Maundy Thursday. The days and nights so ran into each other that I suppose during those days one lost the sense of time, but this letter was written on the morning of Good Friday. The doctor and I were sitting in our dug-out hole in the trench. The relief by the Canadians was going on, and we couldn't leave until it was finished. Very few wounded were coming in as the front line was fairly quiet, but with us it was getting worse and more and more the Germans' guns were shelling, trying to knock out a battery of ours just behind and in line with our piece of trench. I couldn't sleep and could only wait for the next and the next and they came very near. After much prayer and your psalm with its great meaning, I took out my paper and wrote to you. It relieved the strain, one stopped waiting for the next shell, so you, my dear helped me to be saner and more collected. Then came the glad news that relief was complete, and we walked out of the trench out to the early beginnings of day, gradually leaving behind the noise and ugliness, the sorrow and agony of the last few days ...

Today we left early, up about 5.30 a.m. and marched about three miles to the place where we met our buses, old London buses and motor lorries, to take us up country to our new area. It was a jolly ride and the country is beautiful. The bright green of early crops is springing up in glowing green squares, making the cultivated land look like a chess board in the making. The trees and hedges are starting their spring clothes, the sky blue-flecked with clouds, and the air bright and warm. Our men happy and chaffing in their buses and much enjoying the ride. So for twenty miles we went until we came to the village where we are now staying. We are all in very comfortable billets, I must tell you more tomorrow. I mustn't go on yarning anymore, for I have many letters to write to the relations of our dear fellows who were killed. These are sad letters and I shall not write much to you about war, for you are my anti-dote to all this, you speak to me of peace and home and love and beauty.

2 April

Last night we moved our Regimental Aid post from the flimsy cottage where we were to a better place where there is more and safer accommodation for the wounded, and for us who are whole it is easier access too. We keep very quiet during the day and as today, it gives me time to think and read through my letters and write. Last night it blew up for a thunderstorm and I feared our men in their ditches and posts would get flooded but it passed over with only a little rain. Now I am sitting by a hedge in the shelter of a tree where the Boche cannot see me from a plane nor from land either. This house is some distance behind our front line and central for all the battalion to come if they are sick or wounded.

I am very sorry to hear that Miss Mary Bournes is ill again. Thanks for the warning about the ten aunts; those I know are so nice that I am not afraid of the others. For the assurance and comfort of the good lady who warned you about men and nightclubs etc. I have not had much chance out here and not much in Deptford either. It is very warm here today. The doctor and I share a mattress on the floor and a pillow exists which I have discarded as it covers the place with feathers and is very dirty and moults unceasingly. There are two small long-dogs here, nice little fellows and probably full of fleas.

2 April

You will not be awed of me when you know me for I am a very ordinary person, only I am full of a great longing to tell you all that cannot be written. You will I know write to me every day for this joy that has come to me brings a light and longing that only your letters can help me to get. Please keep the measles at bay or I shall not get any letters. It is bad to be kept so far from you by the Germans, but worse luck still if I am prevented from hearing from you by German Measles. I wrote to you on Good Friday after a very early morning move from the gun pit where we had placed our dressing station overnight. All day we were shelled and when I went from the dressing post to HQ. I had to take a circuitous way to get to a place which I wanted to reach. Maundy Thursday the 28th was the worst day, for then we thought that our battalion couldn't, with all its bravery, but be swamped, but the line held; in spite of awful shelling, they still held until we heard the news of our relief. There was no three hour service for us that day, but the enemy's power was for the time broken. It was a blessed thing to get away from it all, to have the relief completed in small bodies of men handing over their line quietly, methodically and with never a man wounded or killed.

3 April

You will be happy in knowing that we are quite in safety and rest. We are in another army now and the corps commander has promised I believe to give us a rest if he possibly can, though we know that in these days there will be more work for us to do. Officers and men are in great heart, full of cheeriness and confidence, ready to do anything they are asked to do. Today they are having drill and training, this afternoon football matches and this evening a concert given by our own troupe in a cinema hall lent by Canadian machine gunners. This morning I had arranged for the Eucharist but no-one turned up, unable to fit it in I suppose. I thought 7.30 was a time that would suit them and know that there were many who wanted to come, but it is very difficult in the army these days. I get a bit heartsick sometimes at the futility of my work. It is easier at home, but so important out here to know the presence of Christ and His power. So my dear you will pray that I may have the energy and imagination necessary to draw these men to delight in the highest things. Each morning I shall be in that place which I have arranged for the Eucharist at 7.30 so you will know where I am, so whether I can offer the sacrifice or not, I shall be praying for them and you, and you for them and me. What a co-operative society the world becomes through prayer.

In this room of mine is a picture of the Madonna, a striking one and much more beautiful than most one sees out here. Our Lady stands in a glowing light clothed with blue and green robes holding in her hands the Saviour. On her right stands a little Chinese child looking up with adoration. On her left kneels a little African negro child, both looking at the Saviour's face which is smiling with joy. I like the picture very much.

4 April

Last night I buried a German who was killed just outside this house when the fighting began here. I found it awfully hard to pray at all, yet I expect that man was a patriot as he was taught, likely a brave man who perhaps has a wife and children at home. He thinks he fights for right, we know we do, but in both of us there is such a vast amount of evil, and evil makes war possible and allows it to continue.

Easter Day 1918

Tomorrow we are going further on where we shall I hope have a week's rest. The King has congratulated our army commander, General Bing, on the splendid service of our division. We are all feeling refreshed by a day in God's good country with flowers and trees awake and bursting into new and lovely life.

I am proud of the regiment and the 13th King's Liverpool Regiment and 1st Northumberland Fusiliers who compose our brigade and have been fighting side by side against enormous numbers. Now we are going out for a rest and refitting.

The 91st Psalm I know and love, it is that psalm which I used to strengthen myself and the men of my battalion of St Eloi when the murderous barrage of the enemy was coming round us. After that I felt better and was able to go up to the craters to look to the wounded on the night of the 27th. Pray for me dearest, not so much that I may be safe, as that I may be doing what I have been sent to do.

7 April

Yesterday we moved out of our last place to this one. We got here about 12.30, in the evening. I had to find out where my other battalion was, to fix up a service. It was a wet night. It was light when I started and soon got over there on Kitty, but it was a job getting back as it was a very dark night, but Kitty's sure hooves never let me down and we got back just before 10.00. This morning we left at 9.00 and got over there in time for 9.30 but my battalion was late and I had not started when the next lot was due, so I had to keep them waiting for half an hour and then had to race over here for some of my men. Here we had the Eucharist with hymns ...

Out here it seems so senseless that there should be these divisions between us; we are all carrying the message and we are all hindering the message by not putting our whole hearts into it. At home perhaps one doesn't see the folly of these many ways of telling the message. Out here it outs one's heart, RC's, C of E, Wesleyan and Presbyterian, we are all untuned and jamming each other on the line. What a curse history is sometimes. Centuries ago men hated each other and put each other to death for the sake of religion. Now we are so utterly indifferent that we don't think religion matters much one way or the other. What does God think about it all? It isn't really our own bad will that causes it, is it? I suppose the RCs say we cannot believe and do less than we do, and C of E say we can't take in the Pope, yet somehow I feel so tired about it all, it is such a waste of strength and purpose and good will.

Today we have moved about five or six miles to a mine town, not quite so comfy for the men as the last place, but they are pretty fair. This evening I had to go over to my other battalion to arrange for a service tomorrow. I am longing to be able to talk to them all, they were so splendid. So 8.00 here which another padre will take, I go first to the next place for service at 9.30, back again here from the Kings to the Royal Fusiliers for 11.00 here with celebration after, and evening service at 6.30 and another celebration at 10.00 in the other place and 8.00 and 10.00 here. Bed now, as it's getting late.

10 April

I finished up my letter last night in a hurry and packed up and departed with the battalion for other parts. They are not very far from the place we were staying in. We were needed and so last night and today have been living in what a few days ago were comfortable country sur-roundings. Now the farm is smashed horribly, a dead horse lies in the stable, a few foals still run about, most have been killed by our men for food, so have the rabbits. I suppose if they were not killed they would die sooner or later. Their owners have probably fled far away. Poor souls, what it must feel like to have one's home and belongings blown to pieces by furious shelling in a few savage hours. The cultivated land and orchards ploughed up into great ugly holes. The village is being smashed into fragments, all day long it goes on.

We have had very few casualties today, only two and not very bad. War is a filthy thing, cruel, heartless, wicked. This morning a grey-haired man and a young daughter went back to their farm to try to get back their few cows and a horse. The girl was cool and collected, showing no fear of the shells which were bursting in the village. One of the men told me of another family harnessing the horse to a cart on which all the household stuff they could save was packed, a little child of six was helping to collect things and fit them and get them ready. What a horrible evil it all is. We are in reserve to people who may need us, we don't know how long it may be. We live in little holes dug into the earth in a bank or behind houses or in cellars. There is not much to do. It is difficult to think or pray of any value when subconsciously you are listening to where the shells are coming from.

12 April

Here we are still, as yesterday, waiting in reserve line. I say a line, it is only a line of holes, but in weather like today holes are not such bad places. The sun is lovely and it is only shells that make it uncomfortable. What an amazing foolishness it all is. Think of about 1000 men sitting in damp little holes in cultivated fields which have been spoilt. Imagine us, a little sandbag hut, roofed with a few bits of corrugated iron, on top of which is a little earth and a few bits of turf. This place was made when it was peacetime here, by gunners. There is a little stove in the corner, two sides have two wire bunks on each, we have brought in a table and a nice little mahogany folding card table from a very well furnished farmhouse nearby, which is now a dismal ruin. Two large copper-glazed candlesticks on the table, an alarm clock that came from another house I suppose, a large brass water jug, bread and butter and an odd collection of plates, some French, some enamelled iron, a cardboard pot of jam, tea in enamelled mugs. The Colonel reading letters and eating tea on one bunk. The second-in-command has just upset his cup of tea onto my bed on which I am sitting, with the doctor next to me. Unfortunately for him, the tea ran down along the bed unnoticed by him until he found he was sitting in a pool of tea. His method of getting rid of the pool was to puncture holes in the canvas of the bed to drain the tea out;

not much regard for my bed you would think, but as a matter of fact we are going out tonight. Where I don't know, I suppose to take up a position somewhere not very far away …

19 April

The trees are just bursting into leaf and blossom. Fields are sprouting green corn, beans, peas, others covered with growing clover. Now those farmhouses are many of them broken up with great gaping shell holes, animals lying dead, trees broken down, fields with great blackened pits in them. Some of the farms are aflame, reddening the sky in the distance. War is a filthy thing. I don't see anything good in it.

19 April

We were relieved last night and left our RAP at 11.30. Before leaving I went up to the front line to bury one of our men and two others of another regiment who had been killed. I told you that yesterday the Hun attacked on our right, he also made a heavy attack on the left. Our position did not get it. There was a good deal of shelling, but our artillery was wonderful and probably beat off his attack on us. On the left he made a tremendous effort to get through. A most gallant German officer brought up a pontoon to bridge the canal in face of very heavy fire. He was beaten off but he got his bridge over, and the enemy attacked and was simply mowed down in heaps and entirely beaten. It was a desperately brave thing and failed, but one must admire such reckless bravery. Our men cheered him when the German engineer after placing his pontoon across, got back safely with only about 15 of the 200 men who put it across. Our men of the division on our left were underneath the other side of the canal so his bravery was simply wonderful. This is a bloody war, a horrible waste of good men, indeed of everything.

24 April

Scene – the kitchen and living room of a little French farmhouse, with tiled floor, rubble walls, a good stove, a big cupboard with the usual collection of china ornaments on it, a crucifix, a little image of the Virgin surrounded with china roses and, in a glass case, a Singer sewing machine; a large cupboard which contained the best hats and dresses of madame, two tables and three or four chairs. On either side of this room is another, a loft above the lot, in which are bundles of haricot beans laid to dry in the pods. Nothing else of interest except a very small, neat little hen with five chicks whom she looks after with much care and calls in under her feathers when any shelling takes place. We relieved a regiment of another brigade last night, a good relief with nothing unpleasant happening. This morning early we had one of our company commanders hit, Capt. Lord, who sits next to me in one of the photographs. His farmhouse and company HQ is close to ours and his got the shells when the early morning strafe came on. He was only slightly wounded. I am very glad; it won't do him any harm to have a bit of a rest. He has the MC and will soon have the DSO. He has been recommended for it for his splendid work up near Arras.

29 April

I have been scrounging round a farm today. I expect you don't know the word, it means picking up oddments, cockney for looting, though mine wasn't looting. There had been a camp when it was peace-war here and was shelled out the first day I expect, and the men left various things. I picked up a tin of tooth powder, a sack of wheat and six sacks of oats, about 700lbs of oats which will go down to the Brigade quarter-master tonight. The latter, not the tooth powder. I also found a little red paint and an old tooth brush with which I adorned my tin hat with a great red St George's cross, so that I should know my own chapeau. I painted it with the tooth brush.

I have been thinking about our honeymoon, it is a long way off I fear, but when that good time comes, how lovely it will be to cycle round the country and have a little tent with us and carry it on our bikes, carry a little primus stove, a small pack of luggage each. We will have a lovely camp holiday in the summertime I hope, you and I together enjoying the things and places and beauty that I think you will enjoy. Tell me, do you love the country and cycling round seeing old cathedrals and lovely views and sea bathing and birds and flowers? I think you do. That sort of holiday has always been my ideal, though I have never thought of it in this way of course. I had a cycling holiday in June 1913, or was it 1914, anyway long ago in the pre-war days. I much enjoyed it, but I was lonely, I wanted someone to share all the good things with, but I was by myself. DV I shall never spend another holiday alone, I shall always write to you and try and fix up holidays.

2 May

After breakfast I went to a padres' meeting, rode over on Kitty. A lovely morning and she danced along as if made of rubber. Coming back she nearly pulled my arms out. She is a rascal when she is with another horse, she wants to fly. I visited my other regiment this afternoon. They had a bad time when they came out two nights ago. They had had nine days in the front line and just as they got to their billets, the Boche put over gas shells and, tired as they were, they had to turn out and unfortunately have had a lot of men gassed, not dangerously but they have had to be sent away. It is a hateful thing gas, but I am not at all afraid of it, for these helmets are splendid and one is perfectly safe if one gets them on at once.

The weather today is lovely, quite warm. What a joy it will be if leave does come along sometime when the weather is good.

5 May

I never thought that I should ever write love letters, somehow it seemed a very remote thing, though I had often thought of love and marriage as something very desirable for other men, but never coming my way. I used to love to hear married men out here talk about their homes, they meant everything to them. I always rather envied them, and now I am one of that party looking forward to the time. Don't you think I am too old? You my little girl, not yet twenty-four and I am an ancient piece of history, nearly thirty-nine. I am glad you like old furniture, I shall fit the surroundings if we have any. But you won't sit on me will you? Only treat me as an old curio, though you won't have to keep me in a glass case yet ... Am thinking of you and mother at Lambourne together on a peaceful Sunday. You have been to the Blessed Sacrament this morning in that lovely old church and the sun was shining, I hope, and the birds singing, and the new little leaves laughing in their new green coats. Later the bell is ringing and the people coming in, and the funny old padre walking about in cloth cap and cassock like a farmer with borrowed clothes. He is a kind old fellow with a sad life behind him, and not much hope or joy left.

7 May

It is now midnight, Wednesday morning really. The sick and lame have just gone back to their companies. You would have liked to see them, about nine sitting round the table in the kitchen upstairs, each eating a hot meal of stew made of meat, potatoes, dumplings, leeks. They did enjoy it. They come down with sore feet which are washed and dressed, or festered fingers which are cut open, washed and dressed, or boils treated in the same way. If they are sick and have a temperature then they are sent away to hospital. The kitchen has two stoves so that there are many pots of boiling water for washing ready, but the heat in the kitchen is appalling as the windows have to be blanketed to keep light from going outside to show the enemy the place is inhabited. The doors too are covered with blankets to keep out gas in case a gas shell drops near. He puts over a good many of the latter and when it comes near we put on our respirators and sprinkle chloride of lime about.

7 May

No, my dearest, I wasn't sarcastic, sarcasm and irony are not meant to be the ingredients of your letters. What I said I meant, we really are extraordinarily comfortable; sleeping in clothes and boots is no hardship. I suppose comfort and luxury are relative terms. When you are warm it doesn't much matter what the surroundings are, provided they are more or less clean. When one can get a bath every day, a shave, good food, a blanket to sleep in, it is comfort, much more than one can get in the most luxurious furnished surroundings. A cellar is an amazingly safe place under such conditions. Our men here are as happy as birds, they have been singing all day long, for we have happily been idle for the last twenty-four hours. No wounded at all. We are fixing up baths for men who come in for minor ailments, so the doctor sends them back fed and clean. He is jolly good and all the men love him.

10 May

Now things get busy, transport moves up bringing rations and ammunition, barbed wire and all the other necessities. Am just going out for a walk round to visit the companies up the road. They are all very cheery, but I know are much looking forward to going out. I suppose it will be soon for we have had a good long time in. Everybody admires this abode of ours, it is really palatial – a lamp, an armchair, washstand, table, bedding, clock (which doesn't go). All these things belong to French houses, if they weren't here they would get broken up by shells.

12 May

My own dear love, a few little bits of flowers and best of love. 3.15 a.m. and relief complete. Yours ever.

13 May

Here we are out again and living in a big millhouse where things are very comfortable. The men are not so, they are in canvas shelters, but safer than where we were out before. We cannot afford to lose men by giving them comfort and extra risk. This village has not been shelled, but to put a large number of men in houses together is a dangerous thing in these days, for we are not far away from the line. I suppose we shall have four days out. Tomorrow we have the Eucharist at 8.00; it is earlier than I wished, for the men need more sleep after eight days of no rest, but training must go on and work must be done even at rest.

14 May

During the morning the senior padre came in to introduce another new padre named Keats who is living with the first Northumberland Fusiliers. A nice chap I should think, quiet, quite new out from home and nice and fresh and full of energy and keenness. When they had gone I went round to the battalion canteen, which I am in a way responsible for, found they had a good supply of stuff which was nearly sold out – the usual things: tinned salmon, herrings, soap, some cake, chocolate, cigarettes, tobacco, writing pads and some envelopes. When I was at home I ordered a big lot of the pads and got the first lot. The second parcel of 4 gns worth had not come, but they turned up today and were all sold out by this evening. Tonight I must send for some more. I ordered them at Berrymans, Blackheath Road. Then I got on my bike and cycled up to the same village where our HQ was last, to fix up something and had lunch with the Scots Fusiliers. The colonel is a most amusing man, he knows the place where I used to work in the Free States and knows South Africa well. Then I met the brigade major of another brigade whom I knew. He made me come in for tea. After that I went round to the Kings and fixed up services for tomorrow with them. Then went to an open air concert with this battalion which was quite good and then back to dinner where we had the Colonel and second-in-command of the Northumberland Fusiliers in for dinner.

15 May

I don't feel at all jealous of the man whom your cousin has chosen for you. I wonder what would have happened if I had not written to you in March. I am sorry I disappointed your cousin and her kind plans, never mind, perhaps she will forgive me for upsetting arrangements. After all you and I are the persons chiefly concerned. Don't get filled up with any of that Daily Mail stuff you find in that ridiculous book of Mother's, you know the sort of stuff they write. It amuses me to see some of those comic cuts. I am afraid they are not very truthful. I have not many recommendations, but I always wash when I can and usually shave every day ... I had a letter from the Rector today. St Hilda's has been taken by Mr Shirley, a very good chap. I am glad, I wish it could have been possible for me, but I know I could not do anything else than go on with this ... We shall have heaps of things to talk about and I am afraid a fortnight won't get it all in. It has been a perfect day. We had the Eucharist this morning. They had cleaned out an old brewery place and the men had carefully put down chloride of lime to make it smell less unpleasant. I chose the garden instead behind the brewery. It was overgrown with grass, but the shrubs and trees were perfect and the sun was bright and lovely and I am sure the men felt it was the right place for worship. I enclose some of the leaves from the shrubs around to show you what a wonderful colour scheme it was, and with the thick carpet of grass and the glorious blue sky above there could not have been a more lovely setting for the Eucharist. There were 30 communicants and about 200 altogether. I sometimes wonder whether I ought not to stop in the army as a permanent chaplain, when one gets some regular times and methods and chances one could have such opportunities, only if I did take on army chaplain's work after the war it would be difficult to be near Mother. It would be alright as far as you were concerned as I should have married quarters given.

Whitsunday

I enclose a horrible propaganda leaflet, it does not strike me as being much good, but it may. I saw the small balloons which we send up to distribute these things, some fell over our lines and I suppose many over the Boche. They are very crude. The Boche also sends up balloons to do the same. His are red and ours sparkling like silver, made of silk I believe with a small spirit lamp which makes the hot air expand until they are high enough and then the contents fall. Such is war. It sounds rather like comic opera.

23 May

Today an aeroplane of ours has been sending more little balloons skimming over the Boche lines dropping sheaves of pamphlets. I don't know what those contained. The lot of which I sent you one was a very poor thing I thought. Perhaps it might make the ordinary Boche soldier think that he was swelling the pockets of the profiteer, but I don't think he would be impressed much by such a paper. It is a very Gilbertian war.

We have lovely white, lilac and purple irises on the table tonight and are going to eat asparagus picked in gardens near the line. In every farm there are lettuces growing and we have them every day. The poor old town is still burning, the strong wind helps the fire to spread. There is no-one living there now.

Whitmonday

A hot day with a delicious breeze to cool it. It would be very hot in a town but out in the open one does not feel the heat of it, and I can go to my dugout which is on the side of the canal bank, very cool, damp if you keep the things in all day, but my blanket is out in the sun all day. I have some canvas, straw and a little mattress underneath so I am very comfy. It is made with two passages with a room between. A gunner officer, our intelligence officer, a very nice lad, usually called Fuzzy because of his hair, and I share. I was round the line with him last night. We got to bed about 12.30. Then he had to get up to send in company reports about 4.00 and after that we slept on until about 10.00. Then out and had a cold tub, for we have a pump in the yard and an old tub. Then breakfast. This afternoon I have been strolling about talking to people and had tea with a very nice subaltern of the Northumberland Fusiliers. Now I am talking to you in this abominable scrawl of mine and after dinner I shall go out again to see how people are getting on. It has been a very peaceful day. There has been so much emphasis laid on the horrible part of the war that one forgets the nice part of it. Lovely country, birds, flowers, any amount of laziness really, enormous amount of food.

24 May

We are quite a happy party at HQ. The Colonel is usually cheery, Attewell always so, Peacock, the adjutant, and Mcgregor the doctor are not often otherwise. The Colonel is a varsity blue, soldier in South African war and farmer afterwards, a very keen cricketer and sportsman, a man of high ideals and culture, but not caring for religion. Attewell a schoolmaster, keen on everything, deeply religious in life and thought. Peacock a pushing Canadian, very honest and straight and thoughtful, a Methodist in persuasion, and the doctor is an RC. It is a most cheery mess and always good company. One of the most abstemious I have met. Now we have another member, Honeywell, a boy just from Eton and Sandhurst, very delightful and charming.

26 May

I wonder if your friend's name is Winnie Daw. When I was a kid at Launceston, she came to tea once with her cousin Christina Collard, and I being eight years old, and she, Winnie Daw, about ten or so, I fell very much in love with her. This is a confession, isn't it? I think I got in a row with the gardener, old Connett, for giving her a bunch of flowers. At any rate I was deeply in love with her. She was I thought very pretty then, I am glad she is still nice. Since then I have not seen her. It is funny that your Miss Daw is the same one, I expect it must be. I am not in love with her now, and I do not think I have ever been in that desperate state again until 1918, that's your fault!

27 May

A splendid day but clouds about so it may rain. Had a walk round the line last night. All very quiet, our men working hard, putting up wire and digging trenches. Daytime is quiet and nobody moves more than necessary. Night brings work, and artillery and machine guns on both sides get busy too to prevent things happening. Today two Boche planes have been flying around taking photographs I expect. The air photography has been brought to perfection. They and we can see every bit of progress in making trenches and defences. I have been prowling round the village and finding equipment to send down as salvage. There is a great deal of stuff lying about. I feel as a rate payer when I see this stuff lying about. It costs an enormous amount of money. This village was a good long way behind the line before the offensive as there were all sorts of peace-time camps there. There is a YMCA in Boche hands further up at the other end of the village. We are in a well appointed cellar with all the latest improvements and more air than we had in the last one. I am going to clean out another little cellar for a quiet place for prayer and reading.

29 May

Today I hate the war and all its beastliness. Men killed and wounded last night, and it makes one feel sad.

30 May

Here I am in a lovely wood where our detail camp is. Birds singing round, little oaks, saplings sprouting in their delicious green. I am having a rest today. Came down for a padres' meeting at 10.00 and went to the dentist after lunch. Took funerals and have been loafing since. The battalion comes out tonight so I haven't gone back. We shall be out for a few days, over Sunday I hope. We have had a long time in, and all are ready for a rest. Last night some of our battalion made a raid and captured a prisoner who was wanted for identification of regiment etc. It was very smartly done and the General is very pleased about it. Today an officer and a squad of men have come back from instruction school with great distinction in the way they passed their test. Our transport was congratulated on its excellent turn out, so the battalion is in good fettle all round and everybody is pleased with us, so we are happy ... The General came to our meeting today and told us that he was pleased with our work and said that he was ready to help us in every way that he could, that he liked us to be with battalions and to go into the line and would support us in every possible way.

1 *June*

The weather is warm and beautiful and the hedges are covered with wild roses. HQ is in a good billet, the company officers in separate billets and the men in the companies are in bivouac tents in the open. I wish they were in safer places, there must be difficulty in getting away from the line these days. Every day and night there is the possibility of an attack so we cannot be very far away from the line. It makes one anxious all the time at night. When we are in the line we know and expect to be shelled, but trenches are fairly safe except for direct hits. When one's men are in the open and the enemy does area sweeping shelling we may get lots of men hurt and the strain is never taken off. I suppose one ought to get accustomed to it, but one doesn't. We at HQ are safe and comfortable and have cellars to go to if necessary ... I am very fond of tomorrow's Epistle. It is as real as if it was written tonight. It is a comfort in these days for you at home and for us out here. It helps me tremendously to try to put out my prayers for the men when they are being shelled. Shelling makes me a fearful coward. The truth comes in the Epistle. If one prays with love for other men, one's fear for one's own skin – that is the torment fear – goes. Prayer shifts a fear of one's own self and makes it into a better prayer for the man next to you. St John knew the perfect love which casts out fear. I suppose he must have been afraid when he stood by the Saviour crucified. St Peter's nerves went but St John and the holy women stuck where they were, so I suppose in times of danger if we stick close to Christ, we shall not have that torture of fear, but something of the love which He gives. I am writing this to you and I am going to tell it to the men tomorrow, for I know it's true.

2 *June*

We are out for rest and training. It is not much rest for the men. Last night 250 of them had to go up to near the line for digging a trench, laying cables for communications and filling in again. I went up with them. I rather like to go up with working parties sometimes, it is perhaps eyewash as the army has it, but you must share things a bit and if you as a padre go with them sometimes you can understand them more and they you. You wish God would blind the Germans' eyes, they are blind enough, but blinding is of the devil. How beastly and devilish it all is. Here we get a request from the Pope to respect Corpus Christi in Cologne, and the very same day the Hun airmen bomb Paris and destroy a church. We can never expect anything from the Boche that is not devilish, now he is winning it is the hour of the power of darkness, but we shall win. If there is anything noble or true or right with us we must win. God give strength and vision to General Foch and us to beat him and chase him back again.

Let us get away from the war. I have got such a jolly bright room here. The room next to mine was spoilt by a shell and nobody took this one, but a shell is just as likely if it comes to hit one room as another. Bennett has put pictures on the wall and a table covered with a red cloth, an easy chair, and when I came in there were vases of lovely flowers, one of red peonies, another of cream coloured and in the middle a vase of cream peonies, roses and variegated leaves and a few bits of a beautiful purple flower the name of which I don't know. I got back soon after 4 this morning, had some food and went to bed. Bennett called me at 9.00 and I dressed and went to the place which I had fixed for the Eucharist. Long grass, tufts of reed in it, clumps of bush covered with pink wild roses, patches of broom around. On a little rise I put the table for the altar and dressed it with green cloths and frontal, decorated it with sprigs of wild rose round the cross. There were about 100 men and officers, 30 communicants, all was beautiful. One of our planes droning overhead, frogs croaking in a nearby pond, birds flying round, a sweet breeze and gorgeous blue sky, and bright sun. A gem of a day. There was training on and many of the men no doubt were tired. Tonight I have another service at 7.0.

I am very glad Airlie House is the crack house in everything. Best food, lowest expenditure, that is your doing my clever little girl, singing, lacrosse, cricket, it is all splendid ... Our officers and men are splendid, cheery as anything, hard worked but full of spirit.

Now I must be off for evening service.

3 June

Just paid my month's mess bill, nearly £6 for extras. 155 francs at 5 francs a day, we really ought to reduce it to three, but the army is an extravagant institution. The doctor runs the mess and he has reduced it a good deal. I don't pay much else but 15 francs to my servant, 15 francs to my groom, and messing each month, and odd amounts for washing, and boot polish and cleaning kit for saddlery. The rations are so good that we ought not to pay nearly so much for extras, but the Colonel likes expensive extra things, and when at dinner, we have hors d'oevres, soup, fish, meat, sweet, and savoury, and these days we get almost free vegetables. Yet money soon flies, I wish I could save that £5 for us when the war was over, but I must live in the mess so it is no use grumbling. I get free tobacco and matches as a ration. The rations are extraordinarily good always. Now I am going to have Kitty saddled up and go over to see the Brigadier and have tea with them, then back here for one of our little Bible classes at 7.00. Fondest love my own dear heart.

4 June

After lunch the doctor and I rode out to the range where some of them were training in musketry. This evening our HQ played the Brigade HQ – quite a good game. It made the Brigadier run like a hare and they just beat us. I will send you the rules when I have them written, I think your girls would like it, it is a jolly good game, rather like rounders only better.

7 June

I am sorry the little fusses spoil things so but there is no need for fusses, I am sure, if your boss will take things calmly. It is just the same with COs and company commanders, some get splendid work done and never fuss and their battalion or company is a family party, others fuss all day, don't get any better work and leave people's nerves bunched up and tangled. We are in the same place and by the look of the paper the French are able to hold the offensive now. I am very fit, just been on a stroll along the line. Tea with W company, Attewell's. This morning spent part of it reading my Greek testament and making notes and trying to remember things I learned years ago, so you see we are having a quiet time. The door is still on its hinges. I picked a bunch of little cream coloured roses, they are on my table. My study is the kitchen of a farmhouse, I have swept it out for my quiet room. Next door are two other rooms, one of which is the kitchen and contains a stove where the men do the cooking. The next room the doctor and I use for our meals and across the yard are two little iron roofed shelters, one of which is the dressing place where about five men sleep and next to it is a similar one in which the doctor and I sleep with our two servants and two of the other men. We sleep in these places and dressing is done there, for at night if there is any shelling they are safe and safe also from gas as the doors and windows are protected by gas blankets through which the gas cannot come. We are all very well used to gas and if we use our respirators at once it does no harm. We haven't had a single gas casualty for a long time. The days of cloud gas are over, they only use it in shells and since they started doing that we have also.

7 June

After lunch I went on to the detail camp where the quartermaster and sergeant-major live. The former looks after stores and rations and supplies, the latter trains men to be machine gunners and NCO's and keeps up the standard of the regiment by his work. I saw the cooks busy making rissoles of bully beef, potato and onions for the men in the line tonight. They have a great oven where the meat is roasted and sent up cold. Dripping is all saved for making rissoles. Yesterday the men had rice pudding with dates in it. The pudding is made in quantities and put into empty preserved meat tins cleaned out. The bacon is boiled and sent up with the roasted meat in tin-lined boxes made by the pioneers. The food question is well understood by Warren the quartermaster and our men are very well fed, and the food is sent up clean and not put into sandbags as so often is done with the result that it comes out covered with dust and hairs from sandbags.

I went into Brigade HQ on my way back, had tea with them. The General feels pretty optimistic about beating the Germans, and says the Americans will have hundreds of aeroplanes in action soon.

8 June

A lovely day finished. Our swallows are very busy building just outside the door. Two or three couples building close to each other. Quiet round here and I have been round to HQ and to some of the companies, all very cheery. This afternoon I found a corps car standing outside and the owner of it turned up the next minute – the General with whom I used to live when I was in the Heavies, General East, with his staff captain. They were round looking at their guns and positions. I am very fond of him, he was very good to me. He is a very keen churchman and it was through him that padres were first appointed to live with heavy artillery. His corps went north on 17th January and I stayed with the batteries, but was sorry to lose him. He came in and had tea and is going to send his car over one day to fetch the doctor and me over to dinner. It was very nice to see him again.

9 June

I have been reading Mr Roseveare's two letters in the May and June magazines. I hope some day to be able to work with or near him again. I would sooner be with him than with anybody, I expect some day they will make him a bishop.

10 June

Tomorrow I have to go to a court martial to speak for a man who is on trial for desertion. There isn't much to say for him. I hope his sentence will be commuted, but it is a very serious charge. He had a good record but was away from January 1917 until May of this year. Death is the penalty, but I hope he won't be shot. He has practically no defence to make. I went down to see him this morning.

St Barnabas Day, Captain Lord is back again, looking a bit thin after his wound. The DSO and MC look very nice on him. He and Mattock have both come back very quickly – they are both very keen. We have got four more Military Medals and two DCM's lately and one officer got a bar to his MC. We had a great game of baseball this evening, HQ versus companies and HQ won.

12 June

Nothing particular to say. I cycled over to the place where my brother was buried in the cemetery of a village, you know the name I expect.

Markby, the assistant adjutant, took me over, knows the place well, and recognised all the places where he used to pass up and down to the trenches. Richard's grave I found after some difficulty. The cross had been broken but an RAMC man fixed it up very nicely. The church has been badly shelled and the cemetery too, but all was quiet when we were there. We found an aid station close to the church and the major gave us tea. It is perfect weather, warm and sunny with a breeze blowing. Our mess room is full of lovely roses and quite beautiful. I am late now so shall write again tomorrow.

13 June

Nothing doing today, fine weather and cool wind. I just got to this very dull and uninspiring statement when your letter arrived, bubbling with you and love and all that is nice. I picture you weighing out your scraps of margarine, wading through ration cards and books, battalions of 56lbs. pots of honey. Pyne, the solid matter-of-fact dear old kind heart, rather mothering you, you mothering and looking after your girls. On my dear, your letter is lovely and it shows me you and your busy life. I cannot tell you anything more about leave, but it will come I feel soon.

14 June

The last few days have been pretty full up as we have been out. Now we are in again and there is little I can do during daytime as one cannot get about very much. Too much movement is bad as it attracts attention to the trenches where the companies live. Last night when we got in, I went in to see the Aid Post of the next battalion, and sat and yarned for a bit, had a cup of tea and then came to our HQ until relief was complete. This finished, Major Tower who is now second-in-command, and I went for a ramble round the line. All quiet. Had a yarn with Attewell in his dugout. In these trench dugouts one has to crawl in on one's hands and knees, they are high enough to sit in and the floors are covered with straw. The roofs are made of curved corrugated iron with earth piled on top. Attewell was as cheery as ever.

16 June

I didn't write yesterday. We have been winning back part of the enemy line. You will see in the papers that the attack was very successful. The battalion has received much praise. It began at midnight, and by Saturday morning early we had gained the objective proposed and a good number of prisoners. The other regiments of the division gained all they were set to do. We have not had a heavy casualty list and only one officer and not many men.

17 June

My own dear love,

My leave starts on the 20th. All being well I shall leave here on the 19th and be in Lambourn on the evening of the 20th. I will wire when I get to Folkestone. Ask Miss Daniel to let you off so that you can be at Lambourn on Friday or Saturday. Our show has won us great praise, I am glad it is over and all have been splendid. I wish I could leave them resting. I feel a pig for coming, but I must come. Oh my love, next Saturday.

3 July

What a wonderful holiday ours has been. We met knowing each other as I thought well, by pen and paper, and we did too. I found you as I knew you to be, my most loving and beautiful girl ...

We know now that the fortnight has shown us clearly that in ideas and thoughts and ways we shall be what I always knew – help-mates, life companions, true lovers through and through whatever happens. I am full of thankfulness and happiness and only long for the time when I can claim you as my wife and live for you and with you, both of us working for the honour and glory as He wishes it, of God.

7 July

It is curious how when I was at home, I felt quite remote from France. Now I have just slipped back again into the same old life, only with a difference, that great difference. Then you and I knew each other part of the way, by previous meetings and then a great deal further with letters, but the fortnight brought us right to each other's arms in that wonderful and beautiful first meeting. This morning we had the Blessed Sacrament in the wood. The altar a table covered with a green cloth, all around thick planted young chestnut trees, beneath soft moss and dried leaves and bracken. The sun shining and birds singing, no sign of war, except the man who knelt before the altar. The Kings band played the hymns, and we had a small party from the Kings and Royal Fusiliers who are down training in the camp here. Later on I had Kitty to take me to the cemetery where I buried an officer of the Kings. At 2.30 I went up to the HQ of that regiment on my bicycle and found them all well. I had tea with them and then left to go to a field ambulance place where they have an annexe hospital for sick men mostly. We had a fair number of men and a very nice service and the Divisional band played two voluntaries and the hymns. They play very nicely and have only lately restarted and I hope to get them during the week for the battalion. Then I cycled back to camp and am now waiting for Kitty to take me to the place where we shall be staying for this week. I hope we shall have a good quiet week, I expect we shall.

9 July

I wonder if you ever think that it was worthwhile for me to ask you to love me, I have had your love so generously given, yet one thinks sometimes would it not have been better to leave you and your heart free until I could ask you to be my wife. I did think that it might be better to do so at first, but I know that my love for you must ask you and your answer had to come. Now I am going to write an extract from the letter the rector wrote me when I asked his advice whether I should write to you or not. "I take it that EM had not come into your thoughts at a jump and my reason for suggesting that you should write to her at once, is that I think the girl's heart is at present whole. This cannot last. She is attractive, she must love someone, her nature cries out for love and for someone to love. She is bent on nursing soon, and she ought not to embark on it if a home is for her. I think of her as much as of you, and long for the happiness that will come to both of you." And in another letter Canon Roseveare writes: "She is a sweet girl, the best, and will make an excellent wife. I know her inside and out, and her inside is even better than her outside, which is high praise. She is older than her years of life, and life has disciplined her well. I should advise you, as I gather that you must feel at least all that you say, to get into correspondence with EM. May God guide you dear brother. Meanwhile may He use you where you are and bring you brightness and hope."

9 July

I wrote to you this afternoon and this will go tomorrow. 11.00 p. m. I have just come back from having dinner with my old general with whom I was working in the Heavy Artillery, winter 1916. I met the Staff Captain the other day, and he asked me for dinner and sent his car over for me and it has just brought me back again. I was very fond of General East, a very good churchman and a very keen soldier. One compares the comparatively comfortable times which the heavy artillery have with the infantry. It is the infantry that get the worst of everything. Oh, how I wish they could get more leave, they are so longing for home, and nothing but a wound gets them home, except the leave which comes so very rarely, twelve or fifteen months. Major Attewell has the MC, I am so very glad for him, and his wife and the family too. It will fill them all with joy. He is a splendid man, true and brave and good. I hope you will meet him when he comes home. I hope he will get his leave next month. The doctor has gone, so that brings us one nearer to each other.

12 July

The night before last I went up the line with a big party, who had to do a big digging job. We were out all night and did not get back until 8.00 a.m. It wasn't a very nice place and I don't like having those big parties of 300 men or so. We got a few wounded, but none badly. Yesterday morning I slept after it till 1.00. In the afternoon we had baseball, quite a good game. We play officers and men mixed and it's good fun. This morning I went to see Vischer, the SCF of this division. He is going on leave so I shall have to take his place, but I am not going to the Division, it is too far away from my battalions. I shall stay where I am in the village where all my battalions come out in turn for rest, then I shall be handy for going up the line, so this week I shall mess with the Kings, live in my room here and keep Bennet here too if I can, and fix it up to have Kitty up here with the Kings horses.

16 July

I think your idea of earthenware pitchers is good, unusual too. There are lots of things like that that are much nicer than ordinary fancy things which are common and cheap in idea. We shall have an exciting time when we can really furnish the house. It will be like another wedding. We seem to be doing everything in unordinary ways. Do you like bowls for porridge and soup rather than soup plates? I like the old French bowls, and there are no handles to break off, and plain pottery vases are much nicer than so called artistic ones. They show flowers off much better. We will furnish with strong hefty stuff, it must be good wood and solid, not gimcrack. I like wooden beds and roomy chairs and don't like mirrors over the mantelpiece; we must have one room with a plain blue paper and a frieze of wild roses round the top. The blue will remind us of the Lambourn sky, and the pink roses will always be woven in my memory with you.

17 July

I'm having a visit up with the battalion this afternoon. I must say I feel rather lost stopping down here with the other battalions, but it is good to be with them sometimes. The weather is beautiful today and quite a cool breeze. I am going round with Attewell to see the companies. The news is good, the new offensive has got through, a very little way and 1000 prisoners taken by the Americans. Oh if the Boche could only be badly beaten now, what a difference it may make next year.

18 July

You told me about Miss Davis' concert, she must be a wonderful pianist. I haven't heard anything out here that will bring back the music of those days, those lovely days. But music is only won by hard work, and one day I hope our work will earn us a holiday together, better even than the last one. You said you were longing to put music into my life, you have done it, you have made my life music. Could I have ever known what my love is for you? There was a whole side of me that no-one had ever opened before you. You have opened it. It may not be worth much, but it is real. Keep me dear love full of the music of that wonderful love you have given me.

19 July

This morning we had the Eucharist at 9.30 a.m.; voluntary services I always have now. There were 200 men there I should think and over 40 communicants. Certainly as I look back to the old days there are many more communicants than there used to be when I had the old parade services, with Communion afterwards. I am quite sure that the Blessed Sacrament is much greater to these men than an ordinary service. It must be, it is concrete and near and much more definite than the matins sort of thing. I sometimes wish I had these regiments in surroundings where they could worship in beauty and with full ceremonial. In the army there is so much ritual and ceremonial in everyday life and therefore in religion it is more natural. One has hopes of what peacetime will bring if we can carry on the impression and deepen the effects. I often think that if I were to continue in the army and we had a house near the barracks, we would be able to do great work for these boys. Our home would give them the home life they so much need. They could have a room for their use and we would make them comfortable and happy, but peacetime is a long way off yet.

I think the Rector's ideas in Deptford were so good, because all through he represented the home life as the basis of religion. St Paul's was a wonderful home life to everyone. Oh dearest, when our home comes, we must try to build up our parish life on that same good foundation and make worship a beautiful thing, speaking of the home in Heaven which is foreshown by happy earthly homes.

19 July

God grant that a good time comes soon, but, dearest of hearts, don't be oppressed by the sense of my danger. I want to be ready to do my work and brave to do it. It is an awful thing to live in fear of dying, and if I am killed you will know that my personality isn't dead. One has got to just fight away fear of death, to fear is not to love. Perfect love casteth out fear, because fear has torment. Personality doesn't die, love doesn't die, love remains because it is a gift from God. You will not have me afraid to die. You will love me knowing that it is only by life given that we are given life. You are giving your life to the welfare of those with whom you live. We shall, you and I, try to help and raise the lives of other people. You and I are bound together by a great and sacred promise. One with each other in the sacrament of love.

19 July

I have just had your letter. I'm glad the Bishop had a chat with you but I don't think he quite understands I am not a free agent. I have signed on definitely until May 1919, and unless I should be wounded or ill or incapable of work out here, in either case I am just as much in the army as any combatant officer or man. It simply isn't a question of choice at all, so I am afraid he will have to fill this parish in the autumn. I know that you know how great a temptation it is for a man to leave his work, when home and home life is calling more strongly than it ever has, but I am fit and well. If I tried to get out of my duty here, and I believe it is a duty, it would be an unworthy thing to do. If I were not fit, or in danger of a breakdown it would be different. No, if I am brought safely through this year, it may be better for me to give up the army, but now I have no option at all and a very strong call to carry on here, but against that a great longing for you and home, which is right but not to be used as an argument or temptation for me to leave my present work. As for the advice to be prudent, I think I am these days, so prudent that I am in danger of losing grip. When one reads the New Testament and Acts and sees the tremendous needs of men, one sees one's poor little soul shrivelling up with over-prudence. You would not have me self loving, and in this case prudence means that to me, for I have always been careful to run no risks which are foolish or un-necessary. Dear love I long for you, how much I can't tell you, but the job is here.

Sunday, 21 July

Today at 9.00 I celebrated in a building in a village not far from here. A company of RE there. They turned out well and there were ten to fifteen communicants. The hymns were played by the fiddler very well and singing was excellent. Then I went off on my bike, or rather not mine, as getting there my back tyre burst and I got a swap from the RE's. Loaded with my books and my church kit and a furious wind in my teeth, so I was very hot by the time I got to my next destination. 200 men or so were ready and we had a good service, though the wind was unpleasantly gusty. The accompaniment was a clarinet, well played but hardly strong enough. After lunch I went to the cemetery on Jim my old horse, as I didn't ride Kitty down, thinking a bicycle would do things more easily, and wished many times I had taken Kitty during the morning instead of the bike. I came back to a neighbouring Labour company where they had asked me to speak at a brotherhood meeting. It was held in a tent shelter in the wood. The men run it themselves under the care of the captain of the company. Their brotherhood consists of men of all denominations. They are keen and full of the Spirit. I was much struck with them. They have extemporary prayers, quaint but full of the real thing. I took the Gospel for St James' day, a kind of meditation.

27 July

I have been out all day visiting the line, a beastly day. Trenches in one party have been duck-boarded, in others they are deep in mud. Signals had a car going up to Brigade so I walked up the rest and I had lunch with the Northumberland Fusiliers HQ. Went up to the trenches afterwards and came back through the Kings trenches via the RAP and had tea with the headquarters of Kings. I phoned for my horse to meet me and the groom met me and got home at 7.30 in time for a wash and change for dinner. A busy day tomorrow and it's late, so won't write more.

28 July

Today has been fine and I have had very good services. Holy Communion at 8.00 at headquarters of Division; not many there, the General, two officers, and two men. Left them at 9.00 and went to the Royal Fusiliers HQ and found that training was to go on. I had arranged services and saw the General to ask that battalions out of the line on Sundays, might not have to train on Sundays. The training was cancelled and we had the loft full, 20 communicants. Went on then to the Suffolks, had a big voluntary service at 11.30 in the open, and the mess room fitted up as a chapel for Eucharist afterwards, about 25 there. I had lunch there and walked back to get my horse and groom at the stable and found on the way a Crossfield Deptford boy waiting to see me. One of the extremists of Crossfield Street; his brother used to be a little villain. He was very nice and delighted to get a breath of Deptford air. On then on Kitty to an RE company and found they were only just back from work and having dinner at 4.00 p.m., so I had no service there. Had tea and rode back to service at 6.00 where the band played very well. Came back with Kitty, went to the Pioneer Battalion headquarters to dinner. The Colonel loves an argument and talk, they were a very happy party.

30 July

A splendid day, quite hot. I went over to the 4th Royal Fusiliers in the morning, had lunch with them at HQ and came back here to meet Berry, DACG of this Corps, who sent a message to tell me he was coming at 2.30. Then after he had gone I went back to the Fusiliers again, and had a game of baseball and a chat to the men, had tea, and then it was time to meet some men in the town here for a Bible class and communicants class. Five came and we had three quarters of an hour class. Then Kitty trotted me home to camp. Tomorrow I have a service at 9.30 as the battalion goes up the line. After service, I hope to have a car lent me to go to a Chaplains' conference some distance away, too far to ride. Neville Talbot will be there, and will talk in his breezy way. He is a most refreshing person, and we shall have lunch and then come back. I have to see the General at 2.00 and shall ask him to come to a service in the woods on Sunday the 4th. I thought this job would be dull, but find it interesting. There is plenty to do and arrange, and I can go anywhere, and when I want to I can go up the line and see my chaps in the trenches. Only I miss being at the RAP when they are in the line. I don't see the wounded and don't get the personal touch I had with them in the regiment.

29 July

I am very glad to hear from you and that the term is really ended. I am glad the girls gave you hankies and things and mysterious things that I wot not of. What a weird name Ethlene is, is it a short convenience for Ethel and Kathleen? I am glad too that Miss D. has hurled things at you in the shape of a fiver. It is very nice to feel that all has gone well. I like your picture of the break-up, all the dignified staff, you amongst them, sitting in rich apparel on the stage. The poor girls, all of them sitting in houses in the hall, looking like rabbits in hutches at a big market, or like a collection of Noah's arks.

Letter to St Paul's, July 1918

Dear People at home,

I haven't written to you for some time, partly because it was difficult to tell you what I have known for some time. Now I think it is time for me to tell you that I am engaged to be married to Miss Molesworth, one who loves St Paul's and has often worshipped there. Many of you know her. We hope to be married next leave.

I should be untrue to you if I did not now tell you that when my work as Chaplain is no longer needed out here I shall be probably asked by the Bishop to take charge of a parish. I do not know where or when it will be. I have signed on as Chaplain until next May. I promised when I left St Paul's in May 1915 that I should come back again as Curate. We did not think then that the war would last so long. Since then, as you see, I have made another promise and that has altered circumstances. I told the Rector some time ago of my plans and he thought that my promise to return to St Paul's was no longer binding. Until my last leave I could not well tell you of these hopes and plans. I have told you enough about myself and hope you will understand.

I see by this month's magazine that Mr Reakes is going into the Army as a combatant. I hope I may have the good fortune to meet him out here. The magazine is very interesting and it shows that the life of St Paul's is very keen. I have only just returned from a most delightful leave in the most beautiful country in the world – home. It was very lovely in the green corn lands and on the high downs and in the woodlands of Berkshire. Just before I left, my battalion took part in a very successful attack, which meant taking an important position from the enemy and a good many prisoners and machine guns. Yet side by side with the joy of success and the splendour of bravery is the sadness of losing some of one's friends.

I am writing at the end of a week's rest in a village behind the line. We have all been enjoying rest, games and concerts. Tomorrow before the battalion goes up to the line again, we shall have service and the Blessed Sacrament. For the next week or two while my senior chaplain is on leave he wants me to represent him, so I shall not be living up the line for a while but shall continue to live in my billet in this village and visit my battalions from here. Since my last letter to you we have been living in many different places and have not had such a strenuous time as we had during March and April. We do not know what is coming in the future but whatever happens I know that the officers and men of these battalions will give a good account of themselves. They long for home but are ready always to give themselves for home, dear beyond anything to these gallant men. Every life which is poured out is an offering for your safety and peace. Therefore remember them and their joys and hardships and pains in your prayers and in the Sacrament of Him who came from His home in heaven to win all earthly homes.

Yours affectionately,
Noel Mellish, C. F.

Chapter Thirteen

Armistice

IN JULY I WENT TO LIVE AT DIVISIONAL HEADQUARTERS as the senior padre was going away for a month. Everything was done to help, I had a car whenever I wanted it and my own little mare, who never failed me. There was always a welcome at any Battalion or Company HQ – as I think of it now, I never cease to marvel at the splendid friendship that was characteristic of every rank, from General downwards.

Somewhere about this time in the Royal Fusiliers we were joined by Major Tower, who had been on the staff for a time and was looked upon as a very brilliant officer. His whole being radiated a charm which attracted all to him. He felt that he ought to come back to the regiment and leave the comparative safety and comfort of the staff. He answered his call. During those months from April to August we went back to settled trench warfare, varied by raids which from time to time were made for information, and were commonly called "winkling". One was made by the Kings one night. A barrage was put over for a few minutes, then the men rushed over, all volunteers, collared two Germans and hurried them off, one going without any protest, the other a big fellow wearing the Iron Cross, very angry but refusing to speak. Only two of the Kings were wounded and that only slightly. Another raid was made by the Royal Fusiliers. The German trench was in a cornfield. Our party stole up quietly this time without any artillery and got their man. Unfortunately we had a corporal killed in this raid – such a good fellow and a special friend of mine. The wretched prisoner was brought down, white and trembling, but quite unhurt, his captors thoroughly pleased with themselves. What must have been his astonishment when they gave him hot tea and food, which was waiting ready for them as if he was an honoured guest. Then he was trotted off by an escort to Divisional Headquarters.

The British soldier never learned to hate. He was not given to expressing his feelings; he kept them to himself. Neither did he talk about what he did. Never in any war have such splendid things been done; they were almost commonplace and as often as not those who did most gallant things were killed, or there was no-one left to record them. The regimental stretcher bearers in every action risked their lives every hour in carrying the wounded down to the aid post. The signallers, whose all-important work was to keep open communication between companies and HQ and between Battalion HQ and Brigade, were exposed to the worst of shelling when running out wires and repairing those that were laid. Messages often had to be carried by hand yet the runners got through, passing through fire which cannot be described. I remember one day the CO sending a boy named Green to a company, and just as he was returning he was hit by a piece of shell. He was bandaged up and they were going to carry him off to the aid post; he would not allow it – he must first deliver his message to the Colonel, then having done his work he was carried away.

On another occasion a raid was ordered to get prisoners for identification of the regiments in front. As usual volunteers were asked for and there was difficulty in making the choice, for so many offered. Next day it was noticed that Dennis, an HQ runner, had a black eye. When pressed for an explanation, he replied with some confusion that he and another both wished to go, neither would give in, so they decided it with fists. Such were the men of the BEF.

The middle of August brought a great change. As I was still acting divisional chaplain I moved in great comfort in a Sunbeam car south to Bavincourt, where the Division took up its headquarters. Everywhere the corn was being harvested, old men and grey haired grannies labouring in the fields, and children putting up the corn in stooks. On 20th August the battalions moved up nearer to the front, marching by night to give the enemy no inkling of the change.

The next day I rejoined the Royal Fusiliers in a desolate village, hiding up, no movement of any sort going on. At midnight we left, for we had about five miles to go to reach our jumping off ground for the attack. The Colonel was leading with Headquarters Company, when a dozen shells came over and he and several men were wounded. We got them away as quickly as possible, but it meant a good deal of delay. The Colonel was hit in the lungs, but fortunately later on made a good recovery. The doctor and I went on with the stretcher bearers, but a dense fog had come down. We had some difficulty in finding the way but a machine gun officer came along and he led us by compass till we got to the appointed place. The advance had already begun and I heard that Danvers, padre to the Suffolks, had been wounded. I could not find him in the fog, but I heard later that he had been carried out by his servant – he must have been a giant, for Danvers weighed about 14 stone.

The command of the Fusiliers then devolved upon Major Tower, who, much against his inclination, had been left behind according to orders; it was fortunate for the success of our attack that he was, for he might have suffered Colonel Hartley's fate. How he knew I don't know, but he must have been following up pretty closely, at any rate he took command at once and, under cover of the fog, he led the Royal and Northumberland Fusiliers up the long open slope and rushed the steep railway bank at Achiet-le-Grand and our men were right amongst the Germans before they knew we were anywhere near. Their position was immensely strong, with machine guns between every other sleeper; it could have held up an Army Corps, but the surprise was so complete that the enemy turned tail and bolted. The second Division came through us and continued the chase.

The tide had turned. It was all wonderfully quiet – hardly a gun to be heard and the enemy miles away. We spent the day right in the open, enjoying the rest.

In the evening, Tower, Attewell, the Doctor and I were having some food when Tower got up and said, "I'll just go along to Z Company and see that boy and tell him to keep a lookout on the left." The Company Commander had been killed and there was only a subaltern in charge of the company. Tower went off and we stayed there chatting, but he did not return. The company was quite close, so Attewell and I got up to see where he had gone. He never came back; a long range bullet had hit him in the head and he was unconscious and died the next day. And it all seemed so safe!

Major Tower's death was a grievous loss to us all. His was that lovable nature, so true and courteous, one felt that he lived on a higher plane. I can't imagine anything mean or base in him at any time. He radiated courage and inspired all by his noble character. Major Attewell now took command and we went forward on the following day.

We had no more fighting for a week. One day I saw the wagon of a battery I had been looking for, for there was a young officer in that battery whom I knew. The driver told me the battery's position and I found my friend and we had tea in a gun pit. As we were having tea the Germans started to shell and they knocked a gun out but did no more harm.

A day or two afterwards I got a wire from this boy's father asking me to go and see him at Letreport Hospital.

I found that it was 100 miles away; I started off on a bicycle to a place where the MT were. They had no car they could spare, but had a lorry going to Doullens, so that was a good start. At Doullens I took to my bicycle again and reached the Aerodrome, where the major in charge very kindly gave me lunch and sent me on in a sidecar to Abbeville. Here I found the colonel in hospital going on pretty well, but with several pieces of shell in his lungs. After a talk, I went on, this time getting a lift from a French girl, who was driving a Ford, but she could only take me three miles. Then I boarded a heavy lorry and after a few miles we were stopped at a railway crossing and a Sunbeam drew up with Staff officers in it and one spare seat. I asked for a lift and they took me to within three miles of Letreport. Then I walked for a bit, when a Ford came along loaded more than full with Australian officers. I was pretty lame by this time, as I had sprained my ankle a few days before. They added me to their load and my last lap was on the funicular railway up to the top of the cliff, where the hospitals were.

I reached it at 8 p. m. and found that Martin had sailed for home half an hour before!

The Matron was very kind and fed me and the padre gave me a bed. Next morning I set out in a signals van bound for Abbeville, where I saw Colonel Hartley again, and my luck being in, an RE officer came along and gave me a lift to St Ricquier. After some lunch at a cafe I tramped on until a staff car overtook me. This officer took me another stage on my journey; then an HAC officer carried me another 20 miles, which brought me to Doullens, where, to my amazing good fortune, I found our CRE who, returning past the aerodrome, took up my bicycle and carried me off to Divisional HQ for tea and so back. It was a wonderful journey and would have been impossible but for the kindness one always had in the army. The young officer I went to find made a splendid recovery and rowed in his college boat in 1920.

Extracts from letters to E. W. M. 2 August – 5 November 1918

2 August

I have been pretty busy this week and find the days full. I wish they were longer and then I could get oftener up to the line. There is nobody with my regiments now. Next week I shall try to have two days and two nights up at the line. This afternoon I have been round taking notices and asking various people to back up the commemoration service well. Went first to Q office, that is the management of supply; part of the division. Then went to see the General to show him the form of service. I will send it when it is over. Then on to the Kings to arrange one with them and had tea with them. Had a confirmation class of two and have another of four tomorrow at 10.00. Two of them were on guard today. Then visited 3 Field Ambulance HQ and back here just after 8.00. It is not the time that fills up, but the distance between places, and a bicycle is not good this weather. Kitty is splendid, she is doing a lot of work. Poor old Mary is still unwell, and will be for a good time on the sick list, so Kitty has to do double work, but she doesn't mind.

4 August

I am not going to write anymore now, I have only just finished my sermon and it is nearly 1.00. The first day of the fifth year, and the news is better and better, thank God for it. Can there be another year? I don't think so. Are we ready for peace? I pray we may be.

5 August

Poor old Mary, the grey mare, has gone away. She was too lame to walk, so she had to be put into a float, a deep cart, and resented it very noisily. She couldn't kick it as she wanted to, but she did her best to kick herself out of it. I saw her go off, riding in her carriage, drawn by a couple of strong horses. I don't think Vischer will mind, as she is a very awkward riding horse. I should have been very sick if it had been Kitty, as she is a splendid ride and very nice mannered.

The news continues to be very good. I expect the Boche will shorten his line where he can. He has done so already in places. The French have done magnificently, I wonder if they will beat him on the Aisne and over it? I hope the Boche is demoralised there, he must have had very heavy losses. He must know he cannot win any more, and he is only just beginning to know America and her power, yet there seems no sign of any admission of failure. But it must come. If we could fight him on German soil I believe it would bring the war to an end. The German people don't know what the war means.

Perhaps a good many of our own people at home don't know. It is so difficult to understand it. The French people are most wonderfully brave. Here they are in this village, reaping their corn with insufficient labour, old women with grey hair working until dark to get their harvest. And each day in this village they are shelled, sometimes three times a day, as yesterday, and sometimes during the night. If they leave their homes and bit of land they leave everything. We are out of the village and safe from shell-fire up here.

14 August

Still good news. I am very comfy here, an end of a good hut, curtained off, chair, bed, table and electric light, mess room further on in the same hut. It is a very big well-built one. I have been out in the car this morning to see the land, as it was going, and when I got back I had a visit from Philip Crick who is DACG of this Corps. I took over from him at Rouen in 1915. He is a topper, huge as a bull, very keen. We had Neville Talbot, ACG of the 1st Army and Berry, Dean of Oriel as DACG, and now Crick, Dean of Clare, is with us. They are all top-hole for fellows. Tomorrow all our divisional padres will be coming for our usual Eucharist, and meeting and talk. I got a light tender to go round for them, as it is too far to ask them to cycle. OC signals is very good and gives me all I ask. Everybody is very good.

15 August

After tea went all round divisional area in car and called at Kings and Royal Fusiliers HQ and other places. Home at 8. I shall soon be an ordinary bloke and not a divisional nut who goes about in a car. Lovely country, some villages very nice and old, and some very shoddy and broken down.

16 August

This morning I spent making arrangements for Sunday services. The morning will be Holy Communion at 8.00 a.m.; service with band playing in the chateau garden at 10.00, Holy Communion after. After lunch I shall ride to the place where the Fusiliers and Kings are for an evening service and stay the night if they will have me, and come back Monday morning in time for a meeting in my room to discuss with Crick, the DACG, and the Burial officer about burial arrangements. It is ten miles from here to the village, so I shall not hurry Kitty and tire her too much, for a twenty mile journey is rather much if not necessary. This afternoon I rode over to see the Scots Fusiliers and found they were having sports with the Shropshires in the same brigade and an American regiment. There was a great mixed crowd in the chateau grounds. There were flat races, relay races and jumping, a band race in which all the pipers of the Scots, the drummers of the Shropshires and the buglers of the Americans had to walk a hundred yards making a terrific noise with their instruments. There was boxing, each opponent had to stand in a tub, the tubs being placed on stands which made them wobble. The man who took his foot out of the tub lost the round, they usually over-balanced. The hundred yards was run in heats, one heat being run by three padres, an American RC, Sellers, who is with the Shropshires and me. Sellers left me panting behind him. Then there was a pig crating contest which was asked for by the Americans who brought the pig. The competitors had to rush in from a ring and grab the pig and put it in a box. Only two being allowed to box it. The pig protested vigorously but didn't attempt to run. There was no sport in it at all, and our fellows didn't approve of the unfortunate pig being roughly treated and it was soon stopped. A good tug-of-war ended the sports, the Americans beating the Scots. The Star Spangled Banner was played at the salute and our National Anthem afterwards. There was great friendliness between each battalion.

20 August

It is 4.00 a.m. and we are in a little while going up to a great attack and I hope a great advance. All is very quiet and the enemy I think unprepared. It is all sudden and ought to be a complete surprise.

22 August

Only just a line. We are in an attack and doing well, losing heavily but all are splendid. We have lost our Colonel and second-in-command, wounded, four officers killed and several wounded. We are all doing well and the General is pleased. We hope to be on the way to peace and a great victory.

25 August

We are out again and I have had two letters from you. No time to write but only to send my love. I am quite well and fit. Our loss is heavy, but we have had great success. We are getting back onto the 21st March ground here. The men are superb. We have had a quiet day resting after a strenuous time. The men have had baths and clean clothes and are all looking fit. I am sleeping in a tent with Attewell in a quiet valley far from the battle line, though three days ago it was close to the front. I am living with the battalion again. I suppose Vischer is back as SCF, though I haven't seen him. I have no kit at all except a few hymn sheets and half a dozen hymn books. Haven't any of my kit which I left at divisional HQ. I hope to have it tomorrow. Today has been hot and very dusty. Tonight thunder and rain to lay the dust. Our troops are pressing the Boche back steadily, we shall very soon I hope be on the ground he won from us in March. Our morale is splendid, we shall I hope get a very good position before the winter sets in.

27 August

Now I must tell you what has been happening. On the 20th the
Division had orders to go up, leaving the villages where they were at
rest. At midnight they started and had a long tiring march 15 miles.
I found my battalion on the 21st in the afternoon. At midnight of the
21st we left the place to march up to our jumping off place. When
we were only half an hour away, we were shelled and the CO, Colonel
Hartley, and another officer and a good many men were wounded or
gassed. The Colonel was badly hit. He was in front of the battalion
and the leading companies caught it worst. I was with the doctor at
the end of the column. We were all miles away from the front line,
but these were chance shells, about a dozen, fired at the track I suppose,
to damage transport. The two other battalions of our brigade had no
casualties; they got past before. We were the last to move off according
to our orders. The doctor dressed the Colonel and I helped to dress
the others and we got them away in transport coming down the track.
We went on then, but the battalion had gone on. It was very difficult
to find the way as it was thick mist and fog. However we got to our
next position, with the help of a machine gun officer who led the way
by compass. It was almost impossible for the tanks and cavalry to get
on because of the fog.

28 August

We heard from the Colonel tonight. He is better and has gone to
Boulogne, his servant came back and told us good news of him and
we were all very glad. I expect he is at home now and Danvers the
padre who was wounded is also at home and doing well. This afternoon
I went up with an officer to reconnoitre a trench we have to go to.
It was a long, tedious walk. When coming back we saw an artillery
wagon on the way so got on and had a lift. I was talking to the man
in it and asked him his battery. It is Martin Roseveare's and I know
where the battery is, quite close to where we shall go tomorrow, so I
hope to see him tomorrow afternoon. I am so glad, what luck it is
that we got onto that wagon. I have hoped to meet him for a long
time.

Saturday, 31 August

I am in a lovely place here. I had a wire from the Rector on Thursday
night to say Martin was wounded and here and to visit, so I came
down yesterday by road, begging my way on every sort of vehicle.
Had lunch at an aerodrome and tea at a CCS where Colonel Hartley
is, and on to here by 8.00 p.m. where I found Martin had just gone
home to England. They say he is wonderful, shot right through the
body, but it has apparently done very little damage and he is doing
very well. I am glad. How glad they will be when they see him. I
have had delightful hospitality. The matron of his hospital fed me and
I got a billet from the padre at another hospital. All American doctors.
I slept and had breakfast here and now I am off back again to the
Fusiliers by any transport I can get.

1 September

Now I am at the 3rd Division rest Camp, I sprained an ankle in the
show yesterday, and am nursing it in the fat of the land at 142 Field
Ambulance. I may be here a few days. About 150 men of different
regiments are here, crocked a little. I am quite happy, live in a tent
and mess with the two officers who look after the sick men. We had
a strenuous time yesterday and hope to be out soon.

2 September

I got down here about 1.00 a.m. on Sunday morning. I left the line
on Saturday night. Early on that morning we attacked and I am afraid
we had heavy losses. It was a bad place, thick with machine guns.
Early in the morning I sprained my left ankle while getting into a
little trench. The doctor fixed me up, but it wasn't much use for me
to hang on as I could only hop. I was much annoyed. However now
I am going on very well, it will soon be fit, and I hope to be back
again before long. There are about 150 men here, slight wounds, gas
cases and sickness. None very serious. My own field ambulance is
running it and it is very good. The men are happy and comfy. I have
a ripping little square tent and mess with the MO and quartermaster.
Last evening had a service outside and this morning celebrated in my
tent at 8.00. Nine communicants. Got my servant Bennett here and
he looks after me. Nothing for you to worry about. I expect our

Division will be getting a rest soon for a short time for reorganising. Then on again. There can be no stopping, we must press them on and back before the winter comes in. I expect by now we have the whole of the Hindenburg line. Kemel we have retaken and now we shall soon march on Cambrai.

3 September

My ankle quickly got better under the doctor's treatment and massage, and I came back to the Battalion today and found them out. They have had a very hard time. When I left on Saturday our advance was hung up, and we had had very heavy losses. They attacked again afterwards and got through and did excellently, earning great praise from the General, and took a large number of prisoners, and now the advance has gone on splendidly. Everyone is very cheery though very tired. We have a new CO, a good man with a great reputation, his name is Johnson. Major Tower is dead, such a glorious selfless gallant gentleman, I am very grieved we have lost him and so many of our officers.

4 September

I know it is a bad time for you dearest, but I am well and your letters are a joy. I have been out all day going round and finding out if all our dead are buried. I read the service over the grave where about 30 of our officers and men were buried this morning or yesterday. The place was a dreadfully hard one to take. A sunken road lined with machine guns in good shelter. As our men advanced over the open they were killed and wounded.

Saturday was the bad day. At night the Northumberland Fusiliers came down the sunken road and drove the enemy out. We went forward again and took a number of prisoners with a small number more of wounded. The enemy has been driven miles back. We are out, and shall be for a few days. I must go again tomorrow to complete my work of hunting round for unburied bodies and shall then have a rest. I took a pack-horse and my groom mounted, and brought back a good number of waterproof sheets and blankets to make shelters for the men. They have very little cover here.

7 September

I got back to the battalion after another speedy run in many cars. Started at 9.30 in a signals car from the hospital where I stopped last night. This landed me in the town where Colonel Hartley is in hospital. I saw him again, then I stopped an RE officer in his car and begged a lift which took me on to a small town where they had this glorious church. I went into it and thought how you would love it. It is not so loved as it might be, being spoilt by cheap decorations, horribly out of keeping with its real beauty. I had some lunch in a cafe, a very good lunch, sardines, bread and butter, veal or pork chop and chips, salad and coffee, for five francs. Not really dear for the conditions. Then I hailed a staff officer and he stopped and took me up and carried me on in his car. He was a staff colonel too, but I have unlimited cheek. Then I stopped another who was an HAC Senior Officer, who took me another twenty miles. Finally at the next town I saw our CRE who had his light tender. He took me up as far as the aerodrome where I had left my bicycle. Took up my cycle into the tender in which there were three majors. The colonel suggested that. I had intended to cycle the rest, but was not at all unwilling to go in his car which is a beauty. So I got to divisional HQ, had tea with the CRE in his billet and saw Vischer to arrange things and so on to our abiding place which is a trench, once front line but now far behind the war.

10 September

This afternoon I saw one of our kite balloons and another about half a mile away. Great lumpy white clouds very low. All of a sudden the archies started shelling furiously and machine guns barked. Then out of a cloud cover dashed a Boche plane and shot at the balloon with phosphorus bullets. Off he flew to the second balloon, shells bursting all round him. The observers had seen him coming and jumped out just in time. Then in a second the balloon burst into flame, the flame changing into a great black tail of dropping smoke, nothing left of the balloon. In a few seconds he had reached the other balloon, the same thing happened and he got clean away. Our planes were after him but they couldn't reach him. He got another down that evening the same way. It constantly happens. We, of course, do the same. Sometimes he turns his machine guns on the men as they come down on their parachutes. I believe he did this time, but I wasn't near enough to see that. This is a side of war which is always happening.

19 September

Another attack and a small bit of trench was gained for a while, then retaken by a bombing attack. The Hun's counter-attack, though supported by tremendous gunfire, was absolutely a failure, and our men and officers were highly elated with their success in beating him back. Considering the gunfire we have had very few badly wounded, though about a dozen killed. It cost the Hun a good number of prisoners, about 75 I believe, and numbers killed and wounded. It is a bloody, beastly war, but we must win and we are winning. Today we have heard of 5000 or more taken south of us, and by the direction of our gunfire we can see that there has been a considerable advance there. We are holding at present a place which the Hun badly wants to get back, but I don't fear for a moment that he will get it.

I was out all night going round seeing if there were any more wounded to be brought in. I went with the SB corporal, a very fine chap who fears nothing. It was horribly muddy round the trenches, but all our wounded are safely away. I got in at 4.00 and had my dinner and then a sleep. Now we have finished the grave and I have had lunch. If things are quiet we shall get a party to bury the dead which we haven't been able to up till now. Wounded come first. This is rather a bloody letter I am afraid.

22 September

Now to answer your letter. Looking at it all round, as far as I can see, I don't think Airlie is the best place. It isn't hard work that I mind, it is the strain of the whole thing. You are not so strong as you were before your operation – the pain in your side shows that – it isn't that you have to manage the place, there is undue strain put on you and unnecessary exertion involved in racing about to get food at short notice and taking girls about, often up to town, finding servants and generally doing too hard work. I don't mind your having the work, and the responsibility and care is not at all a bad thing. Your friendship with the girls is splendid, and your friendship and influence with all is very good, but I think that many terms such as last term would give you a breakdown. This must be avoided. With another person than Miss Daniel it could be avoided, but I am afraid it might happen. If you were with someone like Alice, my sister in Guernsey, in such surroundings I should love you to continue such work, but I don't think I can advise or care for you to stay on at Wycombe. Although the war is doing well, I do not feel at all certain that it will be over by next May, nor do I feel assured that I can leave the army next May. If I am as fit as I have been this year, it is my duty to stay on if the war is going on. I don't think that your going to Little Oakley is the best thing either. Of course your people will be glad for you to be there, but the place is too small, there are too few people there, it is a very small horizon. The doings of Mr Bishop, and the eccentricities of Mr Wonter takes too big a place in Little Oakley universe. Your people would love to have you with them, and you would be glad to be there but they don't love the place and neither do you. It is too narrow and mentally oppressive. The third proposal is the office work at Blackheath. I don't see any objection to that work, you won't have too long hours and will get plenty of exercise. It seems to me the danger of Airlie is a physical one, that of Little Oakley a mental one with no chance of spiritual refreshment. Living at Number 22 you will have plenty of work in the office, home work with Aunt Georgie, time for dress-making, church life. Mother will be glad for you to be near too. I should be sorry you won't see much of your father and mother but it may be for another year yet, and Little Oakley is not the place for you and I don't think they would care for you to be there. For it may be a long time yet before we can have our own home. Then supposing I am killed out here, you would have work and would be able to keep yourself. Even if you did not become a nurse, though I expect you probably would choose that very noble profession, we must look all round it as the Rector says.

Now for the joy of thinking of our marriage. Yes, St Paul's is the place for us, I have no doubt about it. I love the church more than any, and I love the people and my life there as well. The Rector will marry us, Joan and Margaret will be your bridesmaids. Will you ask Joan? That would be delightful. Bob Scruby will be my best man, and Violet will I hope be there too. The Rectory would be ideal for our wedding feast, it will all be perfect. You will wear a white dress. As far as I can see I might get leave in November. It will be three months next 4th of October, and leave is going well, both officers and men.

23 September

Last night I went up the line to bury a man and stayed all night with the company. They have a good dug-out as HQ in a nasty place, but the men have no shelter, and it was raining, cold and wretched. I hope we shall be relieved soon. We have had a long time up and have had severe fighting and great strain. Water is short, and the men have wonderful beards, and need a rest and change very much. I brought back about 50 bottles of German anti-tetanus serum which I found in a German aid post, it should be useful. The other night I got three sand bags full of medical dressings from another dug-out which had been used by Germans. I enclose a Belgian farthing I picked up in the German aid post this morning. The motto suits the times doesn't it?

24 September

A quiet day today and only one wounded. An artful Hun plane dropped a bomb into a trench, wounded one not very badly and shocked three. His bombs are much less effective than shells. No wounded today. We were up late last night and I slept till nearly 11.00. After that I spent some time with a few men digging in a reserve water tank into a good safe position, and covered it up nicely with iron protection and any old grass and weeds to prevent its being seen. Nothing to report from this front.

St Michael's Day. We came out here yesterday morning and got here at 3.00. The men had to build up their little shacks to live in out of any old stuff they could find. I am living in a tent with another officer. Today we had the Eucharist in a field near the companies at 10.00 a.m. Then I rode over to the Kings for 11.30; a good number there and the General and about 3 of his staff, about 25 communicants. I got the General to tell the men the latest news and he spoke to them very nicely. I got back just after 1.00 and after lunch had a sleep which I needed. After tea I had a little service in the tent. Tonight we have had orders to move forward again tomorrow. I wish we had one more day for rest and cleaning up. The men have not had baths yet, I have had two, one last night and one today, and I hope for another tomorrow morning. Attewell is back, very fit, and will soon be going home for a three months senior officers course to Aldershot. How bucked his little wife will be. My ordination day today, I hope it won't be so very long before we are together again. Disappointments be gone! My dear it will be love and loveliness, you and your beauty and yourself my own, not a dream but a reality growing more and more real, as we get older with each other and work with each other.

2 October

I had a few lines today written on your washing account, a quaint document which I treasure as a war saving. I must say you are extravagant in having three nightdresses a week, 18 bodices, but you have effected a saving in having only one stocking or does the one refer to collars? Even so it is economical, but 28 handkerchiefs is a large number unless you had a bad cold. Four blouses seems out of proportion to the collar solitary in all its shining whiteness. I had a letter from your mother, she is now at Budleigh Salterton I expect. We must go there some day, you will love the country round. I think if we can we will do a cycle trip round Cornwall some holiday. I didn't enjoy it by myself, but with you it will be perfect.

6 October

Today is your birthday, again I wish you very many happy ones dearest. I had a full morning, 9.30, 11.30 and 12.15 in various places. The first in the old cookhouse in the trench, then up on the rise on the edge of a great hole dug by the Boche as a tank trap. They did these holes about 20 feet deep and 10 yards square, if a tank gets in they cannot get out but I have never seen one get in yet. Then a celebration in another little cut out place in the trench covered by a tarpaulin.

7 October

There may not be much time to write home this afternoon, so I will send home now. Fine weather, a high wind which is good for us. Good news all round which is good for morale. Hope for a letter this afternoon. Everyone very cheery and optimistic, though we are bound to have sticky places yet. Everyone pretty busy getting ready. We had a good draft in yesterday of the right sort, seasoned men. We have had a rest of sorts, nothing in the way of comfort and no baths. We are pretty dirty, though I managed to wash a bit but the vigilant louse is not losing opportunities. However carbolic soap is useful though I don't like it much. But Boche dug-outs are not scrupulously clean.

9 October

Out after another attack today. It was a nasty show and we have lost a number of good officers and men. Three officers killed, six wounded and one missing. Now we are out for a while, a few miles back. The news is very good. I am in my tent shared with Carmichael – Signals – we have both had baths, clean clothes. We have a fine, warm fire burning and it is very comfy. Must stop, I am so sleepy, two nights with very little sleep.

10 October

I have been out over the last battle-ground finding the dead, ten miles each way and a good deal of walking in between. I have found our dead and they are being collected by a party under two good officers. They will make a cemetery and bury them near where they fell. It is wonderful going up there. Two days ago our men were killed, today the Boche is miles away; he is retreating hard. I saw today a battalion march in full column with transport and the band playing, into the village where less than two days ago our men were under close range fire. The country is all open, hardly any trenches and no wire. It is like nothing I have yet seen in this war. We have surprised him utterly and he is beaten and he knows it.

13 October

We have heard today that leave is not given to any officer under five months period. I am next for leave and my name has gone in but no-one in the brigade or division I suppose either, is getting leave now, so I don't think there is much chance of our getting married until December, but that isn't a very long way off after all. Tonight we are actually living in a house. We moved in at 10.00 this morning and the battalion is all in comfortable shelters and dug-outs made by the Germans. The companies are in strong concrete-roofed shelter huts, nice and warm. We are in a house. The doctor and Carmichael, Signals, and I, are in a room with a nice fire going and we all have beds. This place hasn't been so badly smashed and there is plenty of room for men and horses. Kitty and Dick, the doctor's horse, are together as usual under cover in part of a house nearby, and have straw to lie on. We shall be able to have training and games here and the country is not badly holed. The woods nearby are quite beautiful with autumn tints in beautiful colours. I hope soon to see these towns and villages repopulated with their rightful owners. This is a beautiful feature of the war, I should have loved to go into Caudry to take part in the liberation of the people who were there. I have been re-reading your ... to have an old Fusiliers Club, there are hardly any of the old ones left in the Battalion.

22 October

Had a celebration this morning and service. Many hymns and a little service on St Luke as it was the Field Ambulance – such a good lot they are, very gallant and good to the sick and wounded. I used to live with the 142nd Field Ambulance in '15 and they are just as good and still have a few of the old fellows left in. We have had a wet day but the billets are good and we don't mind. No particular news.

24 October

We are in again and have great success and have taken all we were expected to do. It is part of another very big advance, but I suppose it looks small on the map. We hear of great desertions of the Boche over the Dutch border. It may be true or not, but it is likely. I don't think we can expect peace just yet. The Boche is only playing a move and I think we see through his moves now, he must be beaten before peace can come. The enemy guns are busy and offensive but he must be having a very bad time from our guns. He has surrendered in large numbers, we are winning fast, and the map grows more wonderful every day.

I think that if a large number of people will be at our wedding it will be better to have the Eucharist first quietly and then the marriage service later, say at 11.00. What do you think? The time is coming – only a little more than a month. I got two letters last night from you, very welcome too. I am sure the doctor and Aunt Georgie are right. You have had a very hard time and it has taken too much out of you. You are finishing up now at Airlie, you cannot do more than you can. You have given over-good measure and you know these doctor people know what they say. Doctor Russell told me I wasn't to go back before the New Year and see him first. I went back at the beginning of December without seeing him and in January my head began to go wrong and it went on gradually getting worse till June and then they made me go and I had to be away three months or more. So don't think that anyone, least of all I, will be hurt that you cannot go back to Airlie for the end of Term. Miss D., I am afraid, is a Bolshevik and her conduct puts her out of court. You have done all you can so be bien contente.

15 October

It is definite now that I shall not get leave until early in December, five months is a minimum, so you will have six weeks to get ready. Also my 14 days will really finish up your term. I should love to be home for Christmas, but I am afraid it cannot be done. One ought to be out here in one's 'parish'. I suppose December 5th or 6th may see me home, so if this is so you will hardly go back to Airlie. I have installed myself here in a large room, got a piano from another house and have plenty of chairs and a good stove and hope that the men will avail themselves of the room for sitting and reading and have a good fellow who can play the piano quite well. When this is over we shall have to have a room for men to come to in the evenings. I want ... love letters on a battling day. I cannot write much to tell you about it all. It is a beautiful country, the trees are glorious colours, the land cultivated with cabbage and beetroot, and potatoes. Young corn growing and the village is hardly spoilt.

5 November

We had a visit from the General (Deverell) today. He told us the tremendous news that the Boche has retreated to Maubeuge. We thought we should have to fight him to there, I suppose he will make a stand there and will be beaten back again. The Austrian prisoners numbered 300,000 – terrific – and thousands of guns, and the terms are very drastic and will give us the way to attack the Boche through Austria. It is bound to take time, though, before we can get an army through Austria to take Germany in the rear, but it will come. I wonder if the Boche will stand it or no, or whether he will make surrender on the best terms he can get, and they will not be easy terms for him. We have taken ten thousand prisoners on this army front, very few casualties on our side. It shows his men have lost heart.

Now for ourselves, we have had a wet day and a day of rest. I started on the recreation room this afternoon. A good piano and stove, plenty of chairs and quite comfy, two or three lamps and a good many candles to make it cheery and a nice lot of old magazines and papers.

Chapter Fourteen

March into Germany

THESE WERE VERY CHEERING DAYS; the news was consistently good, showing the gradual breakdown of enemy resistance, with thousands of prisoners and guns captured. But that didn't mean that we had it all our own way. I hardly think people realise what it cost us to drive back a huge army which was efficiently equipped even to the end.

It was plain that the German nation was feeling the pinch severely in its resources; for instance, many of their shell cases were thin iron, poorly turned out and not to be compared with the material of which ours were made. Their infantry equipment was in many cases made of paper finely twisted and woven together, their rifles were rough and badly finished, and when we got into Germany we found that soap was an unknown quantity, that which passed for it being a near relation to the famous "Monkey Brand" which would wash neither clothes nor faces.

Yet with all the economic stress they were wonderfully equipped to resist our great assault. Since the initial surprise caused by our introduction of tanks, they had evolved a splendid tank defence system, small guns set low on the ground, and almost invisible, which proved a most effective weapon. They had such numbers of them that in many places our tanks were knocked out in dozens. The Germans had also an anti-tank weapon shaped like a rifle, supported on a stand, firing a hardened steel bullet about an inch in diameter. This gun must have kicked horribly.

We could see that they were being beaten in the air as well as on land, but they were far from finished. One day I saw one of our Kite balloons observing and another about half a mile away. All of a sudden our "archies" started banging while machine guns barked furiously. Then out of a cloud dashed an aeroplane, shot at the first balloon with incendiary bullets and off to the second, with shells bursting all round him. The observers from each balloon were out just in time, but in a second the first balloon burst into flame, the flames quickly changing into a great black tail of dropping smoke, and in a few moments the second shared the same fate. The airman got clean away, though not before he had sent a spray of bullets at the observers dropping slowly like spiders in their parachutes.

One could not help admiring the reckless courage of such men, but the same was happening on both sides.

We moved up to Havrincourt in the middle of September, a place which the Germans hung on to with great tenacity. Scene: our aid post, a narrow tunnel boarded all round and open at each end to stairs leading to the trench.

A draught of air runs through, making the candles gutter and drip in long trickles of grease; bundles of dressings hang on nails in the walls with equipment and coats. The atmosphere very mixed, owing to the combination of meat being fried for dinner, tobacco smoke, brilliantine from the Doctor's hair wafting over to me as I sit near him on the floor, oily smells from the primus stove, the odour of boots and equipment and an all-pervading sub-conscious dugout aroma, all blended together with the smell of creosote with which the place was sprinkled.

Dinner ready, consisting of fried meat and potatoes, kindly left behind by those whom we relieved, stewed prunes into which the cook had managed to spill some Lysol (but only a small quantity) and tea to finish the excellent repast.

I went to get a grave dug, from which earlier we had been driven owing to shelling. We had nearly finished, when suddenly a tremendous barrage broke out and a storm of thousands of shells on the valley behind, where the Boche expected our guns to be.

Half an hour of this and he shifted the barrage to the front line for an hour, then back again to the guns; then the Germans came over, our men meeting them kneeling on the parapet.

Captain Lord withdrew his men from a post and immediately dashed out with a few men and a machine gun and attacked the party which had gained his post and wiped them out. The counter-attack wavered and died out. We got 75 prisoners and very few of our men killed or wounded.

We had a few days rest at the beginning of October, with football and canteen stuff to cheer the men. One day two men escaped from the Germans and got back to us; they had been taken prisoner in March and had been working behind the German lines. They were much exhausted when they arrived, but said they saw the guns and transport in full retreat. This was indeed good news. One night we were marching up when a squadron of enemy planes came over and dropped bombs, but their aim was not good and no one was hurt. Then one of the planes was caught in the beams of several searchlights and our planes closed round him and brought him down in flames. The pilot got out in his parachute unhurt. Several gunners ran up to the plane and then the bombs burst, killing four of them. The other gunners were infuriated and would have killed the German, but a staff officer came up and he was taken away safely. One had sympathy with the men, but the airman only did his job and I was glad he got off.

Early in October we moved on towards Cambrai, the 2nd Division being on our left. It was all open fighting now; we had done with the old trench warfare. Derelict tanks, the mournful relics of the surprise attack on Cambrai, were lying about, but there was no more barbed wire to get through.

We passed through Marcoing and Masnières but on October the 8th at Serranvilles had a check. Our advance lay over open country and all day we were held up and lost many officers – five killed and four wounded – and many men. At night, when another Division went through there was no enemy left. This sort of thing was horribly vexing, we lost so many for nothing. We wanted a tank, for a few resolute men with machine guns in country like that with no cover for us could stop any number of infantry until the flank could be turned; I suppose there were not enough tanks. I wish we could have had two to each battalion, then we could have run through.

It took me two days riding over the country to find all the dead and arrange for their burial. I found that a horrid thing was happening:

our dead were being looted by those behind. It was not done by the fighting men, but by those who followed up. Such a thing I had never seen, it filled me with disgust. I suppose it is inevitable that in a huge army of all sorts and conditions of men this should happen. War is a beastly demoralising thing and those who were conscripted late in the War were of a different type from the earlier volunteer armies. Moreover the longer the war lasted the more we got down to the dregs of the nation. An order eventually came through that looting the dead was punishable with death.

On the 10th October I saw a sight that made my heart jump – a battalion marching in close column, with transport and band playing, into a village, which two days before our battalion was holding under close range fire.

Just after Tower's death we got our new CO, Colonel Johnson. He ought to have had a Brigade long before, but each time he got wounded instead.

In the middle of October Captain Lord went down ill. He had been with the 4th from early 1916 until then. A great record carried through with a devotion which it is an impertinence to praise. The strain of commanding a company for two years is impossible to imagine. No decorations can express the meaning of such work. He wears the DSO and MC, yet they are only symbols for such as can read, of the untiring sacrifice and consistent courage of the man who wears them.

Major Attewell was about this time sent home to the senior officers' school. He also had been a company commander since 1916. Invariably cheerful, known by many as "smiler", he inspired his men with a courage that would not be defeated. A schoolmaster by profession, he looked after his command with all the careful detail that goes to make a school or a company successful. The battalion was fortunate indeed when officer mortality was so heavy to have had the services of such officers as these, who not only led but loved their men.

The division continued to advance and we spent a night at Solesmes and thence to Escarmaines, where five young officers joined us. Next day not one of them remained, all killed or wounded.

At Solesmes I had a talk with one of the French women, who had themselves suffered and had seen how the Huns treated our men who had as prisoners been working near the front. She said they were half starved, feet bleeding through boots worn out. She herself gave one man a piece of bread as he passed, for she saw him stoop to pick up a small potato from the gutter and the guard beat him with the butt of his rifle and slashed at her for trying to give him food.

Never did I see our men ill-treat a prisoner. Often the German prisoners in the camps were cleaner and better fed than our own soldiers in the line. People sometimes laugh at our sportsmanship, yet sportsmanship represents some of the highest traits of character. the man who could go over the top with a football crying "On the ball, forwards" was the man who would feed his enemy in distress and this is commended of Christ Himself. Would that the man in the street would relate this that we call sportsmanship to religion for it is akin to the mind of Christ.

At Ruesnes we were held up all day, with severe losses as usual by machine-gun fire. Their guns were cleverly hidden as we advanced over rising ground and were supported by high-velocity gunfire. After this we were withdrawn and spent a fortnight in quiet places.

On November the 5th the General visited us and told us the good news that the enemy had retreated to Maubeuge and that 10,000 prisoners had been taken on this Army front, with few casualties to us.

The French people were fast coming back again. We lent them lorries and wagons, and strange processions were seen of every kind of vehicle carrying household goods; hand barrows drawn by old men and women, little carts pulled by dogs and occasionally a lean horse in the shafts of a wagon piled with every kind of furniture. The people were as unemotional in success as they had been in retreat – perhaps four years of war had killed emotion.

Our advance was slower now and we had no more fighting. Some days were spent in the neighbourhood of Maubeuge so we were not far from the scene of the first battle of the war. The position allotted to the 3rd Division was in front of Mons while the 4th Royal Fusiliers held the line of the canal at the apex of the salient at Nimy, NE of Mons. There on the Nimy Bridge just over 4 years later RSM Savill and ten survivors of the original battalion showed me the place where Lieutenant Deese and Private Godley won the Victoria Cross by their gallant defence of this position with a machine gun, while the enemy pressed on the first battle with the British army. Deese was killed and Godley though severely wounded recovered to spend the next four years as a prisoner of war.

Now Mons was decorated with flags and vivid placards of welcome to the BEF. After our tour of inspection we went to a cafe to have some dinner which we obtained at a cost. Certainly the welcome to British troops was a financial success for they charged us over £11 for the meal, small cups of coffee costing five shillings each.

On November the 10th we heard that the 3rd Division was to lead the advance into Germany. Early on the following morning we stood in marching order; there was a long wait – then came the news that the Armistice was signed. Companies were dismissed, packs and equipment thrown off and a football was produced. Some of us went into the village church and thanked God. I missed the march into Germany as I went on leave.

In Germany we settled down into comfortable billets which all appreciated and peace-time training restored the smartness of pre-war days.

The inhabitants soon realised that the British soldier was a gold mine and one that could produce not only money, but chocolate and soap. The Brigadier had to give the German men a few lessons in politeness and respect for the British officer by taking off their hats, but there was no friction or trouble.

In the "schloss" at Blatzheim, where the HQ of the Royal Fusiliers was established, the Baroness objected to the hobnailed boots of our servants scratching her stairs! I thought of the gutted houses in France, hundreds of towns blown to pieces, fruitful lands laid waste and tens of thousands of lives poured out. And she complained of a few marks made on the polished surface of her stairs!

Yet the request of the Baroness was respected and there was no further ground for complaint. Imagination conjured up a very different picture if German officers had been living in the homes of a conquered England. If for no other reason, it is worth while to read true histories of the war, especially of the early part of it, for they throw light on the mentality of the Englishman compared with that of the German. Much has been written lately by those who are at pains to vilify the character of the British soldier and the experience of many of these writers was gained in the later stages of the war. We agree that war is a horrible and debasing thing but there is a boundless splendour in the men of our race who fought in it. In countless ways the soldier expressed his true self. With courage which mocked death in its most frightful form he surrendered himself. He wrote home and told his people nothing of his deeds or his sufferings.

He stood for the honour of his regiment, loyal to his mates, sinking self in utter sacrifice. There were exceptions of course, as there are today. When at times the strain was taken off, it needed strong wills and more than ordinary discipline to withstand the attractions which were ready to seduce men from the way they knew was right, and many let themselves go. But the average man in the British army was not the carnal beast he is sometimes represented to have been. From 1915 onwards to the end, the British army was mainly composed of men of the type of the average citizen of today, self-respecting and sober in his habits, loyal to his wife and children, having his home enshrined in his heart. For the response they made to my ministry I thank God, and wish it had been worthy of their need.

This is in no sense a history, but only an attempt to write down a chapter of my life, passed in the bravest company that any could desire. Most of the time was spent with one battalion and naturally I knew that best, but to all the 3rd Division and to the Heavy Artillery with whom I was in touch, I give my thanks for all the unfailing courtesy and kindness I received. In the memory of the gallant comradeship of those who gave their lives and those who live:

I dedicate this book

Extracts from Letters to E. W. M. 6 November – 22 November

6 November

I enclose one of the finest testimonials our Division has ever had. It makes one feel that all those splendid lives which were given in that terrible fighting in March were given directly with this great result. It must be a great Thanksgiving in our General's heart when now after these months it is so plainly stated, and it makes me proud as I have ever been to belong to this division. My dear, I am very glad indeed that you are in good hands and not to go back for ten days. It would be absurd to go to your strenuous work until you are stronger. Miss Daniel must carry on and do the work herself, and with Pyne she will be able to do it. If you were to have gone back after four days you would probably have got a relapse and be very ill. You say I shall think I am marrying a lump of sugar. I do and I want to marry that same lump of sugar, to have that sweetness all my own. I suppose our marriage licence will be my sugar ticket. Read again last night your letter on the 21st March and read by me on the same great day, 27th March. How I longed for that letter. I hope I have come down from that pedestal you put me on in those days. I think that holiday in June, that perfect holiday, put us both on the same natural ground. I never liked being in an exalted position.

7 November

I have been to brigade to ask about leave. No leave is granted to anyone who has not five months service since last leave, so I shall not be able to get home before December 5th. That would mean you would only just get back for the last day of term, which would probably be the 20th. I am afraid you would be uneasy about it and be anxious about the end of term and wouldn't enjoy yourself, so I propose that I should wait to come home until immediately after Christmas. I do not think it is right to leave the battalion for Christmas though I should love above all to be home for the Christmas time.

8 November

This afternoon I went to Solesmes to find out a casualty clearing station where I could get my teeth stopped. I am going to another CCS tomorrow and think I shall probably get them done. I may have to be away from the battalion for two or three days, as our brigade will move forward again in a day or two. I don't expect we shall be fighting again just yet, so I don't mind being away for a few days. I haven't got tooth-ache but my teeth badly need stopping and I must have it done.

9 November

Today we have heard that Maubeuge is ours and Sedan has fallen to America and that the delegates have been given until 11.00 on Monday to declare their acceptance. If they don't, we shall hammer them more unmercifully than of late. They cannot stand it for long for we and the French and the Americans are all pressing them fearfully hard. Every day the French are coming back to their homes and as far as can be done we are giving them lorries to carry them, but only a limited number of course can be used as all provisions, equipment and munitions must be carried beyond railhead, for the Germans have destroyed the use of the railways wherever they have been able.

10 November 1918

Tomorrow will be a day of decision, I think and pray peace. Everything points to the Boche accepting our terms. They deserve all the severity of them. Here the French people are telling us of the sufferings of the British prisoners. Men were bare-footed, gaunt and starving. They used to see them pick up rotten potatoes and eat them. The old lady here says they tried to give little pieces of bread to them, but when the guard saw it they lashed the prisoners. Where the Brigade HQ is there are names of our men written by themselves on the walls, giving their addresses in some cases and their regiments. Tomorrow before I leave I shall take down these names and send them to the Red Cross. We have comfortable billets here. There are several hundred French people here, all the way along, these poor souls returning to their homes. Quaint vehicles of all sorts. One cart was drawn by a cow spanned in with a horse. Some drawn by two cows with horse collars on their necks.

11 November

Today at 11 o'clock the Armistice was signed. We knew it four hours before it was signed. We were to move up this morning at 7.30. About 7.00 o'clock I went round to Brigade and heard the news which had been tapped from German wireless giving permission for the signing of it by the delegates. Our movement orders were cancelled and we have remained here. For those who think, it has brought a quiet thankfulness. I am truly thankful, not for us only, but for you at home who have suffered so much more than we. Now I want to come home, I have a great longing for life at home, but before going there must be a re-adjustment of conditions for home life. The reconstruction of home life and demobilisation of the army will of course greatly affect the work of the clergy. I have asked Crick the corps padre through Vischer, to find out if they are going to keep those of us who have still a period of contract to serve in the army, or whether we shall be allowed to return home to get on with our work while things are beginning. It is so sudden to begin to think about home life as it is going to be. It is difficult to think that peace has begun to come. It isn't peace yet, but it is coming, it is bringing you and me closer together.

12 November

How wonderful it is to think that the war as far as we are concerned began at Mons, and the last fighting was at Mons after all that has passed. It was not our luck to take Mons again, but we have the high honour of being one of the Divisions chosen for the march into Germany, which we shall start on Sunday. We shall take a month to get there. You will be able to follow our progress if you get a Times map of the 9th November, and rule a straight line right across starting from the top arrow. We shall have two days marching, two days rest, so the General says, all the way doing about 12 miles a day. It will be a great experience and quite a climax to all we have had. I wonder how the Germans will behave to us whom they have been taught to hate so long. I expect when they see what a wonderful gentleman the average Tommy is, they will revise their opinion, and know what terrible liars their own leaders have been. At any rate you won't be anxious about my safety. No more shell fire or bombs, and I expect the Germans will not be so foolish as to offer any opposition. I rather suspect they will treat the 3rd Division with an awe and respect, which has I know been held for years by their soldiers. We shall come across no German soldiers, for their army will be forty miles beyond the Rhine, such as is not disbanded. This morning I spent some time in the village church, then got Kitty and went for a canter over the grass. She was very fresh and skittish, she is being clipped tomorrow, she has such a long coat and sweats too much with it on, and has a rug for nights and cold weather. We are playing football every afternoon, and everyone ought to be very fit when we get to Germany. No-one is excited, we all take it very calmly. It is rather difficult to think that there is no more war, no more going up the line, no more killed and wounded. What a mercy it all is. I hope the people at home will settle down to the new conditions of peace and that there will be no discontent and strikes, no grubbing for more money. I hope you have finished your settling up work at Airlie and will have a good fortnight's rest with Aunt Georgie, then possibly you can finish up the term if you are needed at Airlie, and then when I come home on leave we shall be able to get some idea of where the parish will be and still be able to make arrangements for the house and furniture. I wonder what parish the Bishop will offer us. If it is St Marks, I think it will suit us very well. I have just been reading again the Rector's letter, 6,000 people and shall not need a curate. £275 a year. We shouldn't be rich but I expect we shall be able to live on that and I hope by May prices will have lowered a bit.

14 November

We read of great peace celebrations at home. Here we are glad but we are not used to demonstrations, whatever comes we accept it I suppose. We expected it to come sooner or later and when it came, it came quietly, but we didn't clap our hands or throw our caps in the air. Today at Maubeuge the French presented the Guards with a standard. I heard it was a great and touching ceremony. We should have been there but for the difficulty of transport, for according to plan we ought to have relieved the Guards several days before the armistice was signed. But though I am sorry we didn't get anywhere any of the picture shows, I know that our division had a very large share in all the hardest part of the campaign wherever we were and that is enough.

15 November

The papers are intensely interesting. They are starting demobilising the nation, making quick preparations to turn war into peace. I liked the accounts of home rejoicings in London. I think that at home it is more possible to understand peace than out here and more can be done to show the contrast. The service at St Pauls Cathedral must have been wonderful. Oh how I long for a church in which one can have place for worship. I feel a great sorrow that we have not ever been able to use the village churches. Our work has been limited and often nullified by the lack of a building in which there may be the atmosphere and surroundings of religion.

I hope we shall get a nice church with not too much of the church-warden element in it and not too much choir. I always think that a choir if too highly developed overwhelms the singing. I like a women's choir to supplement the ordinary one and give it tone.

I expect you are back at Aunt Georgie's so I am addressing you there now. You said you had your room ready for your successor, so I concluded you were expecting her soon.

Don't be worried about having to leave dearest, it is not your fault nor your plan. I am only glad that the doctor and Aunt Georgie would not let you stay on for you would only have broken down with all the strain of it, and we cannot afford that. Remember if an officer or a man is breaking down, he is sent away to hospital. One of the very best of our officers, Capt. Lord DSO, MC, during the Havrincourt fighting had to give in. He felt he could not go on and he was sent to hospital and then home, so your analogy of officers who get tired and have to go on doesn't stand good. He was much needed in the battalion and has been much missed, but he couldn't do more than he did. Your case is the same.

18 November

We have a nice modern house for HQ, our mess is the dining room, quite comfortably furnished and with tapestry on the walls. My billet is a hundred yards up the road. They are nice people and I have a very comfortable room and a bed with sheets and all, very luxurious. They like us better than the Boche, who here was of a very bad type. The men are all pretty comfy, most of them in one large house ... I am hoping to get a car and drive over to Mons. I should much like to see the place where our battalion greatly distinguished itself and won 2 VC's. Lt Deese and Private Godley, the latter still a prisoner or dead. Deese was killed after five wounds defending the bridge at Nimy, when covering our retirement.

19 November

This morning I got the loan of a box car from the OC signals and nine Mons men and I went up to Mons, about 20 kils from here, to see the place. They recognised the bridges they held, the places they dug themselves into, where they had the first Boche shells amongst them, where Lt Deese and Private Godley won the VC. It was all very wonderful and interesting. Mons is a fair sized town and full of flags, mostly Belgian, crowded with soldiers of all sorts. The shops are in full swing. We had food at a cafe and a very good dinner. Soup, omelettes, beef, potatoes and leeks, and coffee, at a terrific price. I wanted to give them a good dinner and they much enjoyed it and so did I. I didn't look at the menu prices before hand, or I shouldn't have had the courage to order it. So on bended knee I ask your pardon. I fancy the Belgique are making hay while the sun shines. Fortunately I had the money as I had sent a cheque to St Dunstans and put the equivalent of notes in my pocket. You will have to make me go short when you rule the purse.

22 November

We had a visit from the King yesterday. All the troops were posted along the road, not in fighting kit. I expect that was his wish. It wasn't a formal inspection, just a visit. I saw him quite close, his car came along quite slowly and he stopped to speak to the Generals. He looked much better than he did when I saw him in June 1916 ... I wonder what tomorrow will bring in news of my leave. It might be granted, and it might not. Any rate, I will come as soon as I can, but it is not a question of you may, but you must. I am sharing this room with Mattock. He has a little wife at home and I know he and I share the same hopes as you and she. His last leave was in September. He left just before that terrible bombardment the Hun put up when he counter-attacked at Havrincourt, and when he was half an hour away from battalion HQ the shells came crashing all round him and he had practically no place to shelter in except a little galvanised iron bivouac which wouldn't have stopped a bullet even. Mercifully he wasn't touched. What a good providence of God it is that we don't see more than we need ... My dear, the life and the work in front of us is full of joy and possibility. I hope that we shall soon be together, so that we may prepare for that time when as partners we may go into that most holy business of stewardship.

Chapter Fifteen

Wedding and St Mark's, Lewisham

THE LETTERS BREAK OFF HERE as the longed-for leave arrived, apparently on 23 November. Plans for his wedding to Elizabeth had been all worked out but it was impossible to fix dates, and at one time he thought that if leave arrived shortly before Christmas he would have to postpone the wedding as he felt he should be with his battalion for Christmas. However the leave finally came through and on 3 December Mellish was married to Elizabeth Wallace Molesworth by Canon Roseveare at St Paul's, Deptford.

A report from the local paper gives a short account of the wedding:

Miss Margaret Molesworth, sister of the bride and Miss Roseveare, daughter of the vicar, were the bridesmaids. The bride was attired in white crepe-de-chine, trimmed with silver and wore the lace veil used by her grandmother, Mrs John Molesworth, at her marriage. After the ceremony, the wedding breakfast was served at the Vicarage and the bride and bridegroom left for Hampshire, to stay in a house placed at their disposal by Miss Bristow. The bridegroom was the first chaplain to win the Victoria Cross in the war. The bride is a niece of Mr F. N. Molesworth of Town House, Littleborough.

Among the telegrams received was one from Chester:

Love, remembrance and good wishes from all at Saighton this lovely wedding morning, signed, Grosvenor.

Another one from High Wycombe:

Heartiest congratulations and loving good wishes, from Miss Daniel and all at Airlie.

It was a quiet early morning wedding with both families and a few friends and by midday the couple were on their way down to Hampshire where they had been offered a house in a beautiful park near Romsey. To their surprise when they arrived, fires had been lit and a uniformed maid was waiting to serve tea, and had even prepared an evening meal. The following day they went up to the big house to thank their hostess and found to their amazement that she was the 'maid' from the previous day who had arranged their welcome.

The honeymoon passed all too quickly and on 17 December Mellish returned to France and two or three days later rejoined his battalion at Duren not far from Cologne, after a tiring journey by bus, train, ambulance, car and lorry. His letters home now describe life in the army of occupation, and at the same time reveal his growing eagerness to start what he considered his real life's work. As a temporary chaplain to the forces, Mellish was signed on from year to year and could have left the army at any time from 1917 onwards, when his appointment came up for review. During the thick of the fighting he would not consider the idea but when it became obvious that peace must be near and he had already been offered a parish in London by Canon Roseveare, the temptation was great. But after much thought he decided that his duty was to stay with the army while they needed him and even after his engagement to Elizabeth, when the urge to take up parish work in his own home was doubly attractive, duty came first.

Extracts from Letters to E. W. M., 17 December 1918 – 13 February 1919

17 December 1918 – The officers' rest house in Boulogne

We had a very good crossing, very calm, had lunch in the boat and got here at 4.30 ... No news. Same old town, same old crowds of loafers, soldiers and marines. French soldiers, trams, long heavy two-wheeled carts rattling on the cobbles.

21 December 1918 – Cologne

After many days I landed here last night. Here is the programme for
the week. Boulogne about 4 on Tuesday. Left the club just before
6.00 a.m. and got by lorry part way to the starting point and the lorry
had internal troubles and I got onto an ambulance. The train left
about 8.00 and went on in jerks all day up to Douci, where we were
able to get some tea at a canteen about 2.00 a.m. Thursday. Then on
to Valenciennes where I left the train and got to a club where at 9.00
I had some breakfast. I was amazingly dirty, but washing was not
possible there. I walked to the crossroads and after waiting some time
I got a car which was going Mons way and took me through Mons
and on to Charleroi and found a train just going to Namur, and
changed there for another to Liege. When I got there I was glad to
find there was no train until the following day, so Friday night I spent
in a very comfortable bed in a hotel at Liege and had dinner. It was
very good and I got myself clean. Friday morning caught the train at
10.30 and got to Cologne last night at 10.00 p. m. We reported at the
RTO and found that my division is back one hour's journey so I leave
at 12.30 for Duren. Meanwhile I am going to have a look at the
cathedral.

22 December

I had a good day today. The battalion is in three places, HQ in a big
farm with two or three round it, two companies in two villages about
a kilometre away in different directions. I had the Eucharist here at
8.00, then on Kitty to the first service at 10.00 in a village hall, then
to the other two companies at their village in the same kind of hall.
I was a little late there so did not start until 11.15. Back to lunch and
Kitty had her feed too. At 3.00 I rode over to the Kings whose HQ
is in a little village church about 4 kilometeres from here, its name is
Kelst. Had tea with them in their magnificent HQ fitted with every
kind of luxury; electric radiators, electric heated baths, comfortable
and good furniture. A piano and player attached in excellent tune and
every kind of courtesy shown them as indeed is general. It was amazing
when their drums and pipes marched up and down playing retreat.
Swarms of children accompanied them, and all the people turned out
to see with great excitement. To see that makes one feel that the
horrible days of March and the bloody fields of August were a bad

dream. These people are friends and far more hospitable than the Belgians and not out for money. This may be a passing phase, but their property and wealth seems to have been untouched by the war. They have horses and cattle, rich lands cultivated to the last inch. The houses are full of extremely expensive furniture, cases of cut glass on the shelves. If this is a fair sample of Germany, it must be an amazingly wealthy country. My word, the German woman works hard. Twice since I came to the house, and I arrived about 4.30 last night, the paved hall downstairs was washed and mopped up. No doubt our boots and the dirt they bring in are a source of turbulation to the careful housewife. Hundreds of children about, the streets swarm with them. There are four dear little fair-haired girls in the family. They are continually asking for chocolate and there is much fraternizing in the kitchen where our cooks work. All the people greet us as we go about, and the men and boys take off their caps.

Christmas Eve 1918

I don't think it will be very long before we shall be together again. I should not have been happy leaving my battalion at Christmas time, though. It is different from what it used to be, it has so greatly changed during the last year. But they are loveable men, yet I feel my work is at home now with you. Christmas Eve next year I hope we shall spend in our own church and home. I should like to have a Christmas Eve service and a crib in the chapel and carols sung softly.

27 December

This morning we left our last village and moved to Blatzheim. I went with another officer to Brigade and we had a long walk afterwards and got in here about 4.30 very wet, but changed and had a big tea. This is a more compact village. Our HQ is in a great house owned by a Baron somebody. It is in grounds away from the road, a mile out of the village. There is a moat around the house. Unlike the other there is nothing nouveau riche about it. It is all beautifully furnished. A bathroom, hot water, electric light. I have a splendid room with a fire in it, as much furniture as I want and all very good. Very warm and more comfortable than anything one could ever have dreamt of in the last years. This place would do well for an extension of our honeymoon. I shall be quite pleased to stop here for the rest of my time in the army. Is anything settled about your parents' farm at Whiteparish? It would be very nice if they could go back, I hope it will turn out well. I am sleepy having walked about twelve miles, I must write to mother and then go to bed.

30 December

Thank you for the card, dearest. I have in front of me the card you sent me at Christmas 1917. Mr Mellish from Elizabeth W. Molesworth. What a lot has happened since then. The dates – March the 21st when you wrote, the 28th when I got your letter. June 22nd when we met, what a wonderful day, the day you first kissed me and actually gave me your love, and December 3rd when we were joined together in this happy loving union which will be ours for ever. Oh my darling, you have been very good to me, thank you for all.

31 December

This afternoon I went down to football matches. I am on the sports committee, in fact president of it. Tomorrow we have a route march in the morning, football in the afternoon, a concert in the evening. I suppose at home they will have watch-night services. I don't think they are of any advantage out here. In Deptford it is a good thing as it has been a custom. There always seems to me a good deal of unreality about it. Good resolutions seem a kind of fetish with most of the people who came to those services. Still on the whole it was a good thing, I think, and certainly it was as the Rector took it at St Pauls, so if people want it at St Marks, they shall have it. You know all about Sunday School work. Will you get hold of the kind of course you like teaching best? I am keen on getting the KMS and Sunday School good, and I believe that for the Mothers' Union and Mens' Guilds the Christian students' books are the best. Next Christmas I hope we shall have a KMS divinity play and carols. We must get an orchestra going too. There will be lots of lovely things to do. A New Year, it will be a very lovely year for us, won't it.

2 January, 1919

There is a letter in The Times from the Bishop of London about the poverty of the clergy, I suppose it is because the financial side of it is so badly and precariously worked out. There are many parishes of £700 or £800 a year, many of £200. Why don't they do the same as the Wesleyans and have a central board of Finance. It would be a revolution, but it would work far better. These days the clergy must justify themselves by their work. The spiritual is bound to be summed up in terms of material. After all, when a railwayman or a mechanic earns £3 a week at the outside in normal conditions, we shall be much better off than most of our parishioners when we have £275 a year. So if we can live simply on this and save a bit I think we shall be able to provide for contingencies. I sometimes think it would be good if clergy could have a trade as well as their profession. Of course the question of not doing full time would be a difficulty, but as it has been done during the war, a parish priest might be able to put two days work into a factory per week, not necessarily for money's sake, but to get into touch with workmen who at present regard the clergy as a privileged class whose income comes easily. I believe that some day I shall try it when I get to know things in the parish – don't say anything about it. I feel somehow we must get to grips with life apart from ordinary ways.

3 January

I had a good canter on Kitty today to Kerfen to see the Kings about a football match. She was very springy and fresh and enjoyed the soft going at the side of the road. It has been a beautiful sunny day, quite warm in the sun and a glorious sunset. Pink clots of clouds underneath a deep crimson glow. We are sending away about 15 men a day. I am afraid my groom Knowles will go soon, I am glad for him, but sorry for me and Kitty. He loves her and I think he likes me too. I shall take a photograph of him before he goes.

4 January

What a joy it will be to get home and put our house in order. We are very lucky in having such a good start in furnishing. When we get to work it will all be lovely. You will have your work, and I mine and we shall both pool together to the glory of God, and we shall find that people won't be critical, it wouldn't matter if they were. I have just been reading a little book of Talbot's dedicated to the glory of God in gratitude to CMT. That is I am sure his wife. My dear, I haven't brains enough to write any books, but I hope and mean to dedicate my work to the glory of God and in gratitude to EWM. I hope I shall be home by the beginning of February, and with a week put in at fixing up the house and a retreat afterwards to prepare for the work, we ought to be able to make a start at Septuagesima.

7 January

Attewell came back today. He is as fit and breezy as ever, I am very glad to have him back. He said that at the senior officers' school, an officer came down to ask for volunteers for Russia. It was after the armistice was signed. He said "It is dark 8 months of the year, you freeze all the year, you get no extra pay and you may get stabbed in the back. I want 6 officers to volunteer to come with me." Though it was after the armistice and all were looking forward to a comfortable time back with their battalions, there were 48 applications! Isn't it a wonderful spirit? These were all senior officers who had had all the war any man wanted.

I enclose a letter from my old groom who won the DCM at Gheluvelt, hence the name of his tearooms, and was with me all the time at St Eloi and hauled me out of the mud in the crater when I was stuck there. He afterwards left me and won the MM and corporal's and then sergeant's stripes and was three times wounded after he left me. We always had plans to go hopping after the war. Perhaps we shall some day.

10 January

We shall have quite a big household – the goat, eight hens and a cock, a Sealyham pup and about 8 runner ducks. They don't need water except to drink, if geese need too much to eat we won't keep them. We shall have to get our shop-keepers to pay tithe of cabbage leaves to the family. On Monday Vischer is going on leave and he wants me to take over his job while he is away. I don't know if I shall have to live at Duren, it is rather a long way from the battalions, but there is a certain amount of paperwork to do so I may have to go there.

11 January

You asked me what you have improved in, I don't know, for to be candid it isn't in spelling. For "phophecies" is hardly a usual spelling unless of course you spelt it phonetically and had a piece of hot potato in your mouth ... This morning early I got up to catch the 7.20 train for Cologne to the Bishops' conference. Had a walk round the shops before the conference, they are very good but linen and lace and such things are much dearer than at home. The glass shops are beautiful and I should think fairly cheap. I went into a toy shop with Vischer. He bought a doll for his little girl aged four. I had longings to buy a doll and toys for someone who may want one later on. What a lovely time that will be, how I shall love to make a doll's house for someone who will love to play with it in God's good time if He wills it. On my dear, how wonderful married life is, what joys there are to come for us.

14 January

Two letters from you today of the 6th and the 8th. They are coming better now. I got yours of the 9th and the papers came too, done up in a wrapper inside of which was a sketch of a rather pathetic lion. I expect this is a study of Margaret's ... I think in these days she should not waste good material, so why not use the lion as an advertisement. His mane, his finely developed foot, his rather squib-like tail would all be excellent. His reproachful expression and his tongue would indicate that there is something wrong inside. An advertisement should always present new features, and a lion with one leg and face like that would be worth thousands.

19 January

I am on my tour round and am writing from Kelz, the guest tonight of 142nd Field Ambulance. This morning we had the Eucharist at Blatzheim, always voluntary service there and a good number always come. Then at 10.30 my groom had Kitty waiting for me and I rode over to Norvenich calling at the HQ of the Northumberland Fusiliers. We had matins in a hall and Eucharist afterwards. Then I rode back to their HQ and had lunch. Left there soon after 2.00 and called in at the ASC to see one of the officers I know. He walked down with me to the next village, Eshwiler, and then after he had gone, Kitty took me at a good fast trot to Kelz, about 4 miles further on. We had a good service this evening. Now after dinner the colonel has just given me some paper. They are very kind everywhere. Tomorrow at 7.30 we have the Eucharist and after breakfast I shall set off to Duren. It has been fine today but cold, and the roads are very muddy.

This is a comfortable house and they have got me a good billet close by for the night. I like this going round to different units. It is a sort of missionary life at present and a home wherever you go. My kit is very compressed – toothbrush, hairbrush, razor, two handker-chiefs, bit of soap, spare pair of socks. That with my church things is all I need and I don't care to give Kitty more than necessary to carry.

22 January

No news from anyone today, but we had an epidemic of cake. Markby had two, and Beacock two, so we are fat and full fed. I send a photograph of us in HQ. The order is, facing from left to right, Mattock MC, Carmichael (demobilised), Attewell MC, The Colonel DSO, Beesley, Beacock and me, and you can just see Kitty on the left waiting for me with Fell her groom.

23 January

You might get a little sixpenny book on fowls and incubators. I have an idea that we could incubate chickens on our gas stove, provided it was arranged so that no fumes were allowed to damage the chickens. (There follows a drawing showing an arrangement that fitted over the stove, with a pipe coil through which water would always circulate). What would be the cost of the gas? It would be a pity if the eggs got cooked. Perhaps we could train the goat to sit on the eggs or the Sealyham when we get him.

24 January

A year tomorrow we went up to the Hindenburg line and there we remained until the attack in March. What an eventful year. So glad we have not got to go up and do it again.

30 January

Still frozen and snowy but not much on the ground. The papers full of strikes, I suppose things will settle after a while. It is self determination, I suppose. I have been reading the report "Country and Industrial Problems". When one sees the enormous proportions of men in 1914 who were earning less than 30/- per week, one realises that there must be a social upheaval, and for a good long time we must expect it. I don't like the breaking away from Trade Unions, for they represent the best mind of labour and do not stand for disorganisation. Glad you enjoyed Peter Pan. I should love to see it again, it is delightful … I like "marveleously"! It looks so emphatic.

1 February 1919

The news in the papers is not very good these days. Strikes and impending strikes. The army is to be a million strong, a big thing, but it is right and if well paid it will be a very good thing for the nation to have a million young men in the prime of life who are trained and fit. A new pay scheme is out. As chaplain I should get 31/- a week more. The army pay is going to be very much better all round. It is the right thing, then we shall not get the army looked down on as unfit to be compared with the civil professions, and the right stamp of man will come in. But home life for me. The army in peacetime has no attraction for me. I enclose a wire from the ACG, so I shall soon hear when I shall go, or if I shall stop until May. I asked him to let me know definitely, then I can write to Bishop Howe and tell him, so that he can fix up the date for the institution. It is no use leaving it unsettled. I have also sent a letter I had from Colonel Hartley. I didn't know he felt like that. He writes from his heart I believe, but I hardly realised how much he felt, though what he says about me is undeserved. He was a splendid colonel. We have been fortunate in having such a wonderful lot since I was with the battalion. Sweeney – now General; Ottley, RIP, Healey-Hutchinson, home wounded, Hartley, wounded and Johnson who was wounded three times and ought to be a General.

2 February

This battalion is going home soon and will be re-equipped and sent to India before long. When they get home I expect there will be a march through London as it is a London regiment. It will be great to see them going through the city with fixed bayonets. One of the few regiments which is allowed the privilege of marching through London with bayonets fixed, but I expect I shall be a civilian by the time they go home. I hope the farm will become a reality for your father soon. He will be happy on his little farm again.

4 February

I hope soon to hear that your people will go down to Whiteparish. Suppose we gave them £25 of our wedding money for buying fowls etc. Nobody need know, we will just invest it that way. So do if you think good and that will help to bring in a few shillings from eggs and poultry feed. They will be happy there and away from that wretched Little Oakley. If they get the cottage, your father will be able to find work with a farmer nearby. It wouldn't bring in much, but with their own fowls, and his work, and a bit of help we can give them I expect things will turn out very well. Is this too optimistic? Our house and furniture won't take all our money and we can easily afford a bit to help.

19 February

I am so glad you have your coal. Poor souls, it must have been horribly cold in that drafty little place without any fire. I have been converted to the central heating principle. For all big houses, it is economical and heats not only the rooms but the house so you never feel cold in this house. I wonder why they haven't adopted the system in England, as they have here and in Canada. Perhaps they may have it in large new houses. In flats I should think it would be far the best method.

In November 1918 Canon Roseveare had offered Mellish another London parish at St Mark's, Lewisham, and as the war was over Mellish gladly accepted. From then on his letters were full of plans for his work in the new parish with Elizabeth and with domestic details on the decoration and furnishing of their first home together. The endless delays were unbearably frustrating but at last his turn came, and the last letter from Germany is dated 14 February.

On 2 March 1919, Mellish was formally instituted by the Bishop of Southwark as Vicar of St Mark's. But there were still one or two details of his military service to be completed. In July 1919, he received the formal certificate of a Mention in Despatches, signed by Winston Churchill as Secretary of State for War. And on 25 June 1920, Mellish attended at Buckingham Palace with Elizabeth, to be decorated by King George V with the Military Cross, awarded for his service in the last months of the war.

The London Gazette of 12th December 1919 announced this award together with a number of other promotions and awards under the heading:

War Office.

The King has been graciously pleased to approve of the undermentioned rewards for distinguished service in connection with Military Operations in France and Flanders.

Dated 3rd June 1919.

During his two years as curate at St Pauls under Canon Roseveare, a man whom he greatly loved and admired, Mellish had rapidly established the pattern of his parish ministry. Now he was able to throw himself wholeheartedly into his life's work in his own parish with the added joy and satisfaction of sharing it with a partner who complemented him in every way, and herself played a very full part in the life of the parish. The ideals and aims instilled into him, first by his beloved mother, strengthened by his years in South Africa and shaped by his period with Canon Roseveare, had been honed and polished through nearly four years of bloody war and hardship and by intimate contact with men of every type and rank with whom he lived and fought.

Post-war Lewisham was a district of great poverty and doubtless much disillusionment. The land fit for heroes had not materialised and within a very short period wartime heroism and suffering was forgotten and ex-soldiers had become unwanted beggars. Despite this, Mellish inspired courage and enthusiasm in his people, attracted greater numbers to his church and increased the collections for causes such as St Dunstan's Home for the Blind and others to whom he felt a debt was owed. In a letter to Elizabeth during one of her rare absences in these years, he wrote: 'We have quite a goodly number of pictures now, and bills to pay too for pictures and books, but I am not going to have the Sunday School stinted and if people cannot pay for the children to be taught we will go without an organist. I am convinced that necessaries come first.'

In the little spare time that he had, Mellish was able to relax and enjoy his two great hobbies, gardening and carpentry. Over the years he produced a number of pieces of furniture which became treasured family possessions. Among these in the family home there is still a heavy carved armchair, a carved oak coffee table and a finely carved oak bureau with Elizabeth's Molesworth family crest on the front. He was also able to take Elizabeth on a cycling holiday in the West Country as he had planned in one of his letters home from the front. In later years she recalled that they spent one night in a delightful Dorset cottage, where they had a huge supper, a most comfortable room and breakfast for the sum of 5/- each.

In July 1920 to their great joy a son was born and was christened Martin, but sadly the baby died only a month later. One of those asked to be a godfather was Keith Markby, the assistant adjutant of the 4th Bn. Royal Fusiliers who remained a friend for life. A year later in December 1921 a second son, Patrick was born. Again Markby was asked to be godfather and Elizabeth's sister Margaret was a natural choice for godmother. The weeks and months passed quickly and busily. Mellish's idea of spending two days a week working alongside his parishioners in a factory or mill never came to pass. Possibly this was because his bishop did not like the idea of a part-time vicar for this would have been a most unusual arrangement at that time. More likely however, Mellish found there simply was not time for another job which would bring him in close contact with some of his parish while he strove to visit everyone and to be available at all times to all of them. Whatever the reason, there was always more than enough to keep him busy, visiting for six days of the week and taking Sunday services on the seventh.

At the same time the vicarage door was ever open to visitors, friend or stranger, and probably no one was ever turned away without a word of encouragement and a cup of tea. Elizabeth used to tell a story of a man who came begging for money for food. To her strong disapproval, Mellish lent him £2 which he promised to return when he found work. 'You'll never see that again,' she said, but Mellish assured her that the man was genuine and would come back. A few days later he did indeed return and repaid the loan. Mellish was delighted to have his faith vindicated. A day or so later on the strength of this, he lent the man £10 for travel expenses but unfortunately this never came back.

Apart from parishioners, St Mark's vicarage was seldom without visiting friends in those years, either some of Elizabeth's many friends from St Anne's or Wycombe Abbey, or Mellish's army friends. The Sealyham pup that Mellish spoke of in his letters from Germany had somehow become a bull terrier called Max who was fiercely possessive of his family. On one occasion the little maid who worked in the vicarage announced a visitor and said she had put him in the drawing room. When Elizabeth went in, there was a very brave soldier friend of Mellish's standing rigid behind the piano while Max kept him at bay. As his hostess walked in he smiled with relief and said, 'I never knew Hymns Ancient and Modern were so interesting.'

In June 1920 Mellish and Elizabeth were invited to a garden party at Buckingham Palace for VCs and their wives. There were 324 holders of the Cross present, the awards dating from the Indian Mutiny through the Afghan, Zulu and Boer Wars to the latest one in 1918. Each of them was presented in turn to the King and Queen, with the Princess Royal and two royal princes in attendance. This was the first of several royal command appearances Mellish attended. There was the garden party late in the 1920s, again at Buckingham Palace in which Mellish and Elizabeth stood back as the King and Queen walked down through the two rows of guests, stopping to chat at intervals. As they approached, the Princess Royal made her way through the onlookers and said to Mellish, 'My mother would like to speak to you.' In 1929 there was another reunion with a dinner in the Royal Gallery of the House of Lords at which the Prince of Wales spoke of 'the most enviable order of the Victoria Cross'.

After the Second World War Brigadier Sir John Smyth VC founded the VC&GC Association, which held meetings from time to time. In 1956 to celebrate the centenary of the institution of the VC there was a special parade in Hyde Park, at which the Queen with Prince Philip inspected about 300 holders of the Cross, and then addressed them and their relatives. After this there was a march past of the assembled company, some in wheelchairs, led by General Lord Freyburg VC, followed by a garden party at Buckingham Palace.

Mellish thoroughly enjoyed these occasions, partly for the chance to take Elizabeth out and show her off, partly for the pleasure of meeting men of every nationality in the Commonwealth and talking to them, always about past campaigns or their deeds, but never of his own.

Chapter Sixteen

India Mission

IN 1922 THE ARCHBISHOP OF CANTERBURY arranged a Mission of Help to India in response to an appeal from the Church there. This was specifically to both army and civilians in India, and was to consist of about eighteen clergy and lay people, chosen from dioceses all over the country. Mellish was an obvious choice, both because of his experience in South Africa and his patent success as a parish priest in London. Perhaps more than this, his name was a household word still and he would be an honoured and welcome guest in any army establishment in India and would probably know quite a number of soldiers out there. The mission was formally commissioned in a service at Westminster Abbey on 5 October 1922 and the small party sailed from Tilbury dock on SS *Nevada* on the 6th.

So once again after only 3½ years Mellish was parted from his Elizabeth and their small son and took to writing to her almost every day, although the letters could only be posted at ports of call or in India when a mail train was running. The letters show plainly his homesickness and longing to return, but also the excitement of travel to a strange country and the anticipation of a challenge to be met.

The voyage passed pleasantly with deck quoits, concerts, and sports for diversion and plenty of work to do in preparing for the mission. Mellish enjoyed the trip greatly and met several people who became firm friends. In a letter written between Port Said and India he describes the passage through the Suez Canal and mentions that he hoped to find time to stay 'a couple of days at Meerut with General Deverell [his old divisional commander] before I begin at Muttra. It will put me much more au fait with Indian military life and will help me greatly to know where I am and how to work my missions to

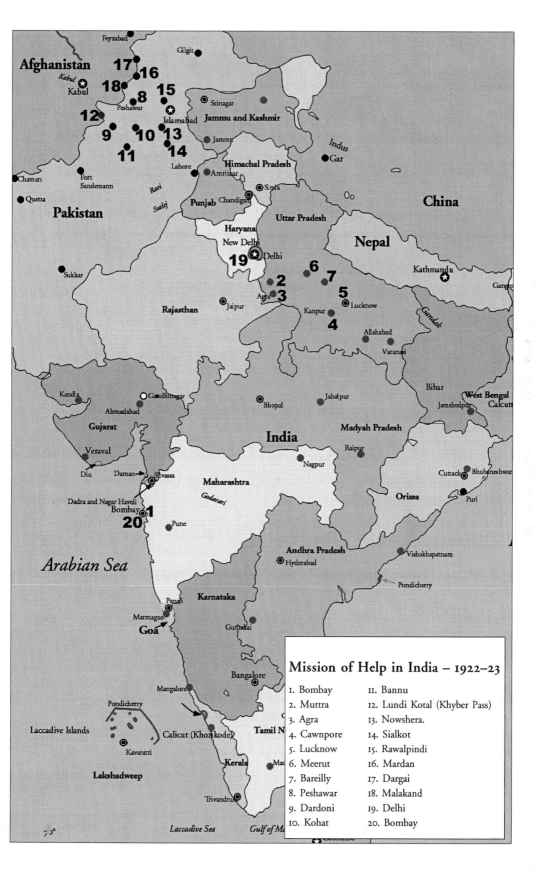

Mission of Help in India – 1922–23

1. Bombay
2. Muttra
3. Agra
4. Cawnpore
5. Lucknow
6. Meerut
7. Bareilly
8. Peshawar
9. Dardoni
10. Kohat
11. Bannu
12. Lundi Kotal (Khyber Pass)
13. Nowshera.
14. Sialkot
15. Rawalpindi
16. Mardan
17. Dargai
18. Malakand
19. Delhi
20. Bombay

the best advantage.' He also made friends with the ship's carpenters and obtained permission to use their workshops to continue with some wood carving which he completed on the voyage. This was destined for his church and he arranged for the carpenters to send it by carrier when they arrived back home so that it could be dedicated in the church by Christmas.

In a letter dated 26 October, Mellish describes the phosphorescence of the water, dolphins playing round the boat and whales spouting:

> I am not at all sorry the voyage is nearly over. It has been an ideal voyage with most delightful weather but the work is ahead and I shall be glad to be starting … It seems such an age since I was at home. As a matter of fact it's a universal thing among us all, at all events the married men, that we are as homesick as a lot of babies, and we are all looking forward to the time when we shall be able to say: "— days more and we shall be home."

Even at that stage he was eagerly planning his return and hoping that a P&O boat leaving India on 3 March would dock at Plymouth so that Elizabeth and he could spend a few days at Budleigh Salterton.

The SS *Nevada* docked at Bombay on 28 October and the party was divided up to spend a few days with various local clergy. To his delight Mellish found that his host was a man named Harby who was at King's with him, in charge of the regimental memorial church at Colabu, a suburb of Bombay.

29 October

He was one of those people who couldn't pass exams at Kings but is a most decided success as a priest, and is doing splendid work here. He has been here two years and like all the clergy looks very pale. It is a moist and sticky enervating climate and very trying for everybody who has to work. His house is a stone bungalow, very well built and delightfully cool. He has four other men living here in what they call a chummery. One is at Grindlays, another an engineer. Harby runs the place and keeps them comfortable and sane. He is a most enlightening person and knows and cares a great deal about the Indians as well as the white people. I am doing nothing here except learn from

Harby's wisdom ... On Wednesday I go off to Muttra where my host will be Colonel Pragnell, commanding 4th Hussars, who was GSO I of the 3rd Division. The 4th Hussars is the only regiment there, so my way is made easy there at once as far as outward circumstances are concerned, and at Meerut Canon Greaves is the guest of General Deverell so it will be easy for him in the same way. This morning at 7.30 we had church parade of the 1st KSLI, the string band playing in the really beautiful church, a memorial to the officers and men who were killed in the Afghan war ...

On Monday we went down to Grindlays and got 300 rupees (a rupee = ¼d). Each missionary has that amount for travelling expenses, and when we want more we draw it. I shall travel as cheaply as I can to save expenses. The diocese is awfully hard up and has to cut expenses as much as possible. I also booked my passage home on the P&O Caledonia on 3rd March, calling at Aden, Marseilles, Plymouth and London, so you will be able to expect me about 23rd March.

On Monday afternoon the missioners were all taken out by launch to an island about four miles away. The metropolitan and local clergy came too and some residents. We had tea on the boat and by small boats we landed and went up by a long steep flight of steps to see a very ancient temple cave wonderfully constructed out of solid rock. We came back in the light of a wonderful glowing red sunset with a delightful cool breeze blowing, having much enjoyed the afternoon.

9 November, Muttra, United Provinces

I came here to stay at the Pragnells on Tuesday. They are very kind a hospitable and I have learnt a great deal about military India from him. They have a dear little boy of 4½, Michael and a little girl of 18 months, a very strong active person called Dina. The Colonel makes it very easy for me to do anything I want to do. That doesn't mean my mission here is any more easy, it is not easy for me to get my message home, but this is not his fault. We have the Eucharist every day at 8.00. There are always communicants, but not many soldiers. It would not do to expect many on weekday mornings for this is the time for training on intensive systems. However permission is given for any to be at church in the morning any day, but I know that men will not take advantage of that if they have to leave their work to others to do. Every morning I take the school children and teach them and each morning I have been visiting with Rigg the married quarters.

There are about 60 married NCO's and men in the regiment here. The hospital and the Anglo/Indian railway community also. They are a small number and very poor. Tuesday afternoon the colonel took me for a short ride, and yesterday I went to watch the polo match and met a good many of the officers. Last night at 8.30 I went to the soldiers' Home (Soldiers Christian Association), an undenominational society. This branch is being run by a Mrs Lindsay, a good woman, and the men much appreciate her work. I took it as a kind of prayer meeting and had Moody and Sankey hymns. There were 40–50 men. That type of thing more attracts them than the church, though I am as free as the most evangelical brother could be, I think, in the mission services. I cannot tell you how the mission is going, but I believe people are praying and that there must be good fruit. I am afraid I cannot get any appeal to the officers. Rigg is an awfully good fellow, but he rather prides himself on hitting hard and though he doesn't see it, it has hit his officers right out of church, and the Colonel is pretty sore about it. The situation is strained. The poor people and the NCO's and families are very fond of Rigg. The officers and their wives are not. The weather is very pleasant, warm but dry by day and nice and cool at night. I sleep on the verandah outside my bedroom.

15 November, Agra, United Provinces

I have plenty of collars so don't send them if you haven't already. I bought a few in Bombay, but as a matter of fact I use the dog collar. It shows who I am and is very comfy. I left the Riggs at Muttra this morning. The former have been most kind and couldn't have helped me more. All the Muttra people are most hospitable and kind and they came to the services very well I think, better than the soldier people by far. The Colonel and Mrs Pragnell were very regular. Now I am in the care of Miss Greene, a friend of the Riggs. She is a school inspector and lives here. She is taking me out now to see Agra fort and the Taj Mahal, a most beautiful and world famous tomb made of white marble. I enclose some photographs and have some more excellent negatives of others but no prints yet.

Thursday, November 16, Cawnpore

I just have a few minutes to send you my love from Cawnpore. I had a wonderful afternoon and evening at Agra yesterday, being piloted about by Miss Greene who knows the place well. I left Agra at 10.20. I spent the night from 11.30 to 5.00 this morning in the waiting room at Tundla. I had a good sleep there and boarded the train which landed me at Cawnpore soon after 9.00 this morning. Maynard, the chaplain, kindly sent his servant to meet me and escort me to his bungalow, and after a good wash, shave, and breakfast took me round the church which is the memorial of the massacred victims of Nana Sahib. A very beautiful church built mainly of white stone and marble. Then to the well from which the garrison got their water at the expense of some gallant lives before the entrenched position was taken. After this we went on to see the famous well down which their bodies were thrown, now encased in a beautiful carved stone wall. Over the well is a great white marble angel. From here we went to see some people named Saxby who came out with us on the boat. Near their garden is the cross which marks the steps on the Ganges down which the captives were taken and placed in boats, after which at a given signal the mutineers hidden on the banks fired volleys into the defenceless occupants. The women and children who were left alive were then thrown into a house and murdered by butchers when even the soldiers refused to do any more murdering. Now I have a little space to write before tea and then catch my train for Lucknow which I should reach at 6.20. On a mud bank on the Ganges I saw two crocodiles basking in the sun this afternoon. This is just for you, only to send all my love, no news in it, but just to tell you I love you and long for you and hope and pray that you are well and happy, sweetheart. If you can, send me some addresses for good schools for boys whose parents are out here. A Mrs Newland of Muttra asked me if I knew any. Her boy is 6 years old and she doesn't want to pay any more than £30 per term. Major Newland is a doctor in the Indian Medical service.

Sunday, 19 November, Lucknow

Next week will be my Christmas letter. It seems totally unlike Christmas time here. The days are so bright with lovely hot sun, yet not at all too hot. The nights are becoming decidedly cool, a difference of 30–40 degrees between midday and night. The people who have been out here over the hot weather feel the cold more easily than I, but I am wearing my cape at night and wore my overcoat in the train coming here. I had a most interesting journey from Muttra, it took about an hour to Agra. Miss Greene gave me lunch in her bungalow.

It is quite the best I have seen, very airy and cool and a pale cream wash on the walls. She has beautiful Indian curtains over all the doorways and very nice rugs and mats on the floors and her walls are covered with beautiful watercolours of English country done by a friend of hers. Bungalows out here are built with very large high rooms. The doorways are all arches with folding doors in them which can always stand open. The archways are hung with curtains, usually of Indian work. The floor is generally covered with a grass woven matting over which mats of Indian work of beautiful designs or carpets of Persian or Bokhara work are put. Each bedroom has its bathroom leading out of it and as there are no sanitary arrangements such as we are used to at home the bathroom has to serve a double purpose. Before I write any more dear sweetheart, don't lift or help to lift any heavy things and let Orton or French do a bit, you must not do too much. They can help themselves more. I wish I hadn't allowed you to keep on the Vicarage, I am afraid it is too much. At any rate tell Orton from me that he must make it as easy as he can and not bring in extras for meals.

Tuesday, 21 November

My programme has been 7.45 half an hour to talk to band boys then in to the Blessed Sacrament. At 9.30 I have a half hour service at the detention barracks where men are kept for military misdemeanours. They sang very nicely and were quite cheery. I met two old friends, two sergeants of the Northumberland Fusiliers who were there on the staff as warders. Good chaps too. Then I had a talk with some of the men and then visited the staff married quarters. At 12.00 I went to visit the venereal ward of the hospital and talked to about 15 men who were there undergoing treatment. They are practically prisoners and are not allowed out of the hospital grounds in that area. They get all pay stopped while they are there and it takes a good long time to effect a cure. Then I went off to have lunch with the Bishop of Lucknow who came here yesterday and is staying with Cohn, the civil lines chaplain. The days are pretty full. Yesterday I went to the headquarters of the 15th Lancers (Indian Cavalry) to talk to them for half an hour about the mission and to give my message. I went into lunch with them afterwards. On Friday I go to the 16th Lancers to speak at their regimental lecture room on the same to the officers and men. Palmer does the same with the Queens and Cheshires and we have our daily mission service at 6.30. Tomorrow we go to lunch with the Governor and on Thursday I am invited to dinner at the mess of the 82nd Punjabis (Indian Infantry) and on Saturday to dinner with General Havelock and Lady Hudson. So the days go on, always meeting fresh people and trying to get our message over. Mrs Bell is visiting married quarters and has had one large meeting of ladies and is having another at Lady Hudson's. The first week in Peshawar, Mrs Bell, Masters and I are to stay with Sir William Maffey, the Governor. I have several letters to write so I will finish for today.

22 November

This morning I have taken time off and have been out to see the historic remains of the Mutiny, the Residency and other places which were defended and finally relieved. I enclose a postcard of the ruins which is very holy ground to the Englishmen here in India. After passing through the teeming bazaar and seeing the ruins we went to the Art and Craft school and saw beautiful work being done of all sorts, wood, metal, wool. I saw a lovely pink silk sari or veil sort of thing embroidered with gold, just your colour, but it cost £4 so I refrained. I will send you a Kashmir shawl when I get to Peshawar.

Thursday, 23 November

Yesterday we had lunch at Government House, you will see who was there. He had a talk to Palmer and me and was very pleasant. The evening mission congregations are growing. We had more than usual last night, mostly men. One way and another I find this going out to dinner rather a trial, but I suppose it is part of the job and we have a chance of talking to people and getting a hearing for our message. It is delightful weather, cool at night and lovely and warm but not too hot by day. I hope you are well my sweetheart and think much of you. I have written to General Deverell to ask if I may spend a night with him on Tuesday and leave on Wednesday for Peshawar. I hope to arrive on Friday 1st. Address letters according to the list of places which is unaltered.

> Peshawar 2nd December – 24th December
> Nowshera 6th – 15th January
> Rawlpindi 20th – 29th January

Kohat 3rd – 12th February
Sialkot 17th – 26th February
Bombay 26th February – 2nd March
then I hope home.

Tuesday, 28 November, Lucknow

I am going to General Deverell until Thursday night and expect to get to Peshawar on Friday night ... Poor old Masters is still ill. He ate something which poisoned him and he has been unable to do anything yet and is still in hospital at Bareilly. I heard from him today, he doesn't expect to be able to do anything until the middle of December. I doubt it then as he has lost a stone in weight and he is 56 years old or so. Palmer and I have been most awfully kindly received here. They can't do too much to show their appreciation and good-will and the numbers have been quite good. We felt that they were stirred up. Mrs Bell looks very tired and has worked very hard ... I heard from Carden and I am to stay with Marjorie from December 20th to 26th. It will be very nice. I wish you were there with me too. I should love all this a thousand times more if you shared it with me.

Wednesday, 29 November

I got to Bareilly last night travelling in the next coach to Mrs Bell who is making a stop at Delhi on route for Peshawar where we shall both be guests of Sir John Maffey, the Commissioner of the United North Western Frontier province. I left my coach at Bareilly and met General Deverell and got into his and at the next halt went to bed in a sleeper next door. He is just the same tremendous iron soldier, full of energy, and untiring to make his command the very best, and very kind to me and a very devoted husband and father. Mrs Deverell is a very bright, capable, homely sort of woman, with a daughter of about 19, a nice simple girl, I should never imagine swank or unreality could exist in the Deverell household. I had a long talk yesterday with a Hindu barrister. He speaks perfect English, his manners refined and his mind I should say highly cultured. His education was a Christian school, and I think he would be a Christian if it was not for the fact of having to sever himself from his associations. I am sure the spirit of Christianity is growing. The Indians who are educated deplore the degradations of their own people under Hindu customs and religion.

Some day I believe there will be a very great turning to the Lord, if, and I fear there is a very big if, money and success does not come in the way. That is I think the danger. Had a good many opportunities of talking to these people in trains. I shall always go second class for that reason except at night. I am sure they are longing for a higher stake in this country, and the old prejudices are dying. The Gandhi and non-cooperation movement is gradually dying, and the wise rule of such men as Sir Harcourt-Butler is bringing about a real sense of fellowship and understanding ... Now I am going for a ride with the General this afternoon.

3 December, Government House, Peshawar

Our Wedding Day, I wish I could have spent it with you. My love, what a rotten time you are having, and I am being nursed and waited on and have everything of the best, but I would willingly give it all for you, my sweetheart. It would have been such a lovely change for you. Peshawar is a beautiful place, the air is bracing, the trees are of glorious autumn tints and everyone has roses and chrysanthemums in their gardens. Mrs Bell and I arrived at Peshawar at 10. Marjorie and Charlie were at the station to meet us. They both look well, Marjorie a little thinner than she was, Charlie also thinner, very happy together. Marjorie has got over her dislike of the country. Of course she had a bad start with her illness. She has very nice neighbours, the Stevensons. Of course they are poor, their income is considerably less than the latest joined subaltern, but they have a nice little bungalow. The drawing room very pretty and tasteful. I like them both and they are ideal here. Mrs Bell and I are both staying here for this week ... Sir John and Lady Maffey are a most attractive pair, he is 6'5" and very handsome with a clean-shaven face. She is very fair and beautiful, perfectly natural and simple with delightful, friendly hospitality. They have four children, two boys, two girls all at home. I should imagine a delightful family party. He is Chief Commissioner of all this great North-Western Frontier Province. This is a huge house and they do an enormous amount of entertaining. I have a car at my disposal whenever I want it and if one wants anything it is there. We have had wonderful services here, 40 to 50 communicants in the morning at 8.00 and 12 or so after parade service. A large number of people apart from the soldiers at parade service and 200 at evensong. Carden is a very live wire and he runs his parish well. Peshawar is a very live place and it is on the edge of the empire with that spice of danger, which there always must be when in near contact with a savage and wild Khyber people. But apart from that there is a much keener feeling for religion than in many places and the air is exhilarating and the place very wholesome and beautiful. At Lucknow I met another sister of Attewell's. She is out here with a family as a sort of nurse companion ... These days are very busy. The preparation has been difficult as Carden has been ill with scarlet fever. He is a good fellow, keen on his work, but a little bit above himself. He is very much liked by the "uppers" and officers and has an excellent curate in Jones, a quiet simple man of God who is very much loved by the simple people and soldiers. So the two are doing very good work here. Trying to get at the men who are not much inclined to come to church.

Tuesday, 5 December

Today has been pretty busy. Holy Eucharist at 8.00, at 11.30 I talked to the children, then on to speak to the men of the Welsh Regiment, a good turnout of officers and men. I got back to lunch at 2.00. In the afternoon had three sets of tennis. They had a tennis party here. I went down to church at 6.00, had service at 6.30 and after that went to the Border Regiment to speak to the men, only about 100 there, the rest on the frontier. Got back rather late to dinner at about 8.45. Tomorrow I am speaking to the Band Boys at 11.30, Armoured Car people at 12.30, RAF at 2.00, going to tea to meet some people at Marjorie's at 4.00, and speaking at the club at 6.00 and a mission service at 6.30. The club talk I am rather funking, but it has got to be done.

Wednesday 10.00 p. m.

Well it's over; a very good turnout of people at the club tonight at 6.00. I talked for about 20 minutes and then went to the church for a service as usual. We had just finished at 7.20 as the people were going out when an earthquake shock made all the roof rattle and crack. Fortunately it was only slight and nothing fell except dust and I should hope that no damage was done.

Letter from Government House, Peshawar dated 4 December 1922 from Mrs E. Bell

My dear Mrs Mellish,

As merry a Christmas as your son's small sock can contain and a happy meeting for all three of you in the New Year when your husband gets back from his big job here in India. He is very fit and seems very happy. India interests him and he looks at everything in his own direct way and confronts every difficulty with the greatest good fellowship. I cannot tell you how much he is appreciated. It is not every day that a hero is so simple and so convinced as to what is the real Glory of life, and what he says in the pulpit and out of it goes to people's hearts. They have all enjoyed him. Character has wonderful power and these soldier folk are not blind as to its force I think. Mr Mellish's cold soon went on board ship and though it has been hard work he has never seemed over tired. I am glad to be in these luxurious surroundings for a week as it all helps in a long effort doesn't it, though one doesn't want that atmosphere all the time. The Maffeys are charming and I wish you were here too. Indian soldiers find great pleasure in shaking a VC by the hand – an Afridi today was touchingly grateful – and the VC finds equal pleasure in showing us photos of you and your son. The mission is having a wonderful spiritual adventure, but I won't write of that.

Yours very sincerely, Eva Bell.

Sunday, 10 December

I am writing this earlier than usual as I am off to an outstation tomorrow early, shall probably be away from Peshawar until nearly Christmas. The way is open for me to go round the regiments who are round about Bannu, so I am leaving Masters to carry on here. I have done a week's mission here and there are other regiments which I can fit in. Colonel Haswell is taking me up in his car tomorrow about 120 miles or so and I hope to reach Dardoni on Tuesday where there is a brigade. Masters is well again, he arrived on Friday night. He has had a bad time, but has been well nursed and is now ready for work again. I expect to return here about the 22nd and stay over

Christmas with Marjorie and on the 26th go to Lundi Kotal for a week and then return here for a couple of days before going on to Nowshera for my next mission. My present expedition was not in the programme before, but the CO of the Border Regiment invited me to come up to his battalion and is very keen, so as Masters is well I am going. Yesterday afternoon Colonel Haswell took me down to the city in his car to a most lovely shop in the bazaar and I bought a shawl. I think you will like it very much. It is Kashmir wool and very fine and light and is supposed to go through a wedding ring. I have left it at Marjorie's and she will send it off by mail this week. I shall be off too early to do it. I have also ordered a fur for you, a greyish brown, I think you will like. My darling, I wish I could come home with this letter. I should so love to be with you and I am sure you want me. It is dreadful to leave you at this time my sweetheart and yet I feel that there is a great call laid on me out here until I have finished. You will find a little note with this from Lady Maffey. The day I left she gave me a little round basket for you made by the people on the frontier and a toy for Pat from the same place. I will bring them home, but thought I would enclose the note now. It is sweet of her to think of it. We shall have to go and see her sometime when she is at home, you would like her so much. They are both away now on tour, and I am staying with General Luard and his wife, most charming people who are equally kind. During the week I have been getting round and visiting regiments and details. On Friday I had three sets of tennis at Government House and managed to play a fairly medium game with a good partner, though I pitch balls about fairly often. However I am not quite so bad as I thought I should be.

13 December

I am now at a place called Dardoni about 150 miles south west of Peshawar. I came here yesterday with Colonel Haswell who has been down for a weekend to see his wife in Peshawar. We left Peshawar on Monday morning and had a wonderful run in his car, stopping for a quarter of an hour at Kohat and Bannu and reached Idak at 4.00 p.m. Idak is merely a camp full of stores, and the base and general HQ for operations that are soon to take place on the frontier. A road is being made to a place called Raymak, the purpose being to economise in troops and to facilitate eventually the opening up of the country round and to prevent raiding by the Mahsuds who are a war-loving frontier people and have been out raiding and shooting. The roads in this part of the frontier are guarded by armed posts like the South African blockhouses, fenced in with barbed wire on high ground. An expedition is going out to protect this road and hold the country until things are quiet. This is a barren wild mountainous country, the Mahsuds cannot support themselves, are well armed with rifles and maintain themselves by raiding other people. The operations in which your cousin Major Molesworth was taking part are south of this ... I am now living with the 1st Border Regiment. The chaplain, Mackenzie is a splendid chap. We are living more or less on a war basis, everybody in tents except HQ people and the General etc. Mackenzie will be going up with a column to Raymak which is a high plateau about 9000 feet above sea level. It will be very cold. It is not warm here but we have had no snow yet, though there is snow on the mountains. This place is a camp in a small plain surrounded by mountains, it is fenced all round with barbed wire and there are day and night guards. The Mahsuds are a very warlike, well-trained, well-armed tribe. They are giving a lot of trouble by shooting at convoys on the road and small parties, and the expedition is to hold the highest, most important point, Raymak, from which it is hoped the Mahsuds will be controlled. The Borders are a fine lot – splendid lot of officers and a good sprinkling of NCO's and men who saw service in Gallipoli and France ... The mission is going very well here. We have had two tents joined together and each evening have 60–70 men at 6.30. We have the Eucharist each morning at 7.30 in my tent which we also use for church. I sleep in one end of it. This morning, Sunday, it was crammed with about 55 communicants at 8.00 a. m ... I am very glad I came here. It wasn't on my programme but I shouldn't get a chance in February as we had previously arranged on account of the advance. I leave here on Wednesday and have an evening service at Idak and HC on Thursday morning, the same at Bannu on Thursday evening and Friday morning, and I should get back to Peshawar on Friday evening if I can get a car, or Saturday if by train. I am spending Christmas with Marjorie except Christmas morning when I go to Lundi Kotal 30 miles from Peshawar for a service, then back to Peshawar.

26 December 1922

I left Dardoni on Wednesday, December 20th. Mackenzie took me to Idak in his car. We had lunch at Idak with the 101st Grenadiers, an Indian regiment, and at 6.15 a service for men, oddments from Signals and armoured cars; at 7.00 for officers in the club. After breakfast we went on to Bannu about 40 miles where Mackenzie had fixed up for a talk on the mission. I stayed with Colonel Furney and his wife; they are both very jolly people. I stayed there until Saturday. I am going there again in February for four days for mission services. We had a Eucharist on Friday morning and Mackenzie left to go back to Dardoni. Colonel Furney then lent me a horse and I had a couple of hours' ride. It was like a circus as it was market day, all sorts of funnies coming in carrying fowls or driving sheep and cows. The market itself was so crammed with people that it was difficult to get through at all. This afternoon I watched polo. Saturday morning Colonel Haswell called for me with his car and took me back to Peshawar. We stayed and had lunch at Kohat with an RE Major and his wife. Bannu to Kohat is about 45 miles. From Kohat to Peshawar about 35 miles. It was a wonderful journey. We crossed two great mountain ranges by roads that curved twice around the hills often in irregular spirals. Very dangerous for inexperienced drivers, but most enjoyable with a good careful driver like Haswell. We got into Peshawar about 5.30. Christmas morning I had a car to take me up to Lundi Kotal on the Khyber pass about 35 miles away. We had a parade service with the Warwicks and details and the Eucharist afterwards. I had lunch with the Warwicks officers and set out just before three and got in here to spend the rest of Christmas day with Marjorie and Charlie. Had a very nice Christmas evening service with some carols which are wonderfully homey things. Many people there and all singing very happily. I am much longing for the photograph, but above all I am longing for good news of you, about the 9th of next month. I know well how anxious and full of hope you are. I wish I could be with you, but when you receive this you will be well on the way to getting better. Please God a new little person will be sleeping placidly in the cradle. Tomorrow, St John's day, I am going to Jamrud, seven miles from here, for a service for details of troops and then on to Lundi Kotal for a short mission and leave again on Monday to return here. I am to stay with Colonel Luard again until Wednesday, January 3rd and spend the last two days at Peshawar with Marjorie and on to Nowshera on the 5th where I shall be until I leave for Pindi where I shall arrive about 19th of January.

2 January 1923

Thursday morning we left for Lundi Kotal. It is a wonderful journey up through the Khyber pass. Well over a 1000 feet higher than Peshawar and Jamrud. You can see from one of the photos showing a little of the road that it is a very twisty one built on the edge of the mountain looking down often to the valley hundreds of feet below. The road is a wonderful piece of work and the railway still more wonderful. It will take about four years more to build and will run right to the edge of Afghanistan. It is being built by the North Western Railway. All the unskilled labour is being provided by the tribesmen, the skilled labour by people from India, all natives except the engineers. The road through the pass is right through tribes who are only friendly for what they can get out of the Government, but there is very little raiding at present, though the pass is guarded by forts and garrisons all the way. All of the neighbouring tribes are doing very well out of the railway as they are supplying the labour. Lundi Khana is at the very end of the pass and is held by the 1st Gurkha Regiment. We went there last Friday for me to speak to the officers about the mission and had lunch afterwards. Colonel Shaw took us up to the post on the boundary line which separates British territory from Afghanistan. The Afghans are at peace with us and we have an ambassador there. The Amir is a progressive ruler who is developing his country as fast as he can. The danger there is the anti-British influence of the Bolsheviks, but at present all is peace there and the Afghan policy is towards civilization, though they don't love us. Every week a great convoy of camels goes down through the pass to Peshawar carrying carpets and goods. The convoy will arrive at the end of the Khyber tomorrow on its way down.

Tomorrow is Proclamation day throughout India, a parade of all troops as an act of loyalty to the King Emperor. They have a feu-de-joie and play God Save the King. I will send you a photograph of it, I hope. I am staying here until Wednesday as I want to get in more of the mission than at present. The Warwicks are very short in numbers as they are moving to Nasirabad next week and no drafts have come up to them. The work is very hard here, 150 men out every night on guard out of 400 strong. They have been here 15 months and are very fed up with the place. The mission here so far has not got hold at all, but I am hoping for better numbers for the next three evenings. Been round with Jones to all the huts to collect and invite the men, but the work the men have to do is so hard that I am not surprised that they are not keen on coming out. On Friday they went for a 22 mile route march, so one could hardly expect them to be very keen on coming to a mission service after that. On Wednesday I go back to Peshawar and Marjorie until Friday and then on to Nowshera.

If you are able, it would be lovely if you could come down to Plymouth, you will be able to find out from the P&O office when Caledonia is due in and we can spend a few days at Salterton with Uncle Dick and Aunt Edie or stay on our own somewhere near Plymouth. Nelly Goldsmith would certainly put us up at Cawsand; it is a lovely little place, and quite close to Plymouth if you had the babies. It is nice looking so far ahead and it will be a good time to get back to the parish on Easter Eve, though I shall miss Palm Sunday. It would be good for you to have a week away and for us to be together after this long time ...

Tuesday. I must send this off with some photographs. The parade was very good, though the feu-de-joie did not take place. After lunch Jones and I called down to Lundi Khana and Colonel Shaw of the 1st Gurkhas took me up 900 feet to the top of the hill to see an ancient Buddhist wall and remains of a camp.

3 January, Peshawar

I am back again with Marjorie, got back for lunch ... Jones and I went to the 2nd Gurkhas for dinner last night and after dinner as we were leaving the officers gave me a lovely Gurkha kukri, a great hunting knife which is the favourite weapon of the Gurkhas, as a remembrance. Wasn't it nice of them?

An unfortunate thing happened at Lundi Kotal on New Year's Eve. While the 745th Punjabi officers were at mess one of their huts caught fire and it was impossible to save it. Four officers lost their kit and two valuable dogs were burnt alive. Fortunately there was no wind in the camp or the camp might have suffered much more.

9 January 1923

Nowshera is a very common-place and ordinary place, nothing to see and nothing to write about. The barracks are good, the church ordinary and as usual the people are very friendly. Morgan is the chaplain, one of the best, full of keenness and so is his wife. They have a small boy of three years old, a very happy person, quite ugly with ears sticking out like handles. This cantonment is scattered so I am having meetings at different places. The services on Sunday were good and quite a good number of people. This evening I am going to Risalpur and tomorrow to Mardan and on Friday again to Risalpur. On Monday I hope to go to Dargai, Tuesday to Malakand, Wednesday to Chakdara. In each of those stations is a garrison with a few British officers and their wives. Friday I go to Rawlpindi where Delabere and I join forces. It will be interesting to compare notes after our various experiences. Last night I visited the Lancashire Fusiliers barracks for two hours and had dinner afterwards with the officers. The colonel is a tophole person and has a very good battalion of very young soldiers, but very keen and happy. The band boys are ludicrously young, round-faced babies, but they are dear things, very friendly.

Thursday, 14 January

I was asked by Charlie to speak to the students in Edwardes College. There were no Christians at all there, but they could all understand English and they appeared to listen well. Then I went down again to the CMS hospital. Dr Cox took me round, I had lunch with him and afterwards went with him and another doctor who is also governor of the jail to the city. We went into numerous serais, yards in which the caravan people who come down, put up themselves and their camels. I saw some beautiful carpets but had not the money to buy any. You would have loved them. The colours are beautiful and they are cheap compared with prices at home. I could have got two beautiful rugs for £2 each or probably less and they were very tempting. I have bought a fur for you. I won't sent it home as it is safer to bring it. It is a grey-brown winter lynx skin lined with silk. I think you will like it. It is nice and thick and will keep you warm. Mrs Haswell chose and ordered it for me. She does a good deal of buying in the city, and got it cheaper than if I had tried. I have been spending a lot of money on photographs but I think it is worthwhile to let you know by picture where I am and to have mementos of my visits, but I am drawing in my horns now a bit as they charge a lot to develop them, the prints cost 3d each for the cheapest.

Now I have seen the most interesting parts of India it is not worth taking views of places like this as it is very ordinary. Today I am going to lunch with a battery and this afternoon to talk to gunners' married families at 4.00. I had a horse from Colonel Lock on Monday and had a good ride and shall ask for it again when I have time.

16 January

You told me, at least I think so, that the baby was expected on the 9th. I have been daily expecting a wire, but I was rather relieved when you said the 14th in one of your letters. I do hope all is well with you, my sweetheart. I am very glad the doctor has forbidden you to do any more. I am glad your mother is staying with you too. I know it is hard on your dad, but he won't mind looking after himself a bit for your sake. I am longing to have good news of you, my darling. I wish I could be with you, and I hope indeed that we shall never have to be away from each other again.

I am up at Dargai. It is actually out of India, a little fort at the foot of the Malakand mountains in the middle of Swat territory; cheery looking tribesman armed every one with rifles. The regiment here is the 117th Royal Mahrattas. There are eight officers, three wives and two babies, all live in the fort. We had a service in the mess room last evening and Holy Communion at 8.00 this morning. They haven't had a service for a very long time and were glad ... It is lovely up here under glorious hills, looking beautiful with light and shade. The country around it is irrigated by a canal from the Swat River and is intensely fertile and much cultivated. I had tea and dinner with the CO of the regiment, Major Hall and his wife yesterday. Very nice people, they have two children at home and a dear little boy here of two years old, but not so nice as Pat. I have seen none to touch him.

16 January, Malakand

I had the wire just after I got here, I am so glad, my dear, I hope you are really splendid. I hoped it would be a girl but I am very glad and hope the new little man will be as strong as his brother. I shall look forward so much to letters which should tell me more all about you and him on February 5th ... What shall we call the new little fellow? How would you like Andrew? It will be very exciting to get a photograph of him, wait to have it taken until you can hold him yourself.

I came up here this morning and got here to the fort just before 12.00. It is a good height up and the fort itself is right on top of the high ground about 3500 feet up. I came in a tonga, a light two-wheeled cart drawn by two ponies, one in the shafts and the other on an outrigger. The shaft pony trots usually and the other canters. The 6th Gurkhas are here and a few other officers, pioneers, engineers, and there are some families here though I haven't seen them yet. I am messing with the Gurkhas. As usual a very nice lot. Tomorrow I go on to Chakdara, the last and most northern point of my whole tour. It is only a fort with two companies of the 117th Mahrattas in it, commanded by Major Standridge, whose wife came out on the Nevada with us. She is there with her husband. Tonight we shall have service at 6.30 in a little church right up on top of the hill, a little beauty, and so nicely furnished. It is a shame the people haven't had a service for months. Difficult of course for Morgan, but it is quite easy to put in a trip once a month at least and the people at Dargai and here are rather hurt that they have been neglected. I haven't done anything exciting lately; I send the programme of my visit to Nowshera and I think it has been quite a useful time; the soldiers have been quite responsive and have turned up very well to all the services and meetings and the meetings for families have also been well attended. I think this is one of my best missions, and I hope Pindi will be as good.

16 January

I had a very nice service tonight in the beautiful little church which is set right on the top of the hill looking down hundreds of feet into the plain which is green with growing crops, and watered by the silver ribbon of a canal far below.

17 January

This morning Holy Eucharist at St George's church. Afterwards I took the Blessed Sacrament to a Major's wife. She has had a baby and has been very ill, but is better now ... This is really a beautiful place. The hills are so wonderful and majestic, the air bracing and glorious, I wish you could see it all. Now after lunch the Colonel is taking me to Chakdara, ten miles, and I shall stop the night with the Standridges.

22 January
West Ridge, Rawlpindi

Had a very happy trip to Dargai and Malakand and Chakdara. At the last place there was only one woman, Mrs Standridge, whose husband commands the post, and I stayed with them. They were very nice but it is a lonely place for a woman on her own. I left there on Thursday and got back to Dargai and after dinner with Major and Mrs Hall at Dargai got on the train about 11.00 p. m. and slept there, arriving at Nowshera just about 8.00 a.m. Just had time to race over to Morgan's house in a tonga and have a bit of breakfast, pick up my box and catch the train at 9.00 a.m. for Pindi.

Delabere had had a few days visit to Peshawar with the Maffeys and he and I travelled from Nowshera together. He is in Pindi and I at West Ridge three miles out. The chaplain, Gorrie, and his wife, an excellent couple. He is an Australian, served in the war as a private and officer, and was badly wounded. Then became chaplain and is in charge here. She belonged to St Hildas society of Lahore, looking after girls and orphans at a home there. The two of them are doing very good work here. We had splendid numbers at church yesterday, a good start for the mission. I feel that we shall have a really good work here. There are not only two regiments here, Oxford and Bucks and Gloucesters, but a large number of railway people, and it would be a great mistake to leave them out, I felt, and the numbers certainly justify it ... On Friday and Saturday it poured with rain, but now it is beautiful. The hills all along in the distance are beautiful and near Murree are covered with snow. Here it is fine and clear but not so cold. On Thursday night we are asked to dinner by General Bird-wood ...

I had a nice letter from the colonel commanding the artillery camp at Akora about seven or eight miles from Nowshera. I am going there from about Monday to Thursday or Friday and then on to Kohat. I shall try after Bannu to see Marjorie again, but I don't know if I can fit it in. Just over five weeks more out here, then hey for Merrie England and you, my own dear love. The mission is going very well. This is not the society part. Pindi has all the big people, here we have all the soldiers and railway people who are all Eurasians or Anglo-Indians as they call them. They are very slightly dark. They are turning up in church very well. They are the people whom one feels most sorry for. When India becomes more Indianised these people will feel their positions more. They are gradually being turned out of the subordinate government jobs, they will never be able to hold the high posts and the Indians will gradually work them out of the lower positions and their future is very gloomy.

On Friday we are going out to Taxilla where wonderful Buddhist Greek remains are being discovered. Taxilla is a buried city dating back to Alexander The Great.

31 January

On Friday after the Eucharist I had a day off and dear old Proby, the chaplain of Pindi, arranged an outing in cars to Taxilla, an ancient city now being excavated. There are wonderful remains of temples and structures called stupors in which are deposited coins and jewels. A museum has been built there in which are shown plaster and stone Buddhas and beautiful jewels of gold and silver and cut stones. The sculpture is of Greek style and the columns in the temples show Greek Corinthian style.

Wednesday, 31 January

Just had your letter sent on from Nowshera. Lovely to have it and the photograph too. It is a beauty. I am delighted with it. How strong and what a boy he is, he looks two years old, and it is very good of you.

Tuesday, 6 February, Kohat

I have had a very happy time here. The Fagans are very kind. Mrs Fagan has given me a pair of Kashmiri wooden candlesticks for you. They will look so nice fitted with electric lamps. We had good services on Sunday; the Eucharist in this charming little church, a service for the troops, about 60 at their lines two miles away, and a good service in the evening. General Birdwood, a very keen person, had just arrived from Raymak after a journey of 120 miles by car, but came to church though he only arrived half an hour before, and read the lessons. He went back to Pindi directly after dinner. A very energetic person and most delightful to meet. Tomorrow I go on to Bannu 18 miles away where I shall stay until Monday with the Wigrams. He is a CMS padre, and Mrs Wigram is a doctor and does noble work in the hospital

there, carrying on the work of Doctor Pennel who died in harness a
few years ago, much beloved by all the people to whom he ministered.
I have just had my last service here. The people have turned up very
well. It has only been a short visit, but so many are away that Devenish
thought more than three days would be too much, as he is really the
padre here and beloved by the people. He is with the Raymak force
and will remain with them until the fighting is over and the Borders
come back again. This morning I had a walk through the city with
its narrow streets, thronged with people, bullocks, donkeys and camels,
very interesting. This afternoon I had some tennis. We finished up
with a tremendous set winning 13–11. Devenish and Mrs Fagan against
Mrs Herepath and me. Tonight I am going to the Deputy Commissioner's to dinner and leave for Bannu tomorrow at 9.00. Yesterday
Lady Roberts, Bob's daughter came here on her way round the frontier.
They had a parade for her of her father's old battery, and a battalion
which he once commanded. Afterwards Colonel and Mrs Bruce invited
all the Indian officers and all the old soldiers whom they could get,
who had served under Bobs. There was one old man reputed to be
100 years old. A photograph was taken of the group, and I took one
also ... This is a lovely little place, the flowers are wonderful and
masses of violets everywhere. In Mrs Fagan's garden there are borders
two feet wide along the drive and along the road to the church each
side is edged with borders of violets. The flowers are not yet at their
best, but there are violets in thousands, wall-flowers, roses, stocks,
pansies, and the whole place is sweet with the scent of violets. It is
very beautiful with trees too. Fondest love and love to little Pat and
the other.

Monday, 12 February, Bannu

I told you I thought Andrew would be a nice name, Mother suggests
Christopher and that is very nice too, and not so common. Perhaps
you would like Lawrence, I am not too fond of it myself ... I have
just had a wire from Mackenzie to tell me that the brigade to which
he is attached is away beyond Raymak so my plan for going there is
off now. Colonel Harden invited me to go up if they were at Raymak.
I could have gone if they had been there, but they are on operations,
smashing up Mahsud villages. The expedition has been most successful
and the casualties have been very light, but some officers have been
wounded, one very dangerously. One man killed and about 30 or 40

wounded. But considering the nature of the country and the warlike and well-armed people they are fighting, the loss has been very small. It is now 12 noon and I am waiting for a car to take me back to Kohat, on I hope to Peshawar tomorrow, where I hope to see Marjorie again and Wallace if he is still there. I am due to get to Sialkot on Saturday, so I may stop on my way to spend two nights at Campbellpore, where there is a small station and some gunners and their wives. Then Sialkot from the 17th until the 26th, then a night at Ambala and another at Delhi and on to Bombay.

17 February, Flagstaff House, Sialkot

I have just had your letter which has been waiting nearly a week. My darling, I am so thankful that you are better, you must have had a dreadful time. I hate having to be away from you, but the time is very fast coming, now only a fortnight and I hope to be on the way to meet you. Yes, I think Richard will be a nice name. Richard Wallace is a good combination. Richard Andrew would spell RAM so that won't do – he would be called Sheep at school. Uncle Dick and our Richard and it has been a common name in our family, so let's have it. Easter for the christening will be lovely. Looking forward to it intensely. Or perhaps Palm Sunday if I am at home and all is well ... Colonel and Mrs Rankin are both most kind. Just gone out to a concert and I am left to amuse myself. I am delighted to do so though they asked me to go with them. This is the last letter you will get from me for I shall arrive I hope with the next mail after this. How exciting it will be and how glad I shall be to see your dear face again with Pat and little Dick. I can quite imagine Miss Cooper's amazement at our postponing his baptism. Certainly I would wish him to be baptised at once if necessary, but this case is I think an exceptional one. I do not see that I should forego the joy of admitting my little son into the Society of his Saviour, and for being the agent for giving him His grace. I am writing to Cecil to ask him to be his godfather. I cannot get an answer from him, but I feel sure he will agree. He is a dear old thing and would like to do so I think. Though he may not entirely agree with the Christian faith as practised by some. I feel sure he lives it and believes it.

You will see by the programme that I am having a pretty busy time here. McKelore is the chaplain, he is a good chap and does very good work among the men. His manner of talking gets rather on people's nerves. He uses the Studdert-Kennedy style rather cheaply without its depth, and is rather tiring, a fearful chatterbox with a good deal of trumpet blowing, but he is very good with the men and they love him. Some of the people I think are rather impatient of his verbosity, but he is doing good work and keeps his people together. There is, as in all small places, a good deal of gossip and tittle-tattle and perhaps McKelore is a bit weak, but on the whole I think this community is very happy. The services have been good, very good on Sundays, and the meetings quite successful. I am staying with General Rankin, they are very kind and the General gives me a ride nearly every day when he goes round inspecting. They have some very good horses and I am much enjoying the riding. On Monday afternoon the General, Mrs Rankin and Ronda, their daughter of 13, and I, all went out a few miles to see the beautiful snow-covered mountains of Kashmir, which were very clear. The country all round is under growing crops and as there has been much rain it all looked like England except for the beautiful mountains in the distance which on Sunday were lit up by the sun and stood out against the clear blue sky ... I thought of Paul for the baby's name. I don't agree about women not receiving the Blessed Sacrament until they have been churched. Churching is a public thanksgiving marking the return to the corporate life of society after her seclusion. She is not excommunicate because she has borne a child. Why should she not receive the comfortable gift of the Life of Christ before she is strong enough to come out into public life again? I think there is apt to be too much of medieval tradition which has no ancient authority. I would always gladly give any devout mother Holy Communion if she desired it in her home, if she is not strong enough to come to church to receive ... There are lots of mongooses here, one came into the house after lunch. They are rather like weasels to look at. Poor Ronda had some ducks and they were both killed by a mongoose, and yesterday she took me out to show me two new quails and we found them just killed by a mongoose who ran away as we arrived. She is a nice little thing, 13 year old and rides splendidly and is absolutely fearless. Fondest love my own sweetheart, I hope that a month tomorrow I shall be at home. It will be delightful. So much love to you and Pat and to Dick or Paul.

This is the last of Mellish's letters from India so we can assume that he did board SS *Caledonia* at Bombay on 3 March and arrive in England about the 23rd. Unfortunately there is no record whether Elizabeth did manage to meet him at Plymouth for a few days' holiday together. It is certain however that Mellish christened his second son in his own St Mark's Church in April and the baby was duly named Richard Wallace Paul. Richard after Mellish's own brother killed in 1915, Wallace after Elizabeth's cousin, Wallace Aspinall, a splendid regular soldier in the Indian Army, brother of Marjorie Bender with whom Mellish stayed in Peshawar, and Paul, probably after a fighting saint.

Chapter Seventeen

Parish Priest 1918–39

BACK IN HIS OWN PARISH. Mellish was able to take up the pattern that had been interrupted and carry on with his ceaseless work. For him it was literally a labour of love, since he truly loved his parishioners, although some of them caused problems, sometimes he was impatient of their prejudices and very occasionally he was angered. There is only one letter during the next year or so describing a holiday camp when he took a number of boys from London's East End down to the sea. From Crowbourne Farm (undated).

> We settled in yesterday well and the Smiths had taken in all our food and we had a bathe after lunch. The river is quite safe and very jolly. We had our first meals satisfactorily, tea, bread and jam, and supper – cocoa and bread and cheese. Breakfast, boiled rice and honey and sugar, plenty of milk on it. We get lovely milk from the Smiths' dairy. We took down the cash for shopping after breakfast and bought our needs and came back and made dinner. Stewed mutton with potatoes, onions, carrots and cabbage all together, cooked for an hour and then put in a haybox for another hour. All are quite contented and eat well. We rest for an hour after dinner and then go bathing. Two of my boys swam their test of 50 yards today and I went with them. After tea we had a scratch cricket match with a Sunday school treat party which was on the Smiths' farm today. Our boys played very well and are keen. They are a ripping lot and good as gold, full of beans too. We have prayers every morning after breakfast and semi-compline at night. My day is full and now they are asleep I can write.

In May 1924 a third son, Robin, was born. Now with a maid and a temporary nanny to help, the vicarage was fairly crowded. For the sake of his family, Mellish then decided to look for a country living where they could grow up in pleasant surroundings and with plenty of space. And so in September 1925 he became vicar of Wangford, with Henham and Reydon, in the county of Suffolk, a few miles inland from Southwold. At the same time he was appointed honorary chaplain to St Felix School, a large girls' school on the edge of Southwold.

The family settled very happily into a large and beautiful old vicarage near the church. There was of course no electricity, central heating was almost unknown in the country, and cooking was done on a big black iron range or a paraffin stove. However, Elizabeth was highly experienced in domestic arrangements and was an excellent cook. She baked all the bread and cakes for the family while Mellish was able to indulge his love of gardening and produced fruit and vegetables to eat all year round.

The family had been expanded by the permanent addition of Daisy, one of a large family of girls from Deptford, who had moved with them to Suffolk, and Elsie, a local girl, who took over the job of nanny to the three small boys. In addition Jim Allen from Wangford, came in daily to help in the garden. Elizabeth's sister, Margaret, also lived with the Mellishes at Wangford since she had started a small school for infants in the area, and to Elizabeth's great pleasure, her parents finally gave up their small farm near Whiteparish in Hampshire and moved to Reydon where they built a bungalow.

As with every job he undertook, Mellish very soon made his mark on the parish and became a familiar figure through his constant visiting. Many years after he had left, he and Elizabeth met the widow of a well-known artist who was living in the glebe house near the church, occupied during his time at Wangford by a Miss Eden, aunt of Sir Anthony Eden. This lady expressed her pleasure in meeting him at last and explained that for the first year or so after she moved into Wangford she was puzzled by constant references to the vicar which did not seem to tally with what she knew of her vicar. She finally discovered that the people who spoke of the vicar were referring to Mellish and not the present incumbent, even though he had left the parish months or even years before.

One of Mellish's new parishioners and friends was the local doctor,

Dr White, who was very good to the family and became closely involved when Paul developed serious gland trouble in his neck which necessitated several operations. Among his other attributes as a much-loved country doctor, Dr White was one of the very few, if not the first man in the county to possess a steam-powered car. This must have been an object of extreme interest and probably extreme distrust to many, but was perhaps not the ideal vehicle for a doctor since someone had to stoke it up and produce a head of steam whenever an emergency visit had to be made.

Mellish of course had no vehicle, but while he could manage well enough on his bicycle, a splendid old Raleigh which was built to last for ever, he felt that some form of transport would be very useful for the family, for meeting trains at Halesworth, the nearest station eight miles away and for transport into Reydon or Southwold. And so Dolly the donkey joined the family. She was a Billingsgate porter's donkey who arrived by train complete with trap from London. Once harnessed, however, Mellish found that she flatly refused to move in spite of all persuasion and entreaty. Finally he recalled her origins and addressed her with a flow of cockney abuse which must have sounded like home to Dolly and from then on she never balked and pulled her little trap without hesitation.

As the children grew and were able to take their place in the dining room for meals with their parents, it became necessary to find a bigger table than the one used at St Mark's. Moreover there were constant visitors to the vicarage, either local or from afar, so that the house was always full. Mellish started to look around for another table, when he found an old billiard table abandoned in an outhouse near the church, with mouldering legs and baize. Having obtained the churchwardens' ready consent, he stripped off the baize and slate and found beneath them a fine cross-panelled oak top which he cleaned up and reshaped by cutting away the cushions and pockets. He then turned a set of sturdy oak legs and made a solid frame to produce a splendid table about 8 ft × 4 ft 6 ins. which was in constant use for the next forty years. It could, and frequently did, seat up to fifteen people and made a fine and almost full-size ping-pong table on which the boys learnt to play. After several years in storage after Mellish's death, it has now been taken out again and restored to a place of honour in the home of one of his sons.

The years passed quickly and busily, but much as he loved his parishes and the work, Mellish found that living expenses with a growing family were hard to meet. However self-supporting and economical they were, he and Elizabeth found it very hard to make do on the salary of a country parson in a poor and unendowed parish. It is doubtful that he took any steps to alter the situation, but a good friend of his, the Rev. Shirley of Redhill, took it on himself to write to King George V drawing his attention to the difficult circumstances in which Mellish lived. Shirley had been vicar of a parish near St Mark's and knew him already when he was a curate at Deptford. In response to his letter, the King commanded that Mellish's name be submitted to the Lord Chancellor for preferment to a bigger parish. The Lord Chancellor personally took up the case and after a wait of some months for a suitable living the very last appointment he made was that of Mellish to Great Dunmow in Essex. In dealing with the necessary papers, his deputy wrote to Mellish:

I have just been going through my late chief's pencilled instruction from his death bed about yourself to Dunmow. It is pathetic to realize how anxious he was to see you settled before he died.

Among the papers on this presentation is a letter from Keith Markby, the former adjutant to 4th Bn. Royal Fusiliers in support of the application. He writes:

I have known Mr Mellish well for the last ten years. First while I was adjutant to 4th Bn. Royal Fusiliers when he was attached to this battalion as army chaplain. It would be unnecessary to refer to his brilliant work in the army with his record of being the first army chaplain to receive the VC. He had a wonderful influence and control over the men in the army. His high standard of character, lovable disposition, generosity, depth of understanding and keenness and devotion to his work, gives one no hesitation in strongly recommending him for any position where the influence and guiding of other people and steadfast devotion to work is required.

At the time of the appointment, Dunmow was a growing market

town in north Essex, with a branch line station, a bacon factory and sixteen or seventeen pubs. Its strongest claim to fame however was the Dunmow Flitch. This was a mock trial held every four years, at which couples presented themselves to a rigorous cross-examination by a local solicitor. If they could convince the jury that they had not had a single quarrel for a year and a day, the successful couple was awarded a flitch or side of bacon from the local factory.

The rectory was a big, rather rambling house of Queen Anne origin, added to somewhat haphazardly in the manner of parsonage houses, to produce a charming if inconvenient home with seven bedrooms, attics above and cellars below, and a solid range of outhouses for stables and garage. The house was situated about a mile from the centre of the town immediately opposite the church and surrounded by farmland.

The dining room was panelled in dark oak to waist height; the remainder of the panelling had been sold by a needy predecessor and had made its way to the big Hall nearby which was the squire's residence. The kitchen, one of the earliest parts of the house, was heavily beamed, with a stone flag floor and a huge black iron range and even bigger boiler. This was intended to run a primitive form of central heating but as it was so costly to stoke, the system seldom worked. Leading off the kitchen was a brick-floored scullery with a cold tap over the big stone sink. As at Wangford there was no electricity but the house was lit by gas which gave a warm and friendly light. Here Mellish and Elizabeth settled happily with their augmented household, which now consisted of the three boys, Elsie the nanny from Wangford, Daisy from Deptford, and finally Jim Allen whose mother had died at Wangford so that he was homeless and had no one to care for him. In addition there was Dolly the donkey, a large black sow, two dogs and a cat. Jim Allen had his own little bed-sitter in the garage block and took his meals in the kitchen.

Over the years the house was steadily improved, Mellish carrying out most of the repairs and any new work such as cupboards and shelving, while Elizabeth did all the interior decorating and papering. About 1930 an electricity generating plant was installed, charging a series of big accumulators, and some years later this gave way to mains electricity. The kitchen range was replaced by an Aga cooker which was a great joy to Elizabeth and after many arguments a telephone was finally installed in about 1935.

For some time Elizabeth had argued that a telephone was really necessary in case of emergencies such as a burglary, and would in any case be very useful. In due course the burglary took place – a very inefficient and amateur business which yielded little of value. The burglars, having first drugged the dogs, forced a way into the house and picked up a small safe from Mellish's study. This they hauled across the garden on one of the children's sledges and then beat open with a borrowed pickaxe. Inside they found a very small sum of money and some papers and envelopes which they threw aside – one of them containing Mellish's medals which he wore only on special occasions and which were even then of considerable value. Fortunately he heard nothing in the night or he would undoubtedly have gone down to investigate, and hanging on the wall of his study over the safe was the kukri given to him by the Gurkhas. When Elizabeth made the point that now they must have a telephone, he replied, "Well, you've had your burglary now, so why do we need one?"

As in his previous parishes, Mellish soon established the basis of his ministry in Dunmow, first visiting every household, whether church-going or not, and then settling into a routine which involved daily contact with a large number of his parishioners and constant visiting. Although he now had a car, a fine old Clyno tourer, this was only used for outlying calls or for the weekly flower collection and mostly it was Elizabeth who drove it when taking the children out, or for shopping.

When he became vicar, Mellish took over a handsome but rather austere church which looked tall and cold. In the next few years he transformed this into a warm and beautiful place of worship, glowing with rich colour. The Mothers' Union was encouraged to make a huge thick blue rug the full length and width of the chancel, the old pendant lights were replaced with concealed lighting, the Victorian organ gave way to a new, smaller one in a plain oak casing, and the Lady Chapel was completely refurnished and carpeted. Both the high altar and the chapel altar, also from Victorian times in pitch pine, were replaced by handsome oak altars with new rails to match. And perhaps most of all, the church was always generously decorated with massed flowers standing in tall pottery vases, of the type Mellish had seen and admired in some of the French churches. On Saturday mornings it was his custom to take the car and make a round of visits to a number of the bigger gardens in the parish. He would return laden with flowers and foliage which he then arranged in big clusters with the help of a team of devoted assistants, and his own garden contributed largely to produce the colour and beauty he strove for.

On Sundays there were always four services and once a month five, when he went out to a mission chapel a few miles away, as well as a Sunday school for children. On weekdays Mellish spent nearly every morning out visiting unless he had any special meetings. Usually he was out again in the afternoons until tea time and most of his paperwork and writing was done at night since he seldom went to bed before midnight. Early on he installed a small hand-printing press in his study, with hand-set lead type. On this he produced all the parish service sheets, notices, cards, invitations and special appeals which are part of an active church community. Many of the cards for jumble sales, bazaars etc, or for special appeals were decorated with lino-cut illustrations drawn and cut by Mellish, or with little rhymes of his own or others.

Lacking a squire in Dunmow, people turned naturally for advice and help to the traditional substitutes, the clergy and the doctors. There were two medical practices in Dunmow, with both of which Mellish worked closely although he was most personally associated with the practice which treated his own family when necessary. Stanley Hall was a devoted and utterly selfless country practitioner who became a great friend, with the common bond between the two men of craftsmen woodworkers. His partner, Dr Roberts, always known as Bobs, was of the same type and another close friend. Indeed he first met the girl who was to become his wife while she was spending a weekend at the vicarage and it was from there that she was married soon after. Mellish also worked harmoniously with the Catholic priest, a small round saintly Father Brown figure, who trudged for miles round his parish in all weathers and all seasons wearing gum boots on his bare feet. Eventually Father Field retired and was replaced by Father Clover, who continued the good relations which were not so common in those days when ecumenism was an unknown word.

Taking communion to the sick and elderly house-bound was a normal part of Mellish's daily round, and to many of these his regular visits were the highlights of a wearisome life. There were other less pleasant duties, such as comforting the bereaved and dying. One such episode was never revealed until a local paper published an account of how Mellish had regularly visited and prayed with a young farmer of the parish who contracted diptheria and was completely cut off from all friends and family in the small isolation hospital. Despite the risk, Mellish insisted on calling every week during the month the young man lay dying, and was able to give him Communion at the end. Naturally he took precautions to avoid the risk of infection, but he certainly never spoke of this episode, so it must be assumed that the family in gratitude told the story to the local paper.

On the lighter side of life, Mellish took a very active part in the organisation and running of the annual church fete which raised quite large sums for the parish and overseas missions. This was usually held in the Halls' large garden which was on three levels and was immaculately kept by Stanley Hall's wife, Joyce. Opening off the road behind the garden was a long garage yard which sloped evenly from top to bottom. Here Mellish and Stanley Hall constructed a roller-coaster switchback which would have done credit to any professional fair. Light-gauge rails were carefully laid on trestles with upward curves and several downward swoops. The train consisted of a number of open carriages with superbly carved dragon heads and bodies, all brilliantly painted scarlet and blue. As well as this, they made a large wooden horse whose tummy consisted of wide rings. The prize was a coconut placed between the horse's ears and competitors had to straddle his body starting at the tail and work their way up, trying to avoid being rolled off along the body.

In the church itself, Mellish made a big wooden crib for Christmas and bought some finely modelled plaster figures, the interior being lit by a concealed light. Since there were no suitable animals he later made a donkey and a camel to complete the picture. He also bought a set of handbells and arranged for his organist, and friend, Miss Lottie Bacon, to write all the well-known carols to numbers printed on small hand-boards. Then with a team of eager volunteers, Mellish would tour the town each evening in the fortnight before Christmas playing either outside or by request, in some of the larger houses, to collect money for St Dunstans for the Blind.

For Eastertide, he made an Easter tomb of stone slabs with a circular stone rolled away from the central opening, and again some fine plaster figures. This was set up every year and banked with flowers to produce a striking and beautiful effect. Also at Christmas, with the enthusiastic help of a large number of parishioners, Mellish and Elizabeth organised an annual Nativity Tableau. This involved a huge amount of work and rehearsal, making of costumes and arranging of the cast for a series of tableaux interspersed with carols in the appropriate places, with solos and even a harpsichord recital. Naturally enough the vicarage was taken over at these times as meeting place, refreshment room and dressing rooms.

However dedicated he was, Mellish would have been and always was the first to admit that his work in the parish could never have been so successful without Elizabeth's wholehearted and loving help. They were in every way an ideal partnership and perfectly complementary. Elizabeth ran the Mothers' Union, visited anyone in need, and kept open house at all times so that no caller at the vicarage ever felt unwanted. Breakfast on Sundays after the 9.15 communion service became a happy ritual for some of the regular worshippers and an open invitation to any new ones. There was probably never a time when an unexpected caller was not offered a meal if he or she happened to be there at a mealtime.

And during all the years at Dunmow, the house was never free of visitors or long-term residents. Not long after the Mellishes went to Dunmow, Elizabeth's parents gave up their bungalow at Reydon and moved to the vicarage. Elizabeth's mother had probably never truly recovered from the illness which forced her to leave Texas and for some years she had been in considerable pain. Now she was able to spend her last years with her beloved daughter, enjoying all the care and love that any mother could ask. In 1928, Elizabeth's sister, Margaret, had married a charming and very able young administrator in Shell Oil who had taken her out to Borneo. Here two sons were born in due course and happily the whole family had been home on leave in 1932 and had seen Mrs Molesworth only months before she died in April 1933. Elizabeth's father lived on with the family until his own death in 1941. In the intervening years he went out to Texas to see his brother and family there, and travelled to the Far East to stay with Margaret and her family. At home he made himself useful wherever he could, pruning the roses, helping in the garden generally, and when not wanted for other jobs, playing golf once or twice a week at Bishop's Stortford, about nine miles away. He was a great raconteur, and a much-loved and most welcome addition to the family, who never grumbled except about the occasional visitor who tried to pamper him.

Within a year or so, the room occupied by Elizabeth's mother was offered to her much-loved Aunt Georgie, who moved down from London with her devoted maid Ruth. Once again Elizabeth was able to repay with all her love and care the debt she felt she owed from her school days, and Mellish too was delighted to have an old friend under his roof. Later still Elizabeth found that Miss Pyne, the faithful though temperamental old cook from her house at Sycombe Abbey, had gone blind and had no one to look after her. So she too was installed in the vicarage where she remained until her death.

No doubt these permanent visitors contributed whatever they could to the housekeeping fund, but meanwhile the three boys were growing up and had all gone away to boarding schools, and Mellish's salary was still pathetically small. In order to help out, Elizabeth took in paying guests whenever she had a room to spare. Some of these stayed for years and became firm friends who returned later as visitors. The few who did not seem to fit in well with the family were looked after until they chose to leave and then thankfully wished godspeed. In this way Elizabeth ran her considerable household, entertained large numbers of friends and a good many casual callers through the years without ever having to ask Mellish to contribute to the exchequer in cash although of course he supplied the family with all the fruit and vegetables they could eat.

In 1935 a longed-for and much-loved daughter, Claire, was born and now the family was complete. Elsie meanwhile had left to be married and her place was taken by Catherine, until she too married some years later. The faithful Daisy became Claire's devoted nanny and friend, and Aunt Georgie's Ruth stayed on in the vicarage as companion and helper until after the war.

Life at the vicarage was not work all the time. There was a very big garden which occupied a great deal of Mellish's spare time as a labour of love. Every evening in the spring and summer he could be seen in shirtsleeves and without his dog collar, tending, weeding, planting or harvesting. Apart from the vegetable garden and a big fruit cage, there were flower borders and beds to produce colour for the house and the church, and simply to admire. The verandah at the front of the house was always a blaze of colour with massed geraniums and there were roses on the wall and hothouse plants in the greenhouse. Outside too, there was a variety of livestock. Dolly the donkey had to be taken out and tethered each day; for many years there was a goat producing milk, originally for Paul when he was ill but latterly for anyone; and there was the black sow who had a succession of litters. Even when the sow and the goat had gone, there were always a dozen or so hens to keep the family in eggs, and sometimes the odd duck. At one time Mellish was given a bantam cockerel which was put with the ladies, but he soon became fiercely jealous and aggressive, flying up at the eyes of anyone who entered the pen. For some time Mellish endured these assaults warding him off with a tennis racquet until he became intolerable.

Bee-keeping became another hobby of absorbing interest. Starting with a few hives, Mellish gradually built up to eight or nine which he carefully and lovingly tended. He became the local swarm catcher for anyone who wanted to be rid of them and when he was stung, as he often was, he simply regretted that the bee died. In return the bees yielded a generous supply of honey, in a good year up to 60 lb per hive which was extracted in the annexe adjoining the study and run off into big 28 lb catering-size jam tins from the school which Margaret and Rhys ran. Rhys had foreseen trouble on his last leave from Borneo in 1937 and decided that with a growing family it was best not to return to the Far East. He then settled in Exmouth where Mellish's boys were at a fine prep school and took a job as teacher at the school while Margaret took over a small pre-prep school in the house which they bought. When the headmaster died very unexpectedly in 1942, Rhys took over the school as headmaster.

And always throughout his life Mellish could spend many happy hours in his workshop. Usually in the evening he would work at the

big old treadle lathe, probably little different from the ones used in
the time of Chippendale, and at the bench. Model boats and book-
shelves for the boys, toys for Claire, furniture for the home, or tall
oak candlesticks for the church; there was nothing he would not
undertake and carry out with all the skill and craftsmanship he
possessed. A holiday in Southwold gave him the chance to produce
an oak fireside fender for the nursery, carved with diamond panels
depicting larks singing, chicks scratching, lambs gambolling, a sailing
boat and a windmill, all features of the local scene. Later when the
three boys were in the Services he made a fine oak work box for
Elizabeth with her initials in the centre of the front panel, flanked
by the boys' service emblems. In the very last stages of carving an
initial his chisel slipped and rather than turn out a faulty job, he
planed off the complete panel and started again. Mellish often said
that if he had not felt the call to be a priest he would have liked to
earn his living working with wood, and indeed he might have done
so, even in pre-war days when handicraft work was very poorly
rewarded. To him it was complete relaxation and pleasure and he
was never happier than when in overalls and among the clean smell
of new-worked wood.

But for all his busy life and hobbies which could fill every spare-time
hour, Mellish was above all a devoted husband and father who
delighted in his family. Breakfast on weekdays was preceded by prayers
with the whole family and any friends who were staying, and meal-
times round the big dining table were occasions for discussion and
happy family gossip. When the children were small he never failed
to say goodnight to them in their bedrooms and as they grew, he
enjoyed teaching them tennis, shooting with an air rifle and cricket
practice in a net on the big lawn. In the 1930s there were several
private tennis courts in and around Dunmow and first with Elizabeth
and later with the three boys as well, Mellish often took part in tennis
parties in the district.

Although he seldom asked them to accompany him, he was always
delighted to have any of his family with him, either in the garden,
the church or the workshop, and while he carried on with his job
they could try to help or perhaps unconsciously learn. To three
normally curious boys Mellish's study was a slightly mysterious place,

full of books and papers, smelling deliciously of printer's ink, tobacco smoke and honey, with cupboard drawers full of assorted treasures such as old coins, medals, broken watches and cigarette lighters. As they grew older, his sons recalled that it was a peaceful haven where they could either read or work quietly or sit and talk if he was not in the middle of some task. Always there was a welcome and a feeling of serenity and purpose.

Nor was life all real and earnest. Mellish had a boyish sense of humour and a ready laugh and would often break into song or quote from a fine repertoire of verses and sayings. To Elizabeth he wrote little poems on special occasions or in reply to letters she received that seemed to him unusually stupid. Often he produced delightful little sketches to illustrate events, such as one of the boys trying to persuade a very fat horse over a jump, or the antics of the dogs or cats. And every year he arranged a locum and took the whole family off on holiday.

Sometimes Mellish took over a vicarage in a distant parish and did Sunday duty there for the month, but more often the family went to the bungalow in Reydon which Elizabeth's father had kept on for just this purpose. Whenever possible Margaret and her family joined forces so that there would be at least six adults and after Claire and her cousin Helen were born in 1935, seven children. In some years there was a French boy or girl to help teach and learn the language and usually other friends to make up a house full. At Reydon a large tent was pitched in the garden and all the boys would sleep there for the month while the rest of the party were distributed round the three-bedroomed bungalow wherever they could fit. The family recalls splendid holidays of this sort at vicarages at Diptford in Devon and at Sedlescombe in Sussex, where they wore the grass tennis court smooth with use. During an earlier holiday in a friend's house on the Isle of Wight, Mellish discovered that the local blue clay was excellent for modelling. Two of the party were proficient sculptors, one specialising in mice, and one in dogs, while Mellish himself made a series of animals which included a fine tiger. Many years later when they left Dunmow, the front part of this splendid animal was found in the accumulated treasure of years in the workshop but sadly it did not survive the move.

It would be wrong to give the impression that nothing ever went wrong or that Mellish had no troubles. There were all the worries and anxieties that every parent must endure, all the usual illnesses and parish discords, and money was never plentiful, although probably this was the least of Mellish's concerns. But generally the years at Dunmow up to 1938 were happy and productive, and Mellish worked tirelessly with Elizabeth to help his parish and his people. He seldom left the parish if it could be avoided, apart from his annual holiday. But once a year on Armistice Sunday he travelled up to London to conduct the Remembrance service at the Royal Fusiliers regimental memorial in High Holborn and afterwards in the regimental chapel of St Sepulchre's, Holborn. In 1935 he had been invited by the Colonel of the Regiment, General Walter Hill, to accept the position of Honorary Chaplain to the Regiment. Probably none of the honours which he received meant more to Mellish than this and he gladly and proudly accepted, and only once until his death did he fail to conduct the memorial service. In 1959 another Colonel of the Regiment, General Cosmo Nevill wrote:

On behalf of the Regiment I thank you for taking the service at our Memorial and St Sepulchres. You set us all a magnificent example and if I may say so, you are beloved by us all.

Chapter Eighteen

War 1939–45

BUT BY 1938 THE NAZI POISON had spread through central Europe and to many the war to end all wars had been a waste and a mockery and another and worse one seemed inevitable. In September Neville Chamberlain returned from a series of meetings proclaiming 'Peace in our time', and it was agreed that a plebiscite should be held in Czechoslovakia to determine its future. At that time someone dreamed up an idea to see fair play and the British Legion Volunteer Police Force (Czechoslovakia) was born.

A call for volunteers was put out and immediately 70,000 responded from every walk of life, the only common bond that they were ex-servicemen, not one of them under forty, but most a good deal more, and every one a veteran of the Great War. Finally 1,200 were selected and sent up to London to be kitted out and prepared. To those who saw them on parade before moving off to embark at Tilbury Docks, it was a heart-breaking and stirring sight, this gallant band, smartly uniformed in blue police suits and peaked caps, their tunics bright with medal ribbons and decorations from every campaign in the First World War and some from previous campaigns in South Africa and India. Every man in this picked force was leaving wife, home, family, well aware of the danger he faced, yet off parade they were as merry and enthusiastic as a bunch of schoolboys preparing for an outing, teasing, joking and laughing. When they formed up, however, they were as smart a force as any sergeant-major could wish for and there was a marvellous sense of purpose and high morale. And so this pathetic and splendid little army marched off, armed only with ash walking sticks, to see fair play against Hitler's jack-booted thugs.

Mellish had immediately volunteered when the first call came, and was delighted to be picked. When they were kitted out at the Olympia stadium, he was even more thrilled to find that by extraordinary coincidence, he had been allotted the number 505 which was his army number as a trooper in the Boer War.

Luckily, but in some ways sadly, common-sense prevailed after a few days and the BLVP force which had embarked at Tilbury, was landed again and disbanded on 15 October, after a life of only nine days. There follows an account of the Force which was published in the *Spectator* on 21 October 1938.

Fortunately, Mellish wrote his own account as one of the rankers in this very unusual unit, and this paints an equally vivid picture of the Force.

The Legion's Lost Endeavour

Born on the 6th October 1938, dissolved on the 15th of the same month and year, the British Legion Volunteer Police (Czechoslovakia) had a long name and a short life. It did not work, or at least, none of the work for which it was created. Its foreign service snuffed out sadly off Southend Pier. In a few days hurrying events will over-lie its memory in the public mind. But before the grass grows on its grave it is worthwhile considering what it was and what it meant.

It was a democracy 1200 strong. It would be hard to find a walk of life which was not represented in its ranks. The squire and his tenant, the employer and his man, the independent tradesman and mechanic, the Church, the Law, the brotherhood of the pen, all were there. There were men of voluntary leisure and a small proportion, some two and a half percent, of less lucky men whose leisure was enforced by circumstance. There were men both rich and famous, and men both poor and utterly obscure. They came from every corner of the kingdom, and they had but three things in common. All were there of their own free will. All had served their country in the armed forces of the Crown, and all, I think, in time of war. All were inspired by a very special sort of comradeship.

The under-thirties, and perhaps the under thirty-fives, must find this sort of comradeship hard to understand. Since it was begotten on a world's agony, it is to be hoped that they will be spared the schooling which taught it and that they may evolve a brand of their own. But war, with all its waste and horror, did produce something worth preserving. Out of the wreck of individual hopes and schemes emerged a common purpose and an almost involuntary selflessness. Shared dangers and discomforts stripped away veneer and sheared through barriers of caste and creed. Mortal stress taught men, hating the sort of discipline which is oppression, to cling to that sort of discipline which is a life-line. With peace these lessons seemed to sink into obscurity, but the old soldier returning from the wars – and many a man of twenty was an old soldier then – carried beneath the medals on his chest a spark of memory that did not die. When he gathers at rallies and places where ageing men, a little incomprehensible, a little pathetic and perhaps a shade ridiculous in the eyes of youth, march together and sing old songs, he is blowing on that spark and warming himself at it. Probably neither he nor the onlooker, nor even the heads of the British Legion whose greatest care is its preservation, realised fourteen days ago the clearness and constancy of the flame into which that spark was capable of being fanned. I do not think that anyone who stood on the pavement outside Olympia at 3 o'clock on October 6th would have realised it. He must have been struck by the resemblance of the Legion to a rather shabby theatre queue. For the Legionaries had been told to bring a civilian suit to wear on the journey and very prudently their wives had not dressed them in their best. At the turn-stiles, where County Secretaries wrestled with confused contingents, patience was more in evidence than organisation. A lady reporter with a trans-Atlantic accent was concerned to know how our wives would carry on, and I fear that some of our answers never got into print. But once inside Olympia everything was changed.

Olympia in gala dress is one thing, but Olympia in the nude is quite another. Not that it was altogether bare, for on the ground floor were lines of tables. Filing past them, we received haversacks, water-bottles, ties, badges, sticks and papers. At the next series there stood a band of bright young men with yard measures. They were only interested in our chests, and seemed to find almost all our figures what they called "standard", a flattering description to those of us who were painfully conscious of a certain bulbousness of form. In a trice we were possessed of a blue suit and flannel shirt, and on our way in buses to Lambeth where, behind the Lost Property Office, we drew our coats and caps. Then back to our bedrooms or rather, bedroom; for we had about four acres of concrete on which to spread our palliasses, and the furniture consisted principally of notice boards bearing the names of our respective counties. And here, under the levelling influence of the concrete floor, we magically ceased to be what chemists call a mixture and became a compound – a formed body with a common soul and purpose.

Let me for a moment take you on fire-picket duty with me. Not that I want your company, for my mate is company enough. He is an old cavalry-man, lately a gentleman's gentleman. The habits and foibles of the rich and famous are open books to him, but he speaks kindly of them. But mostly he speaks of cleaning scarlet hunting coats, of how he sought and at last extorted from a fellow craftsman the secret of a compound which would really do the trick and yet not rot the stitches. As we talk, we patrol and gaze upon our fellow legionaries, some dead to the world, others tossing uneasily upon their straw. This morning we and they marched through the streets behind a band, and very fine fellows we were, throwing great chests. But now we have laid aside our medals and taken out our teeth. Pressed against a straw-stuffed pillow is a face which I recognise from the illustrated papers. It is the face of a man who has walked with kings. Beside it is another face, one that I know. It belongs to an ex-policeman. What is it, I wonder, which brought them here together? For both are old and both are tired, but both in their sleep look singularly happy.

And now our journey is beginning. We have rolled our blankets, packed our kits, and donned our great-coats and equipment. We did not sleep too well last night, and we got up at half past four although reveille was not till five. We march with the steadiness, but perhaps not with the spring, of seasoned troops. We are terribly anxious to be the smartest trainload. Our RTO, a country squire, spurs us on. "Would you mind, Sir", he says, for he is a courteous RTO, "hurrying up with that roll of blankets?" The Legionary he addresses hurries up. He is a Lieutenant-General. Our train is the quickest one and I am sure that our Lieutenant-General is as proud as is our crossing-sweeper. For surely we must have a crossing-sweeper with us. So to our ships. All the world has read about our ships; how some men in the 'Naldera' slept on the floor, which they did, and how everyone on the 'Dunera' had a cabin to himself, which he hadn't. But the only thing that matters about our ships is that first of all we enjoyed ourselves immensely on them and secondly when Southend Pier began to pall and the rumours of disbandment crept round, we were sad on them. And from them we swiftly and suddenly faded away. That is the short story of what we did, and the little longer story of what we were. But what did we mean?

We meant this. We meant that service, and the most dreadful service of the god of war, could breed a spirit which does not die but only sleeps, ready at call to the service of the God of Peace. We meant that the thing called comradeship, so often talked of, is not a myth, but a reality. We meant that old and ageing men, scattered and perhaps lonely, can find a joy in corporate service greater than any which the satisfaction of personal ambition can bring. It has been said that we were an example, but I do not think we were, for youth must follow new paths. But we were a phenomenon. And, if the mind of youth ever turns towards the day when it too will be old, perhaps we were a comforting phenomenon.

Lawrence Athill

The British Legion Volunteer Police

What were we? I say were – for our life was very short, but very sweet. We were born in a crisis. 70,000 did their best to come to birth, but only 1,200 saw the light. It was a healthy, happy family.

One lad weighed fifteen stone and was difficult to fit in ready-mades. Another stood six feet five with a chest of fifty, he also was an outsize gents. Olympia was our cradle. We came in humble civvies, but after a visit to Scotland Yard we blossomed into policemen in blue suits, speed-cop hats, blue shirts, Legion ties, complete with knife, fork and spoon. Many of us hadn't worn boots for twenty years or so, but a gentle route march helped break them in, and we rather fancied ourselves as we swung along behind the Guards band.

Somehow these days seemed to wash out a score of years; a spirit which we knew then had come back again, as we "mucked in" happily together and forgot the years between. To go on fatigue with a brigadier, to sleep on a straw-filled palliasse between a horse gunner and boatswain's mate, to march in the ranks with a major-general and an unemployed miner is Democracy in a halo. A major, ex-cavalry, commanded my platoon. He didn't know what a platoon was and that we formed fours and didn't walk march, and that in the infantry you don't "make much of your 'orses."

In my platoon were several majors and a brigadier, a chief petty officer, RN, a captain or two, a Canadian "Mounty" who became a subaltern of RHA, a versatile person who started with RNVR, went in RAF and finished up in submarines. The sergeant of my section was a major whose last responsibility had been a 60 pounder battery, but he treated us gently and affectionately like his "hairies". The ribbons displayed on the blue coats of the force provided an interesting lesson in geography and history. Our CSM was round and shiny. He had twenty-five years of soldiering behind him and six sons in the service to carry on the good work. He fathered us all and we loved him. My company commander was a colonel, sometime of the Guards, but I think he was a little proud of us. None of us were very young, but we straightened our backs and flattened our fronts and took up our dressing smartly.

One member of the Force had a narrow escape. Once he was RSM of a Highland regiment. He thought his age was 45, but when the enrolling officer looked through his papers he suggested that he must have joined the Army five years before he was born. At any rate we didn't fall out in marching and we did mild PT without any disastrous results except for a button or two which left the ranks without orders. The only time I saw anything that created alarm and despondency among the troops was on the first night that we took up our quarters on HMT *Naldera*, when ships biscuits were provided for tea. It reminded me of a story of Tacitus (I stand open to correction) of the Veteran Legion who at last got fed up with perpetual campaigning, so in despair paraded before the CO and asked him to run his finger round their toothless gums, and then sang "I want to go 'ome." But we didn't get any more iron rations. I don't know if there were many ex-RF's in the Force, but one there was and the last time I had seen him was lying wounded near Cambrai in 1918.

After all we didn't get further than Southend Pier, and perhaps we felt that it was rather under false pretences that we each received kind messages of good wishes from Their Majesties The King and Queen, accompanied as of old days by a present of cigarettes and chocolate. But whatever we didn't do, we were ready, and that is the main thing. We demobilised at Tilbury, and our fine overcoats and smart hats have long since, like ourselves, been returned to stores.

So now in the name of the late lamented British Legion Volunteer Police, I send greetings to The Colonel of the Regiment and all members of the Association.

Noel Mellish,
No. 505 SAC, 1900, and again No. 505 BLVP 1938.

When in 1939 war was declared, Mellish again volunteered at once, feeling that his experience would be of real value in the army. When he was refused on the grounds of age, he wrote immediately arguing that since he was a non-combatant, age did not matter but his knowledge of men and of war conditions must be of use. This argument was put forward by other priests too, but the War Office was adamant, so he set about making life as easy as possible for all who were distressed or far from home by reason of the war. From the first, Mellish became an Air Raid Warden and Welfare Officer and made it his business to contact any troops in the area to offer help wherever possible, and night after night in the early days of the war, he would put on his steel helmet and go out whenever there was an air raid and stay out until he was sure that no damage had been done and no one was in trouble. On these lonely walks in the blackout and whenever sound of bombs or ack-ack fire livened the nights, he must have recalled vividly the scores of nights when he had sheltered in narrow trenches from artillery bombardments or walked among his soldiers, encouraging and helping them or bringing in the wounded and dead. Perhaps a little of what he felt shows in some lines of verse found among his papers after his death.

Winter 1940

Hours of a screaming chaos, benumbing sense,
Roar of the rending and crashing of all things safe,
Acrid smoke and the gushing of flaring flame
Searing and tearing of mangled human flesh,
Scattered fragments of that which a moment ago was life,
Gaping space, smoking and blackened, once a home.

News in the morning, air raid on London
Lasting for several hours.
Damage to property, some lives lost,
Number reported not large.

The first problem was to deal with evacuees from London. Like a great many country towns and villages, Dunmow was sent its quota of mainly young women and children from the East End. Mellish persuaded the Post Office to hand over its old building when it moved to new premises and with ready voluntary help from the people of Dunmow this was converted into a small club for the London evacuees, furnished with chairs and sofas, tables, crockery, kettles, books and magazines; in fact anything to make a homely meeting place for the exiles from home. For a short time this was fine, but after some weeks of the phoney war the London people became bored and perhaps resentful and in a few months most of them drifted back to London, preferring to face the dangers of bombing to the loneliness and quiet of the country. Before they left however they had turned the club into a disaster area, smashed up the furniture and broken most of the crockery. Undismayed, Mellish cleaned up the place and re-equipped it to become a resting-place for soldiers, where tea, coffee and cake were always available. This must have brought back memories of the many impromptu canteens he had set up and run in the bitter years from 1915 to 18.

So far so good but this was not enough. When a pub in the High Street became vacant, Mellish immediately went to the head of the local brewery, Colonel Gibbons, himself a distinguished soldier from the First World War, and asked for a loan of the premises. This was granted at once, and in a very short time, with a good deal of enthusiastic volunteer help, the premises were transformed into a spacious cafe with kitchen in the rear and reading rooms upstairs. The news spread rapidly and equipment, books, games and crockery were given generously. What these gifts and persistent scrounging could not supply, was bought, where possible second-hand, to fit up a well-equipped kitchen with potato peeler, and chipper, gas cookers and utensils of all sorts. All that was lacking was a suitable sign, and by luck the original pub sign still hung on its bracket outside. Mellish took this down and painted a splendid sign showing St Martin, the Roman soldier on his horse, leaning over to hand his cloak to a near-naked beggar. One night Elizabeth went down very late to see why her husband was so long, and found him sitting stripped to the waist in front of a tall mirror, painting the beggar's back from his own reflection.

So St Martin's Club came into being, and operated for six nights a week with a staff of volunteers working on a rota basis. In the next five years tons of chips, miles of sausages and mountains of eggs must have been served together with oceans of tea, coffee or soft drinks, to any serviceman who cared to come in. After the invasion of Europe in 1944, when there were no longer many troops in the area, the Club was taken on by Ruth, Aunt Georgie's stalwart housekeeper, who had played a major part in its operation throughout the war, and she continued to run it as a permanent hostel for a few soldiers based in Dunmow.

This was but one of the extra activities Mellish undertook during the war, and for him it was a labour of love since it brought him in contact with the troops he would so dearly like to have been serving with. He made a point of visiting every unit of the forces in the area and trying to make life easier for them, and established a regular round of visits to the semi-permanent units such as ack-ack and searchlight batteries. Any soldier was welcome at the vicarage and many of them came regularly for baths, meals, and perhaps temporary escape from camp life. Some of them became friends who kept in touch for many years and later brought their own families to visit.

It was ironic in view of his work for the forces that one day two officers of the RHA, who had been fairly regular visitors to the vicarage, appeared on the doorstep in deep embarrassment with orders to arrest Mellish. Elizabeth was at first dumbfounded and then highly amused at this absurdity. It appeared that someone had reported him for ringing the church bells which were of course only to be rung as an invasion warning. No one ever discovered how the story arose, but eventually the officers were convinced that it was untrue and were greatly relieved to depart without their prisoner.

Of all the forces, it was of course the Royal Fusiliers who claimed first place in Mellish's heart. In 1939, as Chaplain to the Regiment, he sent out a letter through the Fusilier Headquarters to be distributed to all units.

To the Officers, Non-commissioned Officers and Men of the Royal Fusiliers.

I do not know where you are and I am not going to ask. But I know well that wherever you may be, you are now as always, upholding the splendid tradition of the Regiment. I long to be with you but my application for service as Chaplain has been declined on account of age. I must therefore do what I can to be useful where I am. Yet my heart is with the Regiment and my thoughts and prayers are constantly with you.

Believe me that I am proud and grateful to be associated with you even in such a small way. Never shall I forget your comradeship in the days that are past.

> Please accept my loving greetings and sincere affection.
> Sept. 10th, 1939. Noel Mellish.

Early in the war Mellish decided that there should be a special place in the church where people could pray for their loved ones away from home, or remember their dead. In a very short time a section at the end of the north aisle was converted to a beautiful chapel, with a blue carpet on the floor, a few rows of chairs, and an altar table over which hung the Union Jack and St George's Cross. On the altar itself was a book inscribed with the names of every man and woman serving in the forces, and this was flanked by tall candlesticks made by Mellish himself, between which stood the cross he had used wherever he held services in France from 1915 to 1919. This was made from the driving band of a German shell mounted into the nose cap of another shell. On the floor each side of the altar stood the tall vases of flowers which he loved, to make his church a place of beauty and peace. From the day St Martin's Chapel was dedicated, Mellish read aloud every name in the book and prayed for their safekeeping or their eternal rest.

Meanwhile the ordinary life of the parish went on as far as possible. But now there were all the additional calls to be made to comfort the families of war casualties, wounded, missing or dead. And because his people knew that Mellish himself had seen, endured and come through every imaginable horror of war, they took comfort from his presence and assurance. Sometimes, but more rarely, he was able to rejoice with families whose absent sons or husbands had received awards for bravery or had been saved from disasters such as the Dunkirk evacuation.

Always he followed the war news with the keenest interest and kept coloured maps of the various campaign areas in his study on which he could mark, at first withdrawals and setbacks, and later triumphal advances. During the dark days of 1940 when there was little enough to be grateful for, the nation was thrilled by the story of HMS *Cossack's* rescue of over 300 British seamen from the German prison ship *Altmark* in a Norwegian fiord. Mellish was so impressed by this brilliant and daring raid that he wrote to congratulate the Captain, Capt. Philip Vian, later Admiral Sir Philip Vian, and adopted the *Cossack* as a suitable recipient for gift parcels. Thereafter the ladies of Dunmow made up regular parcels of knitwear and cakes for the crew of this fine ship and for over two years these were despatched to the grateful sailors.

Presently a more personal concern was added to Mellish's unfailing concern and care for others. Paul, his second son, became a medical student at St Mary's Hospital in 1940, and was in London throughout all the bombing, taking an active part in casualty work and fire-watching. In the same year, Pat, the eldest son, was commissioned to Mellish's delight, into the Royal Fusiliers, and was posted to the 2nd Battalion, which had lost a number of good men and officers and much of its equipment in the retreat from France. After a spell near Camberley and then months of vigorous training in Scotland, the Battalion sailed for Algiers in March 1943. It was soon in action with the 1st Army and on Good Friday, 23 April, it took part in a major action which proved costly and unsuccessful. The Colonel was killed, one complete company captured and two others were badly mauled. Pat was with one of these companies which were cut off and short of ammunition. Both company commanders were wounded and both wireless sets put out of action. Pat then volunteered to try and get back to battalion HQ, but on his way through a cornfield he was spotted by the German machine guns and hit, first in the leg and later in the back. When the two companies withdrew that night he was not found and was then reported missing. And so on 5 May Mellish received the telegram from the Under Secretary of State for War which had brought grief to so many other homes in his parish: 'Regret to inform you Lt P. M. Mellish has been reported missing.'

No one can know what Mellish and Elizabeth went through in the anxious days that followed but certainly the love and care they offered so freely to others was returned in full measure by their friends, and they received some wonderful letters of comfort. And then on 13 May another telegram arrived: 'Further report received from N. Africa. Lt Mellish now located in hospital having been wounded in action.' In fact Pat had been found on Easter Day and taken to a casualty clearing station and thence by various forms of transport to an American Hospital where he received excellent care.

The second telegram was delivered in person by the postman who knew Pat had been reported missing and wanted to ensure that the good news reached the vicarage without delay. Somehow the postmaster heard about this and threatened to dismiss the postman for going out of his way to hand in the telegram. Mellish was so incensed at the injustice of this reaction to an act of great kindness that he called on the postmaster. What was said we do not know but the postman was certainly reinstated without further ado.

After a long period in the American Hospital, Pat was shipped home, where he spent more weary months in more hospitals. The line of bullets across his back miraculously missed any vital organ and he soon recovered from these wounds, but his leg caused endless trouble and long after he was invalided out of the army, and some seventeen operations later, he finally insisted that it be amputated above the knee. By this time his whole system had been deeply infected with poison from the wound and though he became very agile on his false leg and for many years was employed in jobs in England and abroad, he was seldom without pain and has had to return for hospital treatment at regular intervals even forty years later. There was talk of an MC for the action in which he was wounded but perhaps because the Colonel had been killed and his company commander wounded, no recommendation was put through and sadly no award was made, even though his fellow officers believed that he had been so decorated.

So the war years passed and the news changed from gloom to optimism and then to thoughts of victory. Mellish went on his daily rounds and his nightly vigils whenever there was an air raid or hint of trouble, and comforted or rejoiced with the families in his care. And in all this, needless to say, Elizabeth supported him utterly as she had done all their married life. Her beloved father died in 1941, but his room was soon taken by someone else who needed a home or a friend who came for rest and ease. She never failed to provide copious meals on the slender rations available, and few strangers ever came without being invited in for a meal or a cup of tea.

But there was one other character who has to be mentioned for his constant companionship with Mellish, starting in the years before the war and continuing until his death in 1944. This was Simon, a small black dog with his mother's spaniel ears and his father's terrier body, who except in extreme emergency always ran on three legs only, as a result of a motor accident in his puppy days. Originally a kitchen dog, and a fine ratter, Simon attached himself to Mellish and would follow him everywhere, sitting quietly in the church porch when he was there and going out with him daily on his rounds. They were a part of the Dunmow scene, the tall vicar on his aged upright bicycle and the little dog like a small black familiar, running beside him. When they reached the town, about a mile from the vicarage, each went his own way: Mellish to see whoever was on his list for the day, and Simon to look in on his regular stops – his friends the butcher, the grocer, the chemist and any others who welcomed him with a tit-bit and a friendly word. His rounds finished, Simon would trail along the pavements until he came across Mellish's bicycle and they would then return home together.

At the end of the war, Mellish received a letter of thanks from the Adjutant General to the Forces, General Sir Ronald Adam, written to all Army Welfare Officers in the Home Command, asking them to carry on with their work until demobilization was complete and all temporary servicemen had been resettled. This work Mellish gladly added to his daily round, as he had seen how shabbily ex-servicemen were treated after the Great War, and in common with many others, he was determined that it should not happen again.

In 1946, he was invited to become a Deputy Lieutenant of the County of Essex, and was presented with a handsome scroll. The duties involved were not arduous, and he seldom appeared at official functions, but in 1947 the Lord Lieutenant held a dinner for his deputies. One of them, Sir Carne Rasch, telephoned to ask Elizabeth if Mellish had a set of miniature medals to wear for the occasion. When she said no, he asked exactly what medals he had, and a few days later a complete set of miniatures with their ribbons arrived by special post. Many years later when she told this story at a dinner, Mellish laughed and said, 'That simply goes to show how easy it is to win medals.'

A year or so later Mellish received the further honour of an invitation to become an honorary member of the Royal Society of St George, a movement founded in the First World War:

> to call attention to the greatness of our country and to encourage successive generations to uphold it. Particularly we strive to keep fresh the memories of our great men and women and to use their continuing fame and glory in the bringing up of youth.

Chapter Nineteen

Somerset Retirement

BY 1947 MELLISH, THEN AGED 67, felt that he had completed his work at Dunmow and that it was time to find somewhere smaller and a little easier. Elizabeth was strongly drawn to Somerset where she had lived with her parents when they first returned from Texas, and when a vacancy arose, Mellish was duly appointed as Perpetual Curate to the small parish of Baltonsborough near Glastonbury. In February 1948, he and Elizabeth packed up the accumulated possessions and memories of twenty years at Dunmow and after sad farewells from their many friends, set out to start all over again in a new parish.

Their arrival was not auspicious. Mellish's predecessor was a sad and disheartened person who had virtually given up the struggle. When he left he simply cut the electric light flex in every room so there was not a single light fitting for the incomers to use on a winter evening when they arrived. And outside the back door was a mound of tins and bottles reaching into the garden as far as they could be thrown, which took two local authority dustcarts to clear. Worst of all, a half furniture van load of their possessions had been taken back by the removers to their depository to await a full load. The depository was broken into and somehow a fire started which destroyed the place and all its contents, including some of Mellish's furniture and a great deal of his workshop and garden equipment. In new surroundings, it was almost impossible to list exactly what was missing, and for months afterwards, losses were only registered when particular items were needed or their absence discovered.

But despite this unfavourable start, Mellish and Elizabeth soon settled into their new house and made it into a warm and charming home. The garden sloped gently to a river with water meadows bright with buttercups on the other bank, and, with more time available in the smaller parish, Mellish soon turned this garden into a blaze of flowers and neat, trimmed lawns, all loud with the sound of bees which were happily resettled in their new home.

Once again Mellish and Elizabeth set out to get to know their new parish and in a very short time they had established themselves and restored the congregation which had dwindled sadly. The churchyard was brightened with flowering shrubs and roses, the church itself filled with flowers, and old customs such as ringing out the old year and ringing in the new, were brought back. Parish and choir outings, bellringers' parties, the Christmas crib and the Easter tomb, all contributed to weld the parish into a living unit and Mellish's continual visiting and his understanding of, and sympathy with, the way of life of his farming parish produced a flourishing church community.

As always Elizabeth kept open house, and soon after they moved in, Mellish's half-sister, Alice, who was now alone following her brother's death, came to live with them. They were happy years at Baltonsborough but not without troubles and difficulties. An attack of death watch beetle in the church roof timbers meant that a large sum of money had to be raised for treatment. Then a new heating system was needed to replace the very old and inefficient one, and more thousands had to be found. Mellish himself, with the help of Alice, raised a large proportion of the money needed, by writing to all their own contacts and to every name they could find from exhaustive researches in the old parish registers, tracing families who had emigrated to the USA or to Australia. From the more personal side, Pat, their eldest son, became very ill as a result of the bone infection he had suffered for years, and had to be carefully nursed for some time, but Mellish and Elizabeth bore their own troubles with characteristic cheerfulness and unswerving faith.

Another trouble with a happier outcome arose from Mellish's love of his bees. Some of the hives started to die off and a sickness named American Foul Brood disease was diagnosed. By chance Mellish came across a treatment for this in an American journal on bees and started to feed the diseased hives with a simple chemical solution. Shortly afterwards, however, he was ordered by the Ministry of Agriculture to destroy all his hives as this was a notifiable disease. Mellish replied that it was pointless to destroy his own hives when a large proportion of others in the area were suffering the same disease. He explained that he was trying out a cure which apparently worked in the USA and that if, after a reasonable trial, it proved a failure, he would comply with the order. This did not suit the bureaucrats however, and in due course he was summoned to appear before the magistrates for failing to obey a Ministry order. The resulting trial would have delighted a comedy playwright's heart. After one or two cases of poaching had been summarily dealt with, Mellish stood up in the dock and pleaded guilty to disobeying the Ministry order.

> Yes, I refused to obey because it was a stupid order. If you ordered me to kick this policeman beside me I would refuse that too because it would be a stupid order. If my treatment does not work then I will comply but I should be given time to try out a remedy which has been proved in America.

After due deliberation the magistrates imposed the minimum fine of £25 because Mellish had admitted his refusal to obey the order. Mellish then stated that he would not pay and when told the alternative would have to be a spell in prison he agreed but asked that it should be deferred until after Harvest Festival, 'because my parishioners would not like me to be absent then'. The magistrates were sympathetic and amused but could not vary their sentence and dismissed the defendant, after giving him a month in which to pay.

The case attracted a good deal of local publicity as it was all very good-humoured and the picture of a war hero resisting a faceless bureaucracy appealed to many people. Mellish received numbers of letters of encouragement and cheques to pay the fine, with enough to spare to make a handsome profit. To all these he wrote his thanks and returned the money. But when on the twenty-seventh day he decided that perhaps he should settle the matter and went in to pay his fine, he was told it had been paid anonymously some time earlier. The final outcome was even more satisfactory. The bees responded well to the treatment and were completely cured but the Ministry official never returned to see if the order had been obeyed and no more was ever said on the matter.

It was during the years at Baltonsborough that Mellish was laid up with a badly infected leg for some days and only then that he at last yielded to his family's urgent entreaties to write something about his early life. Unfortunately he had only got to the end of the Boer War when his leg healed and he put the papers aside for parish affairs.

In 1953 after six years at Baltonsborough, Mellish had perhaps begun to feel that it was time to hand over to a younger man. Much as he loved the work, the ceaseless striving to raise money was a strain. His decision to retire was certainly confirmed if not prompted by the wish to help his youngest son, Robin, who had been offered a job looking after a small farm. And so in 1953, the family packed up once more and moved to a farmhouse near Castle Cary in Somerset. Mellish continued to take services whenever he was offered the chance, but for a time anyway he was relieved to be free of parish work and enjoyed helping on the farm, making and repairing gates and fences and devoting his energies to creating yet another garden.

But after only one year Robin moved to another job and became engaged to Nonnie, a Dutch girl who had been in England for some years and had often visited the family. In September Mellish married them at a church in Folkestone and then returned to Somerset where he had been appointed temporary rector at a small village near Castle Cary. Here he and Elizabeth lived in a big old-fashioned rectory for three years until they bought a house at Batcombe, near Bruton. Although he was not responsible for the parish, Mellish undertook all the church services here for two years, but the garden was steep and difficult and the time had come when he felt he should lay down his burden of office.

And so in 1959 after a short search Mellish and Elizabeth finally came to rest in the Court House at South Petherton in Somerset. This was a charming mellow stone house, with a pretty garden behind it, overlooking a stream in the valley below. It had once been used by the infamous Judge Jeffries for his bloody work after the Monmouth Rebellion, but was now divided into two good-sized houses, the adjoining part being occupied by a delightful doctor and his wife and family. Here Mellish and Elizabeth thankfully and happily settled, making new friends in Petherton and the district as they had wherever they lived, and offering a welcome to a host of old friends from the Great War days onwards.

The years between 1954 and 1960 produced a number of family occasions and special services which Mellish gladly undertook. First there was Robin's wedding to Nonnie, then in 1957 the christening of their daughter, Leonie, in the church at Batcombe. Soon after this Paul was married to Veronica, the daughter of a retired colonel in the Gloucesters who had taken up farming in the Mendips. The wedding was in the lovely cathedral at Wells which Mellish knew well from his Baltonsborough days when he regularly took duty there as a priest/guide. In 1959 a son was born to Paul and Veronica in America but they were not able to return that year for a christening. However in 1960 Nonnie had a son who was proudly christened Nicholas Noel by his grandfather in the church at South Petherton. In 1961 Veronica had another son, also Nicholas, and in 1964 Fiona was born in America, but sadly Mellish never met the last two grandchildren.

There were more special services too. Among others Mellish was asked by his old friend Keith Markby to conduct the wedding of his daughter, Rosemary, to the Duke of Bedford's brother. Then there were funerals of some of his old friends or their wives and several times he was asked to preach at regimental services. And of course he never missed the Royal Fusiliers Remembrance Day service at High Holborn.

In 1960 the family suffered a grievous loss with the sudden and unexpected death of Theo Rhys-Jones, known to all as Rhys, the husband of Elizabeth's sister, Margaret. Rhys had made a resounding success of his second career after leaving Shell Oil in 1938 and taking a job as assistant master at St Peter's prep school in Exmouth, where Mellish's three boys had been educated. In 1942 the then headmaster Harold Faulkner, died, also prematurely and unexpectedly, and Rhys took over the school with Margaret. He was a natural teacher, a fine administrator and greatly loved by the boys with whom he could relax without any loss of discipline. He and Margaret steered the school through the difficult war years and shortly afterwards took the major step of moving the whole school to new and infinitely better premises, in a large mansion house standing in a beautiful park outside

Exmouth. Here under their guidance a fine school with a tradition of excellence became even better and was able to expand and flourish. In 1959 Rhys underwent an operation and just as he appeared to be recovering nicely he died very suddenly.

This was a tragic loss but even more tragic was the death only two weeks later of Helen, in a riding accident. Helen was not quite twenty-four, a few months younger than Claire, Mellish's daughter, with whom she had grown up as far as possible since the two families shared holidays regularly. Margaret tried to spare Mellish the distress of taking the funeral services, but he insisted and so twice in less than a month he stood in the bitter January wind in the little churchyard at Woodbury near Exmouth to commit his loved ones to the grave. Mellish felt these deaths very keenly since Rhys was a close friend as well as his brother-in-law. Although Rhys was neither a gardener nor a handyman, he had much in common with Mellish in other respects: a love of books and interest in history; a love of the countryside and of walking; a care for people and the mutual respect of men who were each masters of their particular profession. But there was a happier sequel when in 1961, Christopher, Rhys' younger son, was married in a London church by his uncle. To all these services, whether sad or happy, Mellish brought the quiet dignity and shining sincerity with which he conducted his whole ministry throughout his life.

Wherever Mellish went to live, one of the first priorities was to set up a workshop. At South Petherton the small scullery between the kitchen and the garden was admirably suited for this purpose and here he set up a small electric-powered lathe and his bench and tool racks. In 1958, after Leonie's birth, he had made a complete Noah's Ark set for her – twenty-six pairs of animals and on good Biblical precedent they went in two by two, male and female. Every animal was different and every one was alive, creeping, crouching, stalking or slinking according to its nature. When they were all embarked in the Ark, a large sectional vessel on wheels, they were transported up to Oakham in Rutland where Robin and Nonnie were living, and here Mellish stayed for a few days looking round the estate there and helping with fittings in their house. Then Martin was born in America and so a second set had to be made, this time twenty-eight pairs complete with Noah and Mrs Noah, but all to different patterns from the first Ark. In due course these were shipped out to America to become another family's joy and pride.

Now at the Court House, Mellish divided his time between the garden with his little greenhouse, and the workshop in cold or bad weather. Here he could sit at his lathe and spent many happy hours making or repairing things for friends, wood-carving and turning. These last years were completely happy ones. Mellish was delighted to see friends who came to stay or visit, or to welcome his own family whenever they could come, and utterly content simply to be at home with his Elizabeth. They seldom went away now and though they enjoyed the odd visit they were probably relieved to be back home. He was still able to celebrate Communion either in the church at South Petherton or in neighbouring villages, and though he tired if he had to stand for any length of time, he could always relax with a book.

A photograph taken in the last year or so shows Mellish sitting in his garden against a background of flowers, wearing his workshop overall and with a small Border Terrier on his knee. The old bell captain at Dunmow to whom Elizabeth sent a copy, said that this was absolutely typical of the vicar he knew and loved, showing him as a gardener, a craftsman and an animal lover. Another friend who knew Mellish well in those last years remarked on the expression of absolute serenity on his face, best described in the words of an ancient prayer as 'the royalty of inward happiness'.

In June 1961 Mellish was admitted to Taunton hospital where it was found necessary to operate for cancer. The operation was not a success and Mellish was so distressed to be away from home that he insisted on leaving before he was fully recovered. Back home however, he rallied and under Elizabeth's devoted care he was as cheerful as ever. But the disease was perhaps too far advanced to treat and after a mercifully short period of illness Mellish died on 8 July 1962. Somehow Paul, now a Professor of Paediatric Surgery in Vermont, managed to fly over from the States in time to see him. For Pat and Robin it was an easy journey to the Court House and Claire, his beloved daughter, was able to leave her work in Bath, so that he died knowing that his whole family was with him, and most of all his Elizabeth.

A funeral service was held in the church at South Petherton, on 12 July. The Royal Fusiliers were represented by the Colonel of the Regiment, General Cosmo Neville, and a bugler was sent down by the Regiment to sound a soldiers' farewell, the Last Post and Reveille, which Mellish himself had heard so many times. There were friends from all over the country and of all ages, from Keith Markby, the adjutant of his battalion in the First World War, to children from South Petherton. Elizabeth herself chose Mellish's favourite hymns, Bunyan's Pilgrim song and 'Father hear the prayer we offer', and the service was taken by Mellish's friend and joint honorary chaplain to the Royal Fusiliers, Canon Paul Wansey, who won an MC with the 2nd Battalion in Italy. Paul's address at the service was brief but so memorable and comforting that it deserves a place in this story; together with a letter from General Cosmo Neville to Elizabeth.

We are here today in thanksgiving. All good comes from God. We thank God especially, the faithful Creator, for His gift to us, and to this world, of Noel Mellish. In a few minutes General Cosmo Neville, Colonel of the Regiment, will speak to us, and so on our behalf will give expression to some of the causes of our thanksgiving.

And we are here today, out of love for Noel Mellish. Is it too late to give him our love? The Christian answer is most certainly "No". It is never too late for love, which is the essence of the Eternal God, and is eternal. Through the Eternal God, who is love, we can, if we wish, give him our love, in the Communion of Saints, in every daily prayer, in every Holy Communion.

Many of us will have read in yesterday's Times the account of what happened at St Eloi in March 1916. He went back and forth, through machine-gun fire and shell fire, to bring back the wounded to safety, ten the first day, twelve the next day. That was not an isolated incident: it is an illustration of his whole life.

Where are those twenty-two men now? I suppose somewhere in the regions beyond; perhaps needing his help more than ever. Perhaps already he has sought them out and found them again. He, no doubt, is much further on in the realms of the spirit than they are. But back he goes, back and forth – to bring them home. That is the priest's work: and I have no doubt he is more joyfully and fully engaged in it than ever before.

I first met him, on a leave in the last war. I was invited to Dunmow

Vicarage, and had the great privilege of receiving for the first time from him and from all the family, friendship, care and real affection. Noel took me to his church, showed me his Fusilier shell-case cross, and told me that every day of the war, God willing, he would go there and pray for the Fusiliers, and for me. And he is the same today and every day: for us, and for his family, and for all who have a place in his heart, I am sure he daily does this vital work, and makes this precious gift.

To the family may I say: Don't let his prayers be wasted. In your prayers, you pray for him, and ask God to give him your love: then be quiet, remember Noel's love and prayers for you, and let God give the gift. Especially we find this true in the Holy Communion. In receiving the Divine gift, let us also receive that which is a very precious part of the Divine gift, the Communion of Saints.

"No mourning", the paper says. How right! No mourning, but gifts in thankfulness. So let us give ourselves anew to God's service, whenever we remember him, with love and thankfulness.

9th July, 1962.

My dear Mrs Mellish,

It was with the deepest sorrow that I heard the news this morning.

On behalf of all ranks past and present of the Regiment I send you our deepest sympathy in your very great loss.

We bear the loss with you, because he was at heart a Fusilier and we were all devoted to him. He was a shining example to each one of us. He carried the very highest award for valour in war and showed his ultimate courage in peace. We shall miss him terribly on Remembrance Sunday, yet we shall always remember him.

He was a true Christian gentleman.

Grenia and I send you our personal deepest sympathy and love.

Yours sincerely,
Cosmo Neville.

P. S. I shall of course be there on Thursday.

Splendid and well-deserved tributes from a fellow priest and a fellow soldier, for a true soldier of Christ. But perhaps the most fitting description of this remarkable man and his lifetime of service is contained in the words which Noel Mellish himself wrote in 1918, in a simple, moving farewell to his friend, Major Ronny Tower:

Such a glorious, selfless, gallant gentleman.

Epilogue

JUST AS NOEL MELLISH'S LIFE would have been incomplete without
Elizabeth to share it and add to it, so his story would be unfinished
without the rest of hers. Elizabeth lived on for twenty more years
in the 'sure and certain hope' that she had so often heard her Noel
invoke at the graveside. Of course she mourned an irreparable loss,
but if she grieved, she grieved alone, and outwardly was as serene
as ever. She hated living alone, not because of the solitude, for she
had more than enough moral resources to overcome any fear of
loneliness. Rather it was because after a lifetime of devoted and selfless
care for others, she had no one on whom to lavish her attention.
Throughout her life she was never happier than when surrounded
by a house full of guests or family to care for, and so, for the next
ten years or more, she had an endless flow of visitors. If friends
or family were not available she would make a home for anyone she
felt needed some love or care. Up to the age of eighty or more,
she was still running about, visiting, shopping or doing things to help
'dear little old ladies', some of whom may well have been ten years
or more younger than herself. Her family teased her sometimes with
loving exasperation about her softness for 'such a nice little man' or
someone with 'such a nice wife' regardless of their professional short-
comings.

During the 1960s among others Tubby Clayton of Toc H fame
was a regular visitor to the Court House, together with old school
friends, old pupils and Dunmow friends. Right up to the last year
or so of her life, Elizabeth kept up an enormous correspondence with
family and friends, often rising at four or five a.m. to write a letter
before starting on the day's work. She never missed a birthday or

anniversary from an endless list of dates to remember, and more often than not managed to find a present for every occasion.

In 1964 at the age of seventy, Elizabeth flew for the first time when some friends took her to see the battlefields of Flanders. In 1966 she and Claire sailed to America for a blissfully happy visit to Paul and Veronica in Vermont, and then on to see cousins in Texas before returning home. In 1970 her sister Margaret, now remarried to a delightful old friend from Shell Oil days, took her to Ireland where they visited her mother's old family home in County Mayo. In between these special trips, Elizabeth went away quite often for short stays so that she was seldom short of company.

In 1974 the family arranged an eightieth birthday party for her in the Town Hall at South Petherton, attended by about sixty members of the family and friends. At that time she was still remarkably active and fit, but the garden had become rather too much and she started looking for a smaller house, and in 1978 she moved across the road to a small house with only a little courtyard at the rear. Meanwhile Claire, who had been with her for some time, now took up a job in Bath, so for a few years Elizabeth was more or less alone, and without someone else to cook for she scarcely troubled about herself.

Eventually this neglect took its toll and in 1981 she became very ill, much more so than she would admit to, or others suspected. Finally it became clear that she should not be left to live alone any longer so Claire gave up her job and moved back to South Petherton. For a year or two in Claire's loving care, Elizabeth was able to continue her visiting, her correspondence and her interest in church and village affairs. But slowly she became weaker and in the last year increasingly confused, though as serene as ever and unfailingly happy and grateful for Claire's devotion. Shortly before Christmas 1982 Elizabeth became ill again and was confined to her bed. Once again Paul managed to arrange leave from Vermont and flew over with Veronica and Fiona for Christmas, so that in the last few days Elizabeth was visited by all her family and though now very weak, she knew them and rejoiced. Finally in the early hours of 27 December 1982, she died peacefully, watched over by her beloved daughter Claire.

To her family she was a very much loved mother and grandmother. To her many friends a loving and bountiful hostess, and on the authority of Tubby Clayton himself, quite definitely a saint. Now she went serenely and happily to rejoin her Noel in the Communion of Saints to which her long and selfless life of service to others had fitted her.